IDEOLOGY AND ENVIRONMENT
Situating the Origin of Vedic Culture

Ramendra Nath Nandi

IDEOLOGY AND ENVIRONMENT
Ramendra Nath Nandi

First Published, 2009
Reprinted 2025

ISBN 978-81-89833-83-1 (Pb)

Published by
AAKAR BOOKS
28 E Pocket IV, Mayur Vihar Phase I, Delhi-110 091
Phone : 011-2279 5505 Telefax : 011-2279 5641
aakarbooks@gmail.com; www.aakarbooks.com

Printed at
D.K. Fine Art Press, Delhi

Preface

The present study, a follow-up of an earlier work (*Aryans Revisited*, 2001), is of an exploratory nature aimed at a further stirring up of the debate. The earlier work focused on the nature of social formations, settlement history, maritime activities and early political processes experienced and documented by Vedic Aryans. Compared to this, the present work addresses a much broader issue of the origin of Vedic culture, its social and material milieu, the role of environment and demographic movements on cultural processes, the content and context of a religious ideology and the role of political and religious elites in the creation and propagation of this ideology, besides the interaction between Vedic and non-Vedic-speaking communities and its influence on the Vedic dialect.

The reconstruction of social processes outlined here is based primarily on a correlation of textual and archaeological evidence. But, since archaeological documentation itself derives valuable inputs from various branches of palaeo science, an attempt has been made to examine relevant studies independent of archaeological studies. Linguistic palaeo-ontology, physical palaeo biology and ethno-geography also provide useful information in the concerned areas of investigation. Since each of these disciplines belongs to forbidding areas of specialization, the effort has been to draw upon relatively consensual opinions on specific issues and paradigms.

For textual evidence I have used the four-volume edition of the *Ṛgveda Saṁhitā* edited by F. Max Müller and published by the Clarenden Press, Oxford, during the early 1890s

(1890–92) and reprinted as part of the Choukhambha Sanskrit Series in India during the 1960s. This edition provides the most authentic version of the text together with the commentary of Sayana. Citations from the *Ṛgveda* are in the international numbers and the order is Book, Hymn and Stanza e.g. (1.34.2). Longish text citations may occasionally affect readability, but these also help immediate verification of context and meaning besides retrieving passages in the event of a possible numerical mix-up. Citations of secondary works also appear at relevant places in the text of different chapters. Since scholars are already familiar with the transliteration marks in Sanskrit, no separate chart has been appended in the present work. The list of references, which is already formidable, has been confined to works actually cited and not to all the readings, which too have been beneficial in shaping the present work.

03 September 2008 **R.N. Nandi**

Acknowledgments

It is a pleasure to put on record the names of a host of scholars, friends and well-wishers, at the individual and institutional levels without whose cooperation it would have been difficult to bring this work to its present shape.

I sincerely thank the members associated with the Adhir Chandra Chakrabarti Memorial Committee for inviting me to deliver the sixth Memorial Lecture at Kolkata in April 2000. The brief presentation bearing the title of the present book was helpful in piecing together random thoughts on a new theme. The ideas were further developed in the form of the J.N. Samaddar Memorial Lecture delivered the same year in August at the Patna Museum and also in the course of presidential comments on the occasion of the R.K. Choudhary Memorial Lecture at the same venue a year later. I am thankful to the Centre of Historical Studies, Jawaharlal Nehru University, New Delhi for awarding a visiting fellowship in March 2003, which was a good opportunity to give a final shape to my ideas on the subject and share it with faculty members in the course of a presentation.

My thanks are due to Professor Michael Witzel of Harvard University for a brief online exchange of views on certain aspects of the present study; to Professor P. Oktor Skjaervo of the same university for drawing my attention to the work of D.W. McAlpine on Elamo-Dravidian relationship in *Language* and in *Current Anthropology*; to Dr. Jonathan Adams of Environmental Sciences Division, Oak Ridge National Laboratory, Oak Ridge, USA, for an online exchange of views on palaeo-climate studies; to Professor R.S. Sharma for personally endorsing some of my disagreements with existing formulations and suggesting relevant readings from time to time; to Professor Irfan Habib for his views on Avestan geography and generous gifts of reading materials in reprographic version; to Professor Shireen Moosvi and her disciple for seeing me through the relevant volumes of *Encyclopaedia Iranica* in the Central Library of Aligarh Muslim University and to Dr. R.S. Bisht for inputs on the archaeological possibility of textual evidence in the *Ṛgveda*.

I am thankful to Dr. P. Gupta, physician scholar and social activist, for clarification of certain medical terms and concepts and to Dr. A. Dasgupta of the Department of Sociology, Patna University for discussions on social theory. Mr. Ram Swarup Singh of the Central Library, Archaeological Survey of India, New Delhi and Dr. Parmanand Sahay of the I.C.H.R. Library, New Delhi were of great help to me whenever I was looking for normally inaccessible titles. I am thankful to Mr. Syed Ehtesham Rizvi, Senior Technical Assistant, American Institute of Indian Studies, Gurgaon for helping me to scan relevant readings available in the library.

Contents

Introduction

The Aryan Debate

The discourse on the origins of Vedic culture is now more than two hundred years old, but certain basic questions remain unresolved till date. For instance, who were the Vedic Aryans, were they indigenous to India or did they come from outside South Asia? If they came from outside South Asia, when did they come, why and from where? What was their social organization, economic life, political structure and religious belief? Is there any evidence in the *Ṛgveda* hymns that the Vedic Aryans were nomad pastoralists or cattle pastoralists devoid of any form of exchange relations, unrelated to city life and territorial states, as many of the Vedicists and historians would like to believe? Perhaps the idea of pastoral nomadism in relation to Vedic Aryans has been blown out of proportion, either wilfully or unwittingly. Stockbreeders, sedentary or nomadic, have always been a part of South Asian life, interacting in varying measure with people around, peasant communities, urban societies and trading agglomerates besides people living in the forests, on the hills and along the coast, frequently preceding, coexisting with and succeeding each one or all of these. Moreover, stockbreeding is not the exclusive domain of pastoralists. For reasons of multiple use, the sedentary peasant communities relate to stockbreeding thrice as much as pastoralists, nomadic or sedentary. Also, consider the argument that since nomads (read Vedic Aryans) were constantly on the move, they did not require any permanent residence and, accordingly, have not recorded any words for 'house' in their text. One wonders what the twenty-odd vocables signifying different types of human habitation are doing in the text. And, what about the prayers to a god of homestead land to make the pillars of a house strong enough so that the house can last several generations with prosperous bipeds and quadrupeds?

The idea of a people entering South Asia in 'waves' (Müller, 1859) or trickles (Witzel, 1995) does not fare any better. The event is attributed to the 'expansion' of the battle-axe culture or the expansion of agricultural activity, both from Europe. A migrating people equipped with battle-axes remain elusive in the context of north-western South Asia and the contiguous region of Iran and South Central Asia. The narrative of ten kings' battle in the *Ṛgveda* refers to warriors equipped with heavy battle-axes *pṛthūparaśavaḥ*, (7.83.1). But the venue of the conflict was the valley of the river Ravi and the warriors are said to have arrived from the east (*prācā*). Which is the country east and south-east of the river. Besides, this would push the upper limit of *Ṛgveda* compositions by a few thousand years. As regards the suggestion relating to the expansion of agricultural activity, it ignores the fact that the practice of agriculture began simultaneously in Egypt, Anatolia, Mesopotamia, and Baluchistan in the north-west of South Asia about the middle of the eighth millennium BC. As for the 'time' of the so-called migration, there are as many dates as there are scholars, the time ranging between 9000 BC and 800 BC. The 'homeland', which could be anywhere and everywhere in the whole of Asia and Europe, also seems to be a non-starter.

Ideas on the origin of Vedic culture broadly fall into two categories, one which harps on the theory of culture supplanting from outside South Asia and the other, which straightaway identifies Vedic Aryans with the Harappans. The former opinion, though still much circulating has been dismissed on the basis of hard evidence, textual (Erdosy, 1989, 40-41), archaeological (Possehl, 1999, 38-41; Kenoyer, 1998, 74; Shaffer, 1993; Jarrige, 1984), linguistic (Kuiper, 1991, 96; Misra, 1992) and physical palaeo-biological (Kennedy, 1995, 60). The other view, which equates Vedic Aryans with the Harappans also does not explain that if the two were the same people, what was the need for the Harappans to compose a massive oral literature of intense religious nature, propagate an ideology of nature worship and project an exclusive social identity for the followers of this ideology?

Confusion reigns supreme in other areas as well. For instance, there is little agreement among Vedicists themselves about certain basic aspects of Aryan life as described in the hymns of the *Ṛgveda*. For instance, Vedicists of earlier generations like Christian Lassen *(Indsische Alterthuskunde, 1883),* Max Müller (SBE32), Zimmer (*Altindisches Leben*, 22 et seq.), Macdonell and Keith (1912) describe with varying degrees of detail diverse maritime activities of Vedic Aryans including costal sea faring and overseas trade. Compare this with J.P. Mallory's observation (Mallory, 1989, 45) that the Vedic Aryans were a group of illiterate people, non-urban, non-maritime and least interested in any form of exchange relations. Mallory does not provide any additional textual evidence to dismiss the views of Max Müller *et al*. or contest the reading of so many *Ṛgveda* passages cited in favour of maritime activities of Vedic Aryans.

Paradoxically, the scholars who criticize others for circumscribing textual evidence on Aryan sea faring, themselves do this when it comes to explaining the term *pur* and the urban association of Vedic Aryans (Macdonell and Keith, 1912), little realizing that some sort of association with urban places would be inevitable for a people who frequently related to marine navigation for overseas trade and for exploiting the treasures of the sea. This was also imperative for a people whose major divinities, Indra, Varuṇa, Aśvins and Maruts, were associated with the high seas in some way or the other. Such a perception is surprising in view of the absolute consensus among scholars that the term *pur,* which occurs more than eighty times in the *Ṛgveda,* always represented a fort, a rampart or a stronghold. Where would the Vedic Aryans come across strongholds or forts except in the Greater Indus Valley during the Bronze Age? In the Greater Indus Valley, fortified settlements, which served as the centre of political power and resource accumulation and were made of mud, mud brick or stone, would be commonplace between 2500 BC and 1500 BC. In this context, an idea has gone round that since Vedic Aryans had nothing to do with urban places, they tried to destroy these whenever they came across any such structures. The 'destruction' of massive stone or brick ramparts is easier said than done and can never be the intent of a people who viewed these settlements as a source of wealth, power and security, and fervently aspired to possess as many of these as they could. The conflicts relating to the capture and occupation of fortified resource centres would perfectly fit a situation in which availability of resources became scarce, triggering conditions of small-scale but widespread political disturbances and social unrest.

Mercifully, there has been some rethinking, though inadequate, on the chronology of *Ṛgveda* hymns. One study, which draws on the internal evidence of the hymns suggests that the earliest compositions can be dated between 1900 BC and 1750 BC and the latest ones to 1250 BC (Witzel, 1999). Match this with the latest archaeological studies which stretch the lower limit of Harappan urban places to 1500 BC and even later (Shaffer, 1995, 138). Evidently the Vedic Aryans and the Harappans shared a common geographical area and historical heritage for at least half a millennium, if not more.

The graphic accounts of geo-climatic disorders like earthquakes and the deflection of the south-west monsoon, droughts, famines, epidemics, hegemonic conflicts and a constant fear of death and destruction, which may push the upper limit of the synchronism by a couple of centuries, also underline the compulsions for the Vedic-speaking segment of the Harappan population to develop a new religious ideology, claim an exclusive social identity for its members and project a binary classification of social groups into a higher Ārya Varṇa and a lower DāsaVarṇa segments.

Ideology and Environment

All through history, there has been an organic relationship between man and environment. A human group cannot exist without an environment and an environment without a human group does not mean anything to human history. The environment may be hostile or hospitable, and generate appropriate reactions and responses among the people who occupy it. These reactions and responses relate to the thought processes of man, collective or individual, a set of normative ideas concerning the dos and don'ts of human action in a given environment. These ideas can be deciphered as much from the archaeological record of a region or sub-region as from oral texts preserved by the concerned people. The absence of oral records in prehistoric cultures merely suggests the absence of a mechanism of oral transmission rather than the non-existence of any such text. The absence of such mechanisms also suggests the absence of any compulsion to communicate these ideas to other peoples around and/or to the succeeding generations. When such texts do surface in prehistoric times, one must realize that the people who created these texts wanted to communicate certain ideas to peoples across time and space and to that effect had also developed a system for circulation and transmission of these ideas. Since ideas do not originate in a social void, it is also necessary to look for the events and experiences, which motivated these ideas, and to correlate this information to the archaeological record lying around. Such a perspective is likely to smoothen many uncertainties in the history of north-western South Asia during the Bronze Age.

Ideology

The earliest Vedic literature of South Asia, which took a concrete shape in the north-west of the subcontinent possibly during the Middle Bronze Age, is one such oral text, which represents an ideology of nature worship, a liturgical dialect for communication and transmission of the ideology, a formalized mode of behaviour and a distinct social identity for the faithful and endless accounts of conflicts with non-believers, who are called enemies. It is argued that ideologies are found in all societies in which there are systematic and ingrained inequalities between groups and that those who hold power may depend mainly on the influence of ideology to retain their dominance, but are usually able also to use force if necessary

(Giddens, 1997, 583). Since ideology is a mechanism for exercising symbolic power, hiding, justifying or legitimizing the interests of dominant groups in the social order (Thompson, 1990), the formulation and propagation of a new religious ideology through a vast body of oral literature calls for deeper probing and contextualization. A close observation of the bardic compositions reveals that the groups, which had lost their earlier position and were trying to regain it, employed both these methods. Who were these groups and what were the surroundings? Even a cursory look at the nature and intensity of conflicts related in the text should suffice to highlight a gripping social crisis in the area. Textual evidence of a severe economic regression caused and compounded by persistent geo-climatic disorders and the resultant social displacements and raging hegemonic conflicts can be partially reconstructed from the archaeological records as well. Clearly, the second half of the second millennium BC, traditionally projected as the age of the *Ṛgveda,* does not hold water for such developments but the same information becomes instructive and insightful when viewed in the context of the decay and degeneration of Harappan society during the Middle and Late Bronze Ages.

The hegemonic conflicts, which involved fights amongst Ārya chiefs, between Ārya and Dāsa chiefs and between Ārya chiefs and a coalition of Dāsa, Vṛtra and Ārya chiefs show that political interests frequently compromised on religious differences. But at the social and religious levels, the ideology underlined the interests of a class already dominant in the society or trying to become one through a knowledge–power mechanism to consolidate such dominance. In the earlier urban dispensation, the knowledge related to management skills in the production, collection and distribution of merchandise besides political management of power and subordination. In the post-urban scenario, the knowledge related to the management of minds ravaged by persistent geo-climatic and social disturbances. Viewed from this angle, the earliest composers of *Ṛgveda* hyms appeared just about the time the events were taking place and not long afterwards, when these events had become part of a relatively unrelated past.

A useful concept which helps to analyse the interrelation of conflict and consensus is that of ideology, values and beliefs which help, secure the position of more powerful groups at the expense of less powerful ones. We have always to examine the connections between consensus and the goals their members pursue which often reflect a mixture of common and opposed interests (Giddens, 1997, 571). All this holds good in relation to social churnings taking place in the north-west of South Asia during the middle and late Bronze Ages. Conflicts already inherent in the accumulation of social goods within fortified settlements flared up with the disintegration of a collaborative political economy based on trade and towns and violence became the order of the day. In the chaotic situation, erstwhile social groups were trying to reposition themselves and retain or regain as much political and economic clout as possible. Invocation of a new religious ideology, which symbolized the elitist notion of good and bad, progressive and regressive, lionizing the erstwhile Harappan power groups and marginalizing all others appears to have come very handy. The groups, which were developing this mechanism called themselves noble or Ārya and the groups that were sought to be relegated to an inferior position were called enemies or Dasyu. This appears to have been the motivation for the formulation of a two-tier hierarchy of the higher Āryavarṇa and lower Dāsavarṇa. Many of the erstwhile professional groups, which were trying to reposition themselves in a fast-mutating social hierarchy, also elevated their icons to the status of a divinity. Some good examples of this process are Aśvins, the twin physician brothers, Tvaṣṭā, the artificer *par excellence*, Ṛbhus, master chariot makers, Paṇis, bankers and financiers of the third millennium BC besides numerous chiefs who gratified the poets with munificent charities. The new religious dispensation cut across ethno-cultural boundaries and tried to integrate as many diverse groups of people as possible under a common religious umbrella without perhaps any conscious attempt to resurrect the values and prospects of an erstwhile urban phenomenon.

Naming the ideology, attention may converge on two crucial words, Deva or Devtā and Ārya. Deva or Devtā (lit.

'that which shines'), which represents anything and everything between the heaven and the earth is the subject of every hymn or rather every stanza, and therefore central to the whole corpus and the system it propagates. Accordingly, the new religion can be described as the ideology of Deva worship or just Deva ideology. The importance of this idea is stressed by the old Avestan literature which distinguishes between Deva or Deuu and Ārya or Airya. The former is severely denounced but the latter is implored to join hands with the followers of Ahura Mazda. This distinction suggests that the Deuu were different from the Airya, though such distinction is, by and large, inapplicable to the social horizon of *Ṛgveda* poetry. As for the term Ārya, it relates to the followers of the system and not the system itself.

Environment

Set as they are in the background of the Harappan civilizational process, the majority of hymns cannot but describe the turns and twists of an erstwhile globally interactive urban system in its decadent stages. The fortified places, some ruined, some dilapidated and some others still serviceable, provide a perfect setting for the Harappan urban places about the close of the third millennium and the beginning of the second millennium BC. The sluggish nature of merchant activities either through caravan trade or through marginal coastal voyages documented in the archaeological records, also corresponds fairly well to scattered textual data on such activities. But the most important correspondence relates to catastrophic geo-climatic events and the consequent social upheavals not merely in the Greater Indus Valley but also in the adjoining areas of Afghanistan, Iran and South Central Asia. From the tenor of narration in many of the stanzas, these events appear to have been the first-hand experiences of bardic families, which formed part of the Harappan demographic composition.

The decay and disintegration of the Harappan civilization and the consequent destabilization of the civil society structured on the system of urban networking created conditions of social unrest affecting all sections of the society. In many cases the turmoil was expressed symbolically or passed unrecorded. The turbulence was, however, loud and clear in two segments of society: the political elite in the resource centres and the peasants in the distant countryside. For the political elite, perched precariously on meagre supplies of peasant goods, the main purpose was to expand their authority in the immediate neighbourhood through the capture of resource centres (*pur*) in the area. The bardic accounts relating to the capture of fortified resource centres simply appear to revisit similar events in the Harappan context. This would be a logical consequence of the breakdown of a power structure in which every group used to extend its cooperation to the favourable authority in the existing federal political economy. As for fortified resource centres, these varied from very large citadels to middling ones made of stones, burnt bricks, mud bricks or mud dotting not only north-western South Asia but also Afghanistan, Eastern Iran and South Central Asia during the Bronze Age.

In the countryside, the unrest took a different form involving the two segments of peasantry, one benefiting from the hydraulic enterprise of the state and the other living far away from the benefit area. Conflicts over sharing river water by parties living upstream and downstream or on either bank of the river have always been a constant of agrarian history. Peasant groups which lived far away from the river would be already hard-pressed for a share of the river water, the damming of which would only compound their difficulties. The Harappan state tried to raise productivity in the fields by regulating the flow of water through construction of dams fitted with sluices. In the bardic imagery, these dams appeared to represent the demons Vṛtra and Ahi who obstructed the flow of river water. At one place, the former is described as *nadīvṛtra* (one who holds back the river or stream, 8.12.26). At another place, his close associate Ahi is characterized as *abjām* (7.34.16), meaning born or lying in the water (Gonda, 1959). In most instances, Vṛtra represents a dam probably of the Harappan *gabarband* type. The peasants who captured land and the water from the enemy or damaged the barrages on the river, particularly the sluices, would do so only if they had the expertise of field agriculture and control drainage.

With the regression of the hydraulic enterprise of the state, larger groups of peasantry were left to fend for themselves with the help of large and deep wells or underground channels bringing water to the fields from distant foothill fountains or other sources of water. However, these devices may not have been adequate in view of the hyper-arid conditions and the disappearance of the southwest monsoon from the area. With the groundwater level continuously going deeper and beyond the reach of the peasantry, the spectre of famine loomed large in the countryside. In the context of a deprived peasantry, it would be a small step towards describing the conditions as the doings of a demon of drought, Śuṣṇa, and arch enemy of Indra mentioned nearly forty times in the text and thrice together with kuyava meaning bad harvests.

People

The people who were involved in these multiple processes of resource generation, resource control, cooperation, competition and conflict at different periods of Bronze Age history in the north-west of South Asia belonged to diverse ethnic and sub-ethnic communities in disparate geographical regions with divergent social formations. The large number of archaeological cultures strewn all over the area show distinct modes of life represented by habitational remains in the form of structures, artifacts and subsistence goods. Some of these lie beside modern human habitation, some lie beneath such occupation, some have disappeared altogether and some lie in forlorn plains, hill tracks or forests. At the same or different points of time, these communities could have represented nomadic cattle keepers, large-scale peasant communities, trading agglomerates, small and big urban enclaves besides professional groups of miners and gem-cutters on the highlands and colonies of fishermen and shell workers along the coast, the likes of which would be commonplace in north-western South Asia during the Bronze Age. During the mature phase of urbanization, these divergent social formations formed parts of urban networking to the extent needed on either side. But during the decaying stages of Harappan civilization, these groups broke loose from the urban order or maintained a marginal relationship to the extent beneficial to either party. Pastoral communities, marginal trading groups, even semi-urban communities would be around, but the society as a whole was agrarian with insulated peasant localities as the foci of production.

The ethnic and sub-ethnic groups associated with different archaeological assemblages in the entire area cannot, however, be identified except vaguely, by associating the remote ancestors of the present inhabitants with the creation of these ethno-cultural identities. Textual data created and circulated about the Middle Bronze Age and afterwards may provide some degree of correspondence between archaeological cultures and their makers. It has already been argued that the *Ṛgveda* encapsulates multiple social processes over a long period of time involving divergent peoples at different levels of social development (Nandi, 2001). These peoples appear to have represented diverse ethnic or sub-ethnic categories, some of which are named and can possibly be associated with definite geographical regions. A large number of these groups are mentioned in connection with the ten kings' battle (7.18). They are the Bhalanas or people inhabiting the Bolan valley, Śivas (Siboi of the Greeks) who occupied the sibi region east of the Bolan valley and Pakthas (Greek paktues), the ancient inhabitants of modern Pakhtoonistan. The Biṣāṇin or Śṛngin appear to have represented a branch of horn-hooded Scythians. Elsewhere the text refers to Gāndhāṛīs (1.126), people of the Gāndhāra region in the Swat valley, probably the creators of the Gāndhāra Grave Culture of early and mid-second millennium BC. Similarly, Vasiṣṭhas and their clients tṛtsus are distinguished by their white robes and braided locks of hair knotted on one side of the head (7.83.8), reminding us of *Kācchikā cūḍā* mentioned by Pāṇini in connection with the people of the Kutch region. Śambara and his people, who lived in their pit dwellings in a high mountainous region, can likewise be identified with the Neolithic people of the Karewa culture in the vale of Kashmir during the late third and early second millennium BC. These are only a few of a very large number of ethnic communities which defy identification.

Considering the millennial scale of the *Ṛgveda* compositions, there would be many such peoples and episodes, like the ten kings' battle, which brought diverse ethnic communities together for a common political interest. The people who came together and fought for a common cause appear to have communicated with one another through one or more hybrid dialects, which stood halfway between the ethnic dialect and the vernacular Vedic dialect resulting in substantial exchange of linguistic features from one side to the other. This may explain the presence of several lexical and structural items which do not conform to the majoritarian usage in the existing Śākalya text. The intrusion of Vedic linguistic elements into the ethnic dialects is, however, difficult to ascertain in the absence of textual records, occasional gleanings from their modern versions notwithstanding. In the course of these interactions, many of the non-Vedic communities embraced Vedic rituals and lifestyles and some were even raised to the position of the Ārya.

Language

The presence of several ethnic and sub-ethnic communities in an area presupposes the existence of several ethnic dialects and considerable amount of bilingualism leading to the exchange of lexical, structural and phonological features. However, any evidence of the survival of such a process is unlikely in the absence of scripted or oral texts. The north-west of South Asia has been accredited with a scripted language, the script characterized as Indus or Harappan script and the language as Dravidian. Perhaps neither was a reality (Farmer *et al.* 2004, 48). The so-called Harappan script, which has defied repeated attempts to decipher it, could have been just a sign system intended to fulfil limited political, economic and religious purposes, the meaning and significance of the signs and symbols being well known to the users. The arrangement seems to have worked well in a vast multilingual space cutting across linguistic barriers of communication in conveying selected political, economic and religious messages.

The multilingual character of the Greater Indus Valley during the Bronze Age seems fairly well attested to by a vast body of floating oral text circulating about this time and later. The dialects, which were spoken in the area and have survived in the form of substrates in different portions of the Śākalya text are Prakrit, Munda and Dravidian besides the Old Vedic dialect itself. The proximity of the Old Vedic dialect to Zend may suggest that the Zend was the fifth dialect spoken in the area particularly west of the Indus river. Certain diasporic European relatives of Old Vedic like Tocharian may also have existed in the vicinity. The possibility of a hybrid dialect, Elamo-Dravidian formed as a result of intensive bilingualism between the Elamite and the Dravidian, besides a branch of the Sino-Tibetan family circulating in certain parts of the Indo-Iranian subcontinent, is also in the reckoning. Some of the ethnic dialects current during the Bronze Age may also have disappeared as a result of super-session by other dialects.

A few observations about the Old Vedic dialect, which forms the main basis of the present discourse, may be in order here. Contrary to the common assumption that the language of the *Ṛgveda* was an exclusive liturgical dialect and a guarded preserve of religious functionaries who created it (Trautmann, 2005 Intro, 18), there are all the signs of a genuine historical development in which a whole society of men took part (Arnold, 1905, 21) and the poetry itself was the result of great political and social changes (Arnold, 1905, 1). The most important thing about the *Ṛgveda* compositions is that while all hymns are poems, all poems are not hymns and even all hymns do not have any overt religious justification. A considerable number of the hymns may best be described as legend spells or mythical examples which, on being recited in an analogous situation, were believed to fulfil the desired objective of the reciter (Gonda, 1977, 118). Evidently the non-ritualistic compositions, which account for nearly one-sixth of the ten thousand odd *mantras* or stanzas, occupy a very important position in the whole corpus. These mundane compositions together with a large number of nature poems without any religious significance constitute what Arnold describes as the popular *Ṛgveda* as opposed to the divine *Ṛgveda*. The system of nature worship, so much hyped by scholars, was thus a major and not the only purpose of the *Ṛgveda* compositions. Stanzas belonging to the popular poetry and the religious poetry, which were composed by unrelated peoples in different conditions are, however, found together showing through the artificial nature of the arrangement of stanzas and hymns planned and executed by the redactors, probably several centuries after the original compositions. The composers of the stanzas came from all sections of the society: chiefs, merchants, craftsmen, navigators, peasants, physicians, poison doctors, besides professional poets looking for patronage. Each of these segments reflects in some way or the other its immediate interest, divinizing concerned icons and chanting praises for well-defined goals. The stanzas, one or two-liners, when bereft of metrical arrangements, are no more than simple prose compositions frequently without an important component like noun, verb, nominal declension or verbal declension, reading like half sentences put together by the strangest of similes and metaphors mystifying the whole passage. The sanctimonious aura traditionally associated with *Ṛgveda* compositions thus falls apart.

The large degree of cognatic relationship between European dialects and the dialects of South Asia and Iran also needs an explanation. Since such a relationship can emerge only after a long period of physical contiguity and acculturation, the role of demographic movement from one continent to another cannot be ruled out, notwithstanding the assertion that physical contact is not necessary for language change (Barth, 1972). However, such demographic movements can be established only on the basis of hard historical evidence, like skeletal records of Asiatic people in Europe or of European communities in Asia. The idea of a European origin of Indo-Europeans and/or Indo-European languages remains highly specious in the absence of any explanation of why and when the speakers of Indic and Iranic dialects headed for Europe and, if they did, what is the testimony of their arrival in the physical biology of the white continent. Since Mediterraneans are common to both Europe and Asia, particularly South Asia, one would expect some evidence of the proto-Australoids who constitute the bulk of

South Asian population. But so far, no proto-Australoids have been reported from Europe.

Compared to this, ethnic Europeans are known to have migrated to different parts of Asia right from the time of the Neanderthals, mainly under the heat of inhospitable geo-climatic conditions. The presence of Alpines or proto-Nordics in the physical biology of Asia after 4500 BC shows that similar trends continued during the early Holocene Age as well. This might suggest that migration of ethnic Europeans (not the imaginary Indo-Europeans) must have been an event of the early Holocene Age. This seems likely in view of the geo-climatic conditions in Europe and Asia, the former reeling under an extreme dry-cold regime, which nearly destroyed the habitat economy in large parts of the continent, and the latter experiencing a warmer and comparatively more humid conditions during the same period. Migration to certain parts of the northern Mediterranean, which too enjoyed a favourable environment during the early Holocene Age, is also not unlikely. Long periods of contact between ethnic European dialects and the dialects of the Indo-Iranian subcontinent during the post-early Holocene phase may have given rise to the 'Centum' division of the Indo-European family. Estimates of the linguistic chronology of the Indo-European languages suggest that much of their common vocabulary has a more recent origin, about 7,000 years ago (Swadesh, 1972). However, this was only the preliminary stage of language contact followed by several such episodes of migration not only from Europe to Asia but also *vice versa* during the fourth, third and second millennium BC. During the fourth millennium BC, for instance, there could have been an episode of diasporic return to Europe following the onset of mid-Holocene hyper-arid conditions in vast tracts of Asia. This may have coincided with the arrival of the Centum dialect in Europe, where a new phase of bilingualism between the older ethnic dialects and the newly arrived Centum dialect got underway.

Chapter 1

The Problem of Source and Method

The Problem of Original Text

Doubts relating to the originality of the existing Śākalya text have frequently been expressed on two counts. First, the presence of retroflexed consonants in the existing Śākalaya text and the supposition that the original *Ṛgveda* did not contain any such speech sounds. The other ground for suspecting the originality of the present text relates to additions and deletions of textual materials at the transmission and editing stages. According to some, retroflexion is an independent and well-motivated process which began in pre-Vedic Indo-Aryan. However, they do not explain why it began in the first place. According to others, retroflexion in Indo-Aryan is a result of contacts with Dravidians and/or Mundas, and that such contacts must have occurred during pre-Vedic times. In either case, the development is said to have occurred during pre-Vedic times and, as such, there is not much contradiction between the two opinions. Since the text composition did not take place in a social vacuity, the influence of spoken dialects, Prakrit, Munda or Dravidian, on the phonology of the Mantra dialect would be inevitable. This is logical as well in view of the fact that the Indo-Aryan comprised Sanskrit and a non-Sanskrit segments (Bubenik, 1996, 1), which provide accommodation for all linguistic fraternities, that bear varying degrees of cognatic relationship with Sanskrit. In other words, Prakrit, Munda and Dravidian can be treated as close linguistic relatives of Vedic Sanskrit and exchange of linguistic elements between the non-Sanskrit and Sanskrit segments is a perfectly normal linguistic process. It is also likely that many of the speakers of these dialects were actually involved in the process of text composition. This rules out the likelihood of an *Ur* text of the *Ṛgveda* being supposedly unblemished by retroflexed speech sounds.

The area where the *Ṛgveda* hymns were composed already has the tendency to cerebralize certain dentals, like n/ṇ, l/ḷ, s/ṣ. The linguistic scenario of pre-Vedic and Vedic times at least till the time of editing of the *Rgveda* was divided into two groups: one used cerebrals or retroflexed consonants and the other was more comfortable with non-retroflexed consonants like dentals and palatals. The mere existence of two parallel sets of speech sounds within the same or different linguistic communities is no evidence for assigning higher antiquity to one of these and associating it with the hypothetical Ur-*Ṛgveda,* as Deshpande does (Deshpande, 1993, 130). Deshpande (Deshpande, 1993, 137) himself almost suggests this when he refers to the Kāṭhaka tradition of using dentals as well as cerebrals in the same vocable (*panyāt/paṇyāt*) and the *Maitrāyaṇī* preference for the cerebral ṇ (*paṇyāt*). The *Kāthaka Samhitā* merely suggests the absence of any strong difference in the doctrine of retroflexion among editors at the earlier stages of Black Yajus reconstruction. By the time the *Maitrāyaṇī Samhitā* was being constituted, the editors had firmly settled for the doctrine of retroflexed sounds in the concerned vocables. If conjecture is the logic, it can be argued that the Indo-Aryan language and its most dominant representative, the Vedic language, always contained retroflexed speech sounds as a normal feature of phonology and, that the occasional substitution of retroflexed sounds by non-retroflexed ones was the doing of those composers or editors who were more used to non-retroflexed sounds as a matter of habit rather than as a matter of design. It is common knowledge that even within a single linguistic community, speech sounds take quite different forms. Consider the various phonological versions of English spoken in different parts of India. Similarly, each of the different Indian languages shows wide sub-regional and local variations, both lexical and phonological. The importance of retroflexed sounds in the Vedic language is fairly well suggested by the amount of respect and credibility which the author of *Prātiśākhya* and Pāṇini associate with the editors mentioned in the *Aitareya Āraṇyaka* and also by the fact that these editors described ṇ as the strength and ṣ as the breath of the *Samhitā*, which put Prajāpati together with the help of metres. From the tenor of description, the term *Samhitā* in this context appears to represent the whole 'continuous, undivided text', rather than a *sandhi*, 'joint, euphonic combination, juncture' suggesting gathering together of parts.

The question relating to the omissions and additions at the time of editing also has to be considered in a larger perspective. According to Bloch (Bloch, 1920/1970), the editors of the *Ṛgveda*, as we have it, partially adapted to their own dialects various religious texts composed in another dialect. If we accept Bloch's opinion, retroflexed consonants, should register their universal presence in the text. Second, how would one explain the increasing influence of retroflexion in the middle Indo-Aryan? Was it also because of the editor's hand? It is a queer logic that speakers of non-Vedic dialects always turned out to be editors and redactors but never composers or authors of Vedic texts. Commenting on pre-redactional textual transmission, Oldenberg (Oldenberg, 1890/1962, 27) observes that 'in some cases isolated details of the additions of prior epochs were caught and clung to with felicitous acumen, in others, no hesitation was had in wiping out of existence entire domains of old and genuine phenomena to suit half-correct theories, so that the most patent ingenuity of mode to restore in part what has been lost'. He further observes (Oldenberg, 1890/1962, 26) that the collection was re-corrected on repeated occasions often injuring, effacing or destroying the existence of special hymns. However, the marginal nature of these changes would be inconsequential in a text of ten thousand odd stanzas and historical reconstructions based on the text. A much more radical example of the speculative deconstruction of the text is furnished by Esteller (Esteller, 1968, 16; 1969, 17), who thinks that the present Śākalya text is a 'Palimpsest', a written-over text, which was 'woven twenty-five centuries ago by the skillful and well-meaning but deformingly reforming, updatingly defacing (and thus palimpsesting) Pandita-mentality of the Samhitākāra agency in the Śākalya Śākhā tradition'. This is to allege without much good reason that the redactors made 'conscious' grammatical changes and changes in the word order, reducing the text to a document of the Pāṇinian Age. Even this would not affect the intrinsic value of the contents for reconstructing social processes of a much earlier period. But speculative deconstruction such as this has rightly been under the scanner and rejected (Abhyankar, 1969; Mehendale, 1975).

The hymns of the *Ṛgveda* are in the nature of folk literature, which circulated long before these were assigned a liturgical value, about the beginning of the second millennium BC and much later put into a ritualistic straightjacket. The three stages allow for considerable addition and alteration in the stanzas or the hymns, some deliberate and some blamed on loss of memory. Besides, the families of poets who belonged to different geographical regions and cultural traditions made room for their own preference in the compositions. It was these families of poets or priests, which subsequently grouped into separate Vedic schools and the texts preserved by them surfaced as separate recensions of the *Ṛgveda*. Since the entire process reached a finality about the time of the later Vedic *Samhitās*, around 1000 BC, all additions and subtractions relating to the text took place between 2000 BC and 1000 BC. Taken together, these would have little impact on the overall text composition or historical reconstruction based on it.

Arguing from a so-called 'indigenous' perspective, one would like to suggest that right from the beginning of the Early Bronze Age the Dravidian and Munda speech area extended from South Asia to Iran and probably as far west and northwest as the Near East and eastern Europe. Indo-Aryan and Indo-Iranian were entrenched in the Indo-Iranian subcontinent from about the same time. The sharing of common linguistic features, like retroflexion by Indo-Aryan, Dravidian and Munda would be a normal feature of language development in the region. Retroflexion, though regressive also appears in the Nuristani and East Iranian languages (Hock, 1993, 96), the regression being the result of ethno-geographical and cultural separation, progressively consolidated by historical changes. Another innovative feature of the Vedic language is the use of the postposed quotative *iti*, which too seems to have been paralleled by the Avestan *ūtī* (Hock, 1993). There have also been claims of loans from Dravidian into Avestan as well as Vedic, which have been constructed as coming from the Indo-Iranian period (Southworth, 1990).

The Problem of Text Variation

From the methodological angle, data recovery is frequently threatened by uncertainties of time, space and context. The present ordering of hymns and stanzas is based on purely ritualistic interests, which defies thematic classification of historical materials. Metrical and linguistic considerations relating to the so-called early and late portions of the text further complicate this. There are no good reasons to believe that the present arrangement of hymns was handed down in this shape to priestly posterity. On the contrary, the existence of several recensions of the text of which as many as six were known to Pāṇini (Vasu, 1891) would suggest variations of a substantial nature, in both content and classification of the hymns. Since recensions of a text originate from variations in the reading, the existence of half a dozen recensions of the *Ṛgveda*, raise serious doubts about the uniformity of textual matter. The omissions and interpolations came on record as attempts were made to write down the work. A comparison of the first *aṣṭakā* of the Bāṣkala recension with the commentary of Skandasvāmin, one in the Grantha script and the other in the Malayalam characters, shows that passages included in the Grantha recension are omitted in the Malayalam recension and vice versa (Raja, 1935). Similarly, in the Śākalya recension, the hymns are arranged into ten *maṇḍalas* with widely varying numbers of *sūktas* whereas in the Bāṣkala recension the hymns are arranged into eight *aṣṭakās* of more or less even size. Since both Śākalya and Bāṣkala appear in later Vedic texts, the reconstruction of the existing text may have taken place about the beginning of the later Vedic age. The chief compulsion behind this must have been the priestly urge to draw upon a standard work for sacrificial purposes.

The Problem of Stratification

Judging by the classification of the hymns, much of which dominated the greater part of the later Vedic period, the present text of the *Ṛgveda* can be divided into four parts. The first segment is constituted by the six family books (Books II–VII) in which Agni hymns are invariably followed by Indra hymns. The next component comprises the eighth book, in which the hymns are arranged on the basis of the composers (*ārṣānukrama*). To this part also belong the first fifty hymns of the first book, which, like those of the eighth, were composed by the members of the Kāṇva family. The eighth book on account of the interpolation of Vālakhilya hymns (8.49-59), may have constituted the final part of the text in the first round of its constitution. The ninth book, which represents the desire of Udgātā priests to collect all the hymns of Pavamāna Soma at one place, followed soon thereafter. Unlike the family books, which follow the order of gods *(devatānukramaṇi),* the hymns of the ninth book are arranged in the order of metres (*chandānukramaṇi*), all compositions in one metre being arranged together. In the matter of artificiality, each of the three segments seems to compete with the others, the contents of the hymns being irrelevant in every case. The tenth book, which is a medley collection of very late and very early materials, may have emerged in the final round of the constitution of the text.

The tenth book, which contains a large number of diverse materials, simulates the appendix of a book. The appendix is where it is not because its materials were scripted after the publication of the book but because the materials could not be organically structured into the main chapters of the book as envisaged by the author or authors. The same reasoning applies to the eighth book which abounds in Pragātha compositions, or the ninth book, which is a guarded preserve of the Soma oblators. Expressions like 'late book' or 'late portions' of the text are clearly subjective and based on the presumption that certain developments like monarchical polity or peasant forms of production could not be earlier than the later Vedic age. This perception is clearly mistaken since the text furnishes quantifiable data from almost every book to show that both these developments were central to the earliest Vedic society of South Asia (Nandi, 2001).

Detailed work done by Oldenberg and Bergaigne on the family compositions shows a well thought-out priestly scheme of classification, of which three determinants are collections of hymns containing *tṛca* compositions, precedence of the Agni hymns to hymns dedicated to other gods, a larger hymn followed by smaller hymns dedicated to the same god (Majumdar and Pusalker, 1951, 228). In terms of historical sequence, it would be highly unrealistic to dub these compositions as the 'kernel' (Keith, 1921, 69) or 'nucleus' (Smith, 1919) of the text of the *Ṛgveda.* The terms 'kernel' and 'nucleus' do not have any chronological significance. These simply mean the most important part or the core of the text. This is absolutely justified by the importance attached to the family compositions in the ritualistic circles of the later Vedic age and afterwards.

Of the three determinants of a hymn, the metre (*chanda*), deity (*devatā*) and composer (*ṛṣi*), the first is the structural basis of a hymn and therefore needs no verification. Similarly, the names or epithets of gods are frequently mentioned in the hymns and cannot be doubted. But the names of composers are only occasionally mentioned in the invocatory passage. Evidently, unless specifically mentioned, as in very few cases, the authorship of hymns remains a matter of conjecture and fabrication. The brief prose passage, which today prefaces every *sūkta* of the *Ṛgveda* comes, in handy for interpolation of the names of composers. In his commentary on the first *aṣṭakā,* Skandasvāmin names several composers who do not find a place in standard lists of composers. The source from which the commentator got these names is also unknown (Raja, 1935). The insertion of the name of a composer into the prefatory of a *sūkta,* which may have been earlier confined to a mention of the metre and the god, was particularly facile since there was no question of interfering with the structure or content of the hymn. Evidently, the *ārṣānukramaṇi* (index of poets) largely originates from the preface of the *sūkta* whereas the indices of gods and metres derive from the content and structure of the hymns respectively.

Despite recognizing that the tradition of bardic genealogies so well formalized in the *ārṣānukramaṇi* (index of poets) does not conform to the evidence of hymns, (Winternitz, 1972, 58), most Vedicists continue to confide in the 'ascription' of certain portions of the *text* to certain families of bardic composers. Despite also recognizing that hymns of a *maṇḍala* represent materials of widely separated periods (Winternitz, 1972, 57), there is no dearth of optimism to project the so-called family portions of the text as the 'oldest and homogeneous' (Keith, 1921). In the hymns of the family books there is nothing to suggest that stray composers named here and there were contemporaries, which alone can lend 'homogeneity' to the family compositions. On the other hand, judging even by the Puranic tradition, there would be a gap of several generations between one such composer and another. For instance, Gṛtsamada, who is named in the second book, belonged to the third generation of Bhṛgu whereas Bhāradvāja, the chief poet of the sixth book, belonged to the seventh generation of Angirā. Even if Bhṛgu and Angirā were contemporaries, the works of their descendants would be distanced by a century or more. Some amount of diligence in the reading and understanding of bardic compositions would suffice to show that far from representing a record of a 'homogeneous' people, the family books are pervaded by a great plurality of social formations, some conterminous and some others separated by time and territory.

A relative chronology of poets and chiefs may help stratify different *maṇḍalas* or parts thereof and the geographic horizons associated with these individuals and the groups to which they belong. This can also ascertain the geographical regions or subregions central to the related compositions. But, owing to divergent perceptions or presumptions, the methodology yields very different results in different writings. According to one scholar (Talageri, 2000), the *maṇḍalas* can be stratified into early, middle, late and very late portions of the text. Examining geographic horizons expressed in this chronological sequence, Talageri argues that the Vedic Aryans expanded from the interior of India to the west and north-west. However, another study (Witzel, 1995a), which employs the same method to establish a relative chronology of chiefs and poets suggests that the geographic horizon of these compositions indicates migration from outside South Asia in trickles, tribe after tribe, clan after clan. So far as the text is concerned, there is no basis to suggest that the Vedic Aryans expanded from the interior of India to the west and north-west or that they migrated from outside South Asia.

Another important basis of stratification relates to lexical, grammatical and metrical variations in the text. These may represent diverse forms of poetry rather than a chronological division of *Ṛgveda* compositions. For instance, certain grammatical features like *adha* and *atha*, *eva* and *evam* are supposed to represent archaic and late features in the text (Macdonell, 1916). These need not constitute any indicators of dialect development in the *Ṛgveda* and the so-called early and later forms often appear in the compositions of the same poet, frequently side by side. There is, however no dearth of structural and lexical variation within the Ṛgvedic dialect, which underlined some sort of ethnolinguistic divergence at the same time or during succeeding periods of *Ṛgveda* compositions.

Attempts to stratify the text on the basis of grammatical and lexical features frequently overlook the preferences of poets in these matters and the suitability of certain words and grammatical forms in literary works intended for exclusive ritualistic purposes. In other words, certain words and grammatical forms are discarded not because the poets are unfamiliar with these but because of the specific requirements of liturgical poetry. Even when such an exercise is undertaken, the so-called early and late grammatical features and vocabulary work at cross purposes. This can be evidenced from the detailed work done by specialists.

Certain grammatical features like the anathematic flexional forms of nouns and the extended use of the perfect, aorist, subjunctive, and infinitive systems, which are conspicuous in the earlier *Ṛgveda*, seem to distinguish the earlier portions of the *Ṛgveda* from its alleged late portions. 'However, the differences of vocabulary lead directly to a somewhat different conclusion. Amongst the "popular" words there are many of Indo-European origin, having to do with the familiar objects and activities of ordinary life, which must certainly have been familiar to the poets of the *Ṛgveda* proper, though seldom used by them. Hence we are led to the contrast between the "heroic" and the "popular" language, and to the possibility that both may have been simultaneously in use for different purposes' (Arnold, 1905, 24).

The Problem of 'Social Location'

Considering that the earliest Vedic literature of South Asia was the product of widespread depredation in nature and society, the information derived from the hymns needs thematic classification and contextualization. Writing nearly a century ago, Arnold observed that 'the ten *maṇḍalas* or cycles have gathered up the work of many periods, and that the original composition of the hymns was probably the work of several centuries. Great political and social changes occurred during the period in which this poetry was produced, but of these there exists no record, except such as is contained in the pages of the *Ṛgveda* itself, or may be distantly inferred from our knowledge of the general history of mankind' (Arnold, 1905, 1). Our knowledge of the general history of mankind has since improved considerably, which may facilitate a reasoned correlation of what is recorded in the pages of the *Ṛgveda* with the information preserved in the archaeological record of northwestern South Asia during the Bronze Age.

Since the compositions were in the nature of folk songs, they could be authored as much by articulate poet–priests as by mundane professionals like chiefs, warriors, merchants, physicians, craftsmen, navigators, peasants, who, depending on the circumstances, could be both composers as well as subjects and objects of the compositions. The generic term poet (*kavi*) is a postscript not always strictly related to the compositions. A hymn describing diverse agricultural activities could thus turn out to be the work of a peasant just as descriptions of sea faring could be the work of a navigator. Sometimes the professional tag is prefixed to the name of the poet as in the case of Bhiṣag Atharvan. The degree of expertise in the Mantra dialect would also vary accordingly. The poet–priests who wished to invoke and motivate divine powers used and articulated forms of the dialect employing select metres, vocabulary and word structures. Other composers, whose main interest was to document the experiences of everyday life, used a more earthy dialect using a different set of metres or a combination of such metres, a mundane vocabulary and word structure. This may have been the basis for distinguishing between divine poetry and popular poetry, both of which circulated as simultaneous parallel developments. However, at the time of final arrangement, the two forms of poetry got mixed up with compositions in popular metres like the epic *anuṣṭubha* or the epic *pankti* appearing alongside the more sanctimonious metres like *triṣṭubha, anuṣṭubha* and *jagatī*. The distinction between religious poetry and popular poetry is also evident from the fact that while all hymns are poems, all poems are not hymns and even all hymns do not have any overt religious justification.

Many of the hymns are descriptions of nature, without any sacrificial motivation. A considerable number of the hymns may best be described as legend spells or mythical examples, which, on being recited in an analogous situation, were believed to reactivate their inherent truth or power so as to produce the effect desired by the reciter (Gonda, 1977, 118). In certain cases, parts of the hymns must have served more specific purposes, like controlling weather conditions, preserving reputation, continuance of life, funeral ceremonies, neutralizing the enemy, preventing fear of fire, neutralizing witchcraft, reviving the dead, counteracting poisoning, safe crossing of rivers, safe journey through the forest and so forth. Evidently the non-ritualistic compositions, which account for nearly one-sixth of the ten thousand odd mantras or stanzas, occupy a very important position in the whole corpus. Thus there are 'all the signs of a genuine historical development, that is of united efforts in which a whole society of men have taken part, creating an inheritance which has passed through the generations from father to son' (Arnold, 1905, 21). A study of the text undertaken from such a holistic perspective at once sidelines the interest of certain scholars in delimiting the 'social location' of the text as, for example, when it is stated that the work was 'produced and perpetuated by a category of religious specialists and reflects the outlook and interests of that category and not those of all segments of society in that time' (Trautmann, 2005 Intro., 18).

The Problem of Identity

The study of the old Vedic social processes has frequently been affected by an imprecise understanding of certain ideas and expressions like the Vedic community, the Ārya and the religious system developed by the Ārya. The Vedic-speaking community was just one of several ethnolinguistic communities which inhabited north-western South Asia during the Bronze Age. Even the Vedic community itself comprised several divisions demarcated by cultural boundaries in separate geographical subregions. Probably five of them were already known to the earliest composers of *Ṛgveda* hymns and were frequently described as *pañca jana, pañca śreṇi, pañca kṣiti, pañca carṣaṇi, pañca kṛṣṭi, pañca hotṛn* and so forth. The expression *pañca* or five, which may just be a fascination for prime numbers, nevertheless underlines the presence of several culturally divergent Vedic-speaking communities. The cultural divergence may relate to differences in physical appearance, lifestyle and language. The practice of widely divergent modes of the disposal of the dead (10.14-16; 10.18), like cremation, burial and exposure, besides a combination of two or more of these practices, may suffice to underline the cultural diversity of a people despite the use of a common language. As for divergent physical features, Kaṇva, one of the apical *Ṛgveda* poets and a prime composer of the eighth book, is frequently described as *kṛṣṇa* and *śyāva* (10.31.11), both meaning dark skinned. A chief of the Swat valley, who was a great promoter of Deva worship and was named Trasadasyu or the terror of enemies, describes himself as a dark-skinned chief (*śyāvaḥ praṇetā*, 8.19.37) and an Ārya (8.19.36).

Even the language was not as homogeneous as it seems to

be in the first appearance. A closer examination of the textual material reveals that apart from a more or less frozen liturgical dialect, there was a vernacular Vedic dialect which stood half-way between the liturgical dialect and the different non-Vedic ethnic dialects in disparate regions. The vernacular Vedic dialect developed variant forms in each of these regions, though the variations may have been limited to a few lexical, structural and phonological features resulting from the long process of bilingualism between the speakers of the vernacular Vedic dialect and those of the non-Vedic ethnic dialects. The Kaṇva poets of the eighth book spoke a variant of the Vedic dialect which is already noticeable in their compositions. These variations were confined to declensional deviants of both roots and radicals. Puru, who, like Kaṇva belonged to the Swat valley and was likewise exposed to the influence of a local dialect was also denounced by the purists of the Vedic speech as *purum mṛdhravācam* (7.18.13), meaning 'Puru who spoke a perverted dialect'. The presence of variant forms within the Vedic dialect is also evident from the expression vivāca carṣaṇaya (6.31.1; 6.33.2), *vivāca* meaning diverse speech forms and *carṣaṇaya*, a plural of *carṣaṇī* always used to signify the Vedic-speaking community. If *vivāca carṣaṇaya* meant diverse forms of Vedic speech, *vivāca mṛdhravāca* and *vivāca aśiva* (10.23.5) signified the diversity of non-Vedic dialects. Non-Vedic dialects were also characterized as *vadhṛvāca* (7.18.9) or unproductive speech. The expression relates to a speech form, which, if applied to the prayer liturgy, would produce no results.

A distinction also needs to be made between the Vedic community and a system of nature worship developed by some of its members who called themselves Ārya. Considering that the linguistic features of the Indo-European family do not go beyond 5000 BC (Swadesh, 1972), the Vedic speakers appear to have inhabited the north-west of South Asia from at least the Chalcolithic times, if not earlier. Compared to this, an articulated system of nature worship was not earlier than late-third millennium BC when this part of the subcontinent was struck by persistent geo-climatic devastations, a severe economic regression and widespread social upheavals which ripped apart the social fabric. The new religious system was supposed to restore some semblance of order in the society and recover the lost prestige and position of the erstwhile dominant classes, rulers, merchants, master craftsmen, physicians and miracle healers and, of course, poets and priests. Gifted as they were with high literary skills, the poets and singers who came from every section of society, they naturally related their compositions to diverse social processes which were happening around them. Viewed from this perspective, many of the compositions may go back to the mid or early third millennium BC and even before. As for the poems describing the pristine beauty of nature, these cut across time and space and according to the requirement of the society, could be invested with ritualistic significance as and when needed.

The term Ārya, which occurs nearly thirty-seven times in the *Ṛgveda,* has frequently been understood in the sense of an ethnic group. An ethnic group is an aggregate of people who shared a geographical area, a common language, a homo-geneous culture and were conscious of its distinction from other groups of people (Bromley, 1975, 11). The identity can also be the result of self-ascription (Barth, 1969, 10) as in the case of the Ārya. However, the underlying unity of the Ārya was one of religious affinity rather than of geographical or cultural homogeneity which is not touted anywhere in the text. Cultural differences and variations of the Vedic dialect, besides divergent physical features like skin colour are, as noted above, not far to seek in the bardic compositions. Perhaps, as an inclusive religious system which could accommodate all peoples irrespective of physical features, languages and lifestyles, the claims of the Ārya to be recognized as an ethnic group would be as strong or weak as those of the members of any of the world's major religions today. In the Iranian circle of old Avestan poets, the term Ārya was already considered an ethnonym, as would be evident from the bracketing of Airya with Sairma, Tuirya and others whom Zoroaster was constantly imploring to embrace the religion of Ahura Mazda. In South Asia, the term developed an ethnic connotation much later, probably about the time of Patañjali during the second century BC.

The Importance of Myth

Apart from the problem of stratification, there are difficulties relating to the tenor of bardic description. The narration of events is frequently crowded and camouflaged by similes and metaphors, some sensible but most others irretrievably mixed up. It is the last instance, which frequently takes the character of a myth. The Vedicists of yesteryears, whose chief concerns were comparative religion and comparative linguistics, not historical reconstruction of events recorded in the text, were no less responsible for further confounding an already complex mix-up of themes, characters and places. Take the case of Śambara and his followers, a non-Vedic people living in pit dwellings in a high mountain country and whom Indra eliminated after a forty-year quest. Not interested in investigating what this mountain country was or what the mountain abodes of Śambara looked like, Vedic scholars conjured up the image of an aerial demon and his aerial cities.

A closer examination of details relating to the Śambara story may, however, lead investigators to Neolithic pit dwellings in the Karewas of the Jhelum valley in Kashmir. Similarly, there is a large number of stories relating to Ahi, Vṛtra and Śuṣṇa all of which signify a long period of hydrological crises caused by low precipitation, blocked (dammed) rivers and widespread desiccation. The blockage of rivers caused by irrigation dams is particularly significant since these relate to the *gabarband* type of dams erected by the Harappans for proper distribution of river water. Low precipitation caused by the disappearance of the south-west monsoon from north-western South Asia was also an event of great importance in the history of this region during the middle and late Bronze Ages. A logical consequence of low precipitation during the age of mid-Holocene hyper-aridity would be large-scale desiccation and desertification, which is characteristically represented by Śuṣṇa, the demon of drought. In three passages, Śuṣṇa is mentioned together with Kuyava or the demon of bad harvest.

Since myths are considered to be camouflaged reality, the task at hand is to ascertain how far removed the event can be from the poet who dabbles in it. Sometimes a historical episode gets fragmented and distorted through superimposition of unrelated information within a few generations. However, nothing better can be expected from the poets of succeeding generations whose main purpose was to create new invocations even if it meant the worst type of cut- and paste from earlier unrelated compositions. Since it was believed that only new compositions could please the targeted divinity, it mattered little if such plagiarizing led to deconstruction of events and social processes beyond recognition. This had to happen in the absence of any scripted record of the past, which made even small periods of time become hazy and to that extent prompted the distortion of historical or semi-historical information belonging to a couple of earlier generations of poets. Piecing together bits of information from stanzas throughout the text can, however, be of substantial help in reconstructing the original story.

The Problem of Palaeo-linguistic Dating

The preoccupation of linguistic palae-ontologists with the migration idea in relation to the Indo-European language probably stems from the presumption that migrations bring different peoples together and that the togetherness of physical existence promotes ethno-linguistic devolution and the emergence of a proto-language combining dialectal elements from peoples involved in this acculturation. But such an idea can sometimes be wanting in empirical depth. Linguistic changes and affiliations are brought about by a complex series of cultural processes, many of which do not involve the physical movement of social groups (Barth, 1972). Centuries of physical contiguity do not necessarily lead to the formation of a common dialect. A study of nearly 200 Australian dialects spoken by as many as 600 tribes of Australia shows that 'except for pronouns which are similar across the continent and the limitation that there are only two or three numerals, the most striking lexical feature of Australian languages is the fewness of cognates between languages which otherwise seem closely related. Two languages may share grammatical properties and similarities in speech sounds but hardly share any vocabulary items. A curious feature is that a few cognates have been found to be shared by languages at opposite ends of the continent with no intervening cognates, (Wind *et al.*, 1994).

Here it is important to remember that historical linguistics cannot be a replication of historical processes and that linguists have often been baffled by the presence of strange linguistic elements at the strangest of places. Latest studies have shown that coexisting dialects with structural similarities can be very different lexically, just as dialects with almost the same vocabulary can have very different grammatical structures. Dialects belonging to completely different families and separated by thousands of miles are found to have striking similarities in syntax, such as English and Chinese (Wind *et al.*, 1994). No wonder the field of comparative linguistics in general and historical linguistics in particular has been characterized as a 'disaster area' forcing acknowledged linguists to opt out of it (Wind *et al.*, 1994).

The skills of a palaeo-linguist relate to textual stratigraphy and the correlation of the strata with known historical information. There is no problem in stratifying a language on the basis of phonological, lexical and grammatical principles. But the strata so determined cannot produce any hard historical dates in the absence of correlation of internal evidence with known historical events. The concept of dialect devolution, which is commonplace in historical linguistics, has its own intrinsic merits in determining the phonological and grammatical changes experienced by a particular ancient dialect. But it also needs to consider that dialect is a social product and may not experience any change if it remains socially frozen. In other words, dialect change will take place on the basis of internal social dynamics or under the compulsions of external influences, such as population shifts and contact with new ethnic, political or religious elements. From this angle, the Avestan language reflects in good measure the dialectal acquisitions resulting from contact with new peoples and new ideas in new areas. In relation to the *Avesta*, several stages in the devolution of the dialect have been argued on phonological considerations (Hoffmann, 1989), although no hard dates have been put forward for any of these stages. As such, there is no basis for saying that the dialect of the Gāthās or Yaśna Haptangaiti belonged to the fourteenth century BC and not earlier or later.

Similarly, the supposition that the mention of four Vedic gods in a Hitti-Mitannian document of 1380 BC can suffice to fix the upper limit of *Ṛgveda* compositions at about 1500 BC is arbitrary inasmuch as it wishes away the large space of time which intervenes between the beginnings of a language and literary creations in that language. By this token, the large number of West Asian inscriptions, which belong to the early seventeenth century BC and mention numerous old Vedic terms and proper names, the upper limit of the *Ṛgveda* should go back to the eighteenth century BC. Likewise, the mention of two Vedic gods in a Kassite inscription of the eighteenth century BC should push this upper limit to the nineteenth century BC. The Kassites, who lived in north-eastern Iran during the late third millennium BC may have been exposed to the influence of Vedic gods and priests in the Indo-Iranian neighbourhood before arriving in Babylonia to occupy the vacant political space after the death of Hammurabbi in 1750 BC.

From the linguistic angle also, there is little to substantiate 1500 BC as the upper limit of the *Ṛgveda* compositions. It has been convincingly shown that many of the features in the Anatolian documents are identical with Middle Indo-Aryan and therefore much later than Old Indo-Aryan of the *Ṛgveda*. These linguistic features include (1) assimilation of dissimilar plosives, i.e. *sapta* > *satta;* (2) semi-vowels and liquids not assimilated in conjunction with plosives, semi-vowels or liquids, i.e. *vartana* > *wartan, vīrya* > *birya;* (3) nasals also not assimilated to plosives, i.e., *atamna* > *artamna;* (4) frequent anaptyxis, i.e. *indra* > *indara, smara* > *sumara;* (5) initial *v* > *b,* i.e. *vīrya* > *birya, vṛdhāśva* > *bardasva;* (6) ṛ > ar, i.e. ṛta > arta, *vṛdh* > *bardh* (Misra, 1977; Misra, 1992; Misra, 1994). These features were also noticed by Kenneth Norman (Norman, 1995, 280). Hodge also draws attention to *satta,* 'seven', which is the Prakrit form of the Sanskrit *sapta* and remarks that the inscriptions show a Prakritic form of Sanskrit a thousand years before such forms were known in India itself on inscriptions (Hodge, 1981). These observations fit comfortably with the proposal that the Near Eastern kings could have left the Indian subcontinent after the early Vedic period, bringing post-Vedic, Indo-Aryan linguistic forms with them. The most drastic corollary of such a claim, as Jacobi noted, would be a major re-evaluation of the dating of the *Ṛgveda,* which must have considerably predated the appearance of the Near Eastern texts of the sixteenth century BC. In case these texts represent, as indeed they seem to do, a diachronically later as opposed to a synchronically contemporaneous dialectal form of Indo-Aryan, an upward revision of the date of the *Ṛgveda* compositions should be around (Jacobi, 1909; Jacobi, 1910).

Not much concerned with these possibilities, there have been renewed efforts to justify the upper limit of the *Ṛgveda* by drawing parallels between certain passages of the text and the Boghuz Koi document. In the 1960s, P. Thieme (Thieme, 1960; Parpola, 1995, 358*)* tried to equate the Boghuz Koi treaty with a passage of the *Ṛgveda* and argued that all these gods are invoked as protectors of treaties in the *Ṛgveda*, and in one stanza (*RV* 10.125.1) are mentioned together and in the same order. However, the enumeration in 10.125.1 (viz. Mitra, Varuṇa, Indra, Agni, Aśvin) is not the same as in the Boghuz Koi treaty (viz. Mitra, Varuṇa, Indra, Nāsatyas) as claimed by P. Thieme. There is nothing either in this stanza or elsewhere in the *Ṛgveda* to suggest that the poets of the *Ṛgveda* ever invoked these divinities as protectors of treaties. The subject of this composition is not the group of five divinities mentioned together with two more groups of divinities, but Ātman or the world soul, who is the source of the entire creation and who makes everything fall in place including the gods and goddesses. The expressions *aham carāmi* and *aham vibhrami* leave no doubt about this. Interestingly, the passage in question (10.125.1) occurs in the tenth book which is traditionally supposed to represent the latest portions of the *Ṛgveda* and, accordingly, should be assigned to 1000 BC rather than 1500 BC.

Dates in Archaeology

C^{14} dates, which till recently constituted the main basis of chronological determination in archaelogy are invariably accompanied by a large margin of error ranging from ±110 to 150 years. This would mean that any sample recovered from a particular phase can be assigned to any date during a period of three hundred years. And, if the sample has a borderline date between two phases, it may make the confusion worse confounded in terms of chronological sequence. C^{14} samples can work fairly well in relation to large time frames such as those we have in the geological ages and their subdivisions. The samples may also provide a good starting point for broad historical time frames such as early third millennium BC, mid-third millennium BC, late-third millennium BC, early second-millennium BC and so forth. Each of these time frames spans a little over a quarter of a millennium which encapsulates a complex process of incubation beyond the reach of scholars at the moment. So far no alternative method of dating is forthcoming to stratify each of these periods into smaller units of time and provide an incisive view of processual dynamic which monitored transition from early to the mature phase or from mature to the late phase of the Harappan civilization. Dendrochronological and sedimentological studies, which provide annual graphs based on tree rings and lake layers, are yet to pick up in South Asia on a significant scale.

Despite diligent efforts to calibrate and recalibrate C^{14} dates, the uncertainties associated with the production and distribution of radioactive carbon in the atmosphere make the chronology considerably vulnerable. In 1958, De Bries showed that the atmospheric C^{14} did not remain constant through the ages. Stuiver (Stuiver, 1965) subsequently correlated these variations and those of solar activity perceived from the number of sun spots on the sun's surface. When the solar activity is high, the number of sun spots increases and the cosmic rays deflected by solar winds bombard the upper atmosphere with less intensity and consequently production of C^{14} decreases (Magni, 1993, 1). The process would be reversed when solar activity is low. The production of C^{14} isotopes widely fluctuated with major climate changes, like the one about the beginning of the Holocene. About 8000 BC, which coincides with the beginning of the Holocene Age, a large influx of depleted C^{14} from oceans combined with the decrease in C^{14} production at the top of the atmosphere. Accordingly, C^{14} samples from different periods of early and middle Holocene periods would be C^{14} deficient and calculations based on the decay rates of C^{14} isotopes would produce C^{14} age scales quite inconsistent with current reconstructions.

This inconsistency can be resolved by reference to biological or sedimentological features, which build up annual layers over long periods of time (e.g. tree rings and annual layers of sediment building on lake beds). Recent reconstructions of C^{14} age scale and real age scale on the basis of biological and sedimentological determinations have shown that between 20000 BC and 8000 BC, the gap between two types of determination may range from 500 years to 1200 years (Adams, 1998a). Counting back the annual layers will reveal the true number of years before the present and comparing the C^{14} age of each tree ring or sediment layer will give an age scale for how C^{14} age can be converted into 'real' age (Dahl and Nesje, 1996). According to these calculations, C^{14} 1000 BC would be 1200 BC real age, C^{14} 2000 BC would be 2500 BC real age, C^{14} 3000 BC would be 3900 BC real age, C^{14} 4000 BC would be 4950 BC real age and so forth. However, even this method is not completely reliable, since 'false' double rings can sometimes appear and occasionally a year may not appear in the record. But, a missing year or two would become insignificant when one considers that every C^{14} date is associated with a large margin of error ranging from 100 to 150 years on either side. By this token, the present Harappan chronology seems to go topsy-turvy. Accordingly, the Regionalization Era may now begin about 3500 BC, the Integration Era about 2900 BC and the Localization Era about 2300 BC. In other words, the decay of Harappan cities would have set in around 2200 BC and reached a low point around 1800 BC.

Chapter 2

The Indo-European Problem

Indo-Europeanism and Indo-Europeanists

The idea of an Indo-European language family is the product of West-European intellectual motivations during the eighteenth century, the main basis of which was linguistic affinity between European dialects and Indo-Iranian dialects. The formulation was highly speculative and frequently obscured by ethno-linguistic preferences and prejudices. The most important of these prejudices during the eighteenth century was the attempt to separate Western culture from its Judaic heritage and the desire to substitute the Biblical Near Eastern homeland with an Indian or Himalayan homeland. Europeans of the scientific age, who had freed themselves from the conventional Noachian genealogy and rejected Adam as a common father, were looking around for new ancestors but were unable to break with the tradition which placed their origin in the fabulous Orient. It was the science of linguistics that was to give a name to these ancestors by opposing the Aryans to the Hamites, the Mongols and the Jews (Poliakov, 1974, 188).

The Europeans' quest for a high cultural antiquity, which could match their new-found political and economic supremacy, worked like a propellant in studies relating to comparative religion and comparative linguistics. The pursuit of linguistic and cultural affinities intensified in the wake of the mercantilist activities of Europeans and the founding of East Indian trading companies by several countries. In 1583 an English Jesuit by the name of Thomas Stevens working in India noted the structural similarities between Greek, Latin and the languages of North India. Two years later, in 1585 an Italian merchant Fillipo Sasseni observed that there was much in common between Sanskrit and the European languages because in Sanskrit we can find many of our nouns, especially numbers: six, seven, eight and nine, God, serpent and others'. (Possehl, 1999, 40) By the seventeenth century, scholars were also accepting the similarities between Greek and German, and Franciscus Raplengius argued for the association of German and Persian (Mallory, 1989, 273).

Matters reached a flashpoint when Sir William Jones, in the course of his lectures delivered at the Asiatic Society of Bengal during the late 1780s, suggested that Sanskrit had linguistic affinities to Greek, Latin, Persian and some modern European languages (Jones, 1789/90). Voltaire, who, like many of his west-European counterparts was deeply influenced by the writings of William Jones and the prospect of an Indic homeland, believed that 'every thing has come down to us from the banks of Ganges, astronomy, astrology, metempsychosis' (Poliakov, 1974, 185). The enthusiasm generated by this discovery, which was compared by Hegel to the finding of a new continent (Hegel, 1817), could not but motivate back projections of much later European ideas and institutions into the remote literature of a possible linguistic fraternity. It was in Germany that the European Aryan myth had its beginnings. Schlegel, a German statesman and novelist, already familiar with the writings of Jones and highly impressed by the antiquity and splendour of the Sanskrit language, suggested that Sanskrit-speaking hordes commanded by warriors or priests had left their Himalayan homeland to bring civilization to India, Egypt and Europe (Schlegel, 1808).

As more and more people accepted linguistics as the criterion of racial classification, the idea spread outside Germany, particularly to France through French translations of German writings on the subject. One of the more important French authors was Joseph Ernest Renan (Renan, 1863), whose writings and anti-Semitic stance inspired a series of imitations, all arguing that the origin of the Bible is to be found in India and that Abraham was no other than Brahmā of the *Upaniṣads*.

By far the most overwhelming influence on the European mindset was exercised by the renowned philologist and Orientalist, Friedrich Max Müller, who stated in 1859 that 'the first ancestors of the Indians, the Persians, the Greeks, the Romans, the Slavs, the Celts and the Germans were living together within the same enclosures, nay under the same roof' (Müller, 1859). Though Max Müller never gave up his suggestion of a central homeland, he soon realized the weakness of his observation relating to race-language correlation so much so that he stated in 1888 that any talk of an Aryan race, Aryan blood, Aryan hair and Aryan bones and skulls was as ludicrous as talk of a dolichocephalic dictionary or brachycephalic grammar (Müller, 1888). But the realization was too late and had little impact on a racist European mindset. Curiously, a modern compatriot of Max Müller is not constrained by the observations of his illustrious predecessor and continues to refer to the idea of Aryan blood, Aryan bones and so forth (Witzel, 1995a, 113).

A paradigm shift is clearly discernible in the writings of British imperialist tradition. The English were never enthusiastic about the notion that their biological and cultural origins lay amongst the natives they ruled in India, and few Englishmen read Schlegel's works on the subject (Kennedy, 1995, 34). Towards the close of the nineteenth century, A.F.R. Hoernle stated that the Aryans came to India in two waves of migration (Hoernle, 1880). The idea was fully supported by George Grierson, Director of the Linguistic Survey of India (Grierson, 1907–1909). The idea of a superior European race, which was at the back of these writings, was subsequently highlighted by Houston Stewart Chamberlain, who formulated the concept of Nordic–Teutonic racial supremacy (Chamberlain, 1899). The most ardent exponent of a superior European race was V. Gordon Childe (Childe 1926), who believed in the duality of creative and passive races, the people of the Orient being characterized as stagnant and degenerate while Europeans were held to be superior in the qualities of energy, inventiveness and independence. Childe belived that the first Aryans were racially Nordic and the Nordic superiority in physique fitted them to be vehicles of a superior language. According to him, 'Aryan people first emerge from the gloom of prehistory on the northern borders of the Fertile Crescent of the Ancient East, and that dynasts installed on the upper Euphrates by 1400 BC were Aryans, closely akin to those we meet in the Indus Valley and later in Media and Persia'. The idea of duality of races, superior and inferior, however, was not the product of nineteenth century European mindset since it goes as far back as the time of Aristotle, who argued precisely along these lines.

Many Homelands

As the debate continued to grow, the homeland shifted from Asia to Europe and from Europe to Asia, resulting in a formidable list of regions claimed as the original home of Indo-Europeans. The more important of these included Scandinavia, the Danube basin, the Baltic region, the Central European steppes, (Carpathian plains and Ukraine in Europe and Siberia, and the lower Volga valley between Altai and Kazakhstan), and southern Russia between the Caucasus and Eastern Europe (Turkmenistan, north-western Kirghiz steppes, Pamirs, Bactria, and the Central Asian plateau) and Tibet in Asia. An interesting feature of the debate is that 'all of the reputed homelands of the Aryans are postulated as existing between 30° and 70° North parallels and 5° and 95° East meridians' and that 'the dates of their first appearance range from 8000 to 1400 BC' (Thapar, 1970).

More recently, there has been further addition to the homeland list, the arguments chiefly based on linguistic palaeontology particularly loan connections between Indo-European and non-Indo-European. The supposed presence of Semitic and south Caucasian loan words in Indo-European has led certain scholars to suggest that 'the proto-Indo-Europeans must have been situated adjacent to the Semitic and Caucasian language families, somewhere in the vicinity of Armenia' (Gamkrelidze and Ivanov, 1983, 42). D'iakonov, who proposes a Balkan homeland, however, challenges most of the etymologies proposed by Gamkrelidze and Ivanov (D'iakonov, 1985).

Similarly, Dolgopolsky, who proposes a Near Eastern homeland, more effectively in central Anatolia, also challenges the south Caucasian or Armenian homeland theory (Dolgopolsky, 1989, 17). Sheveroskin, who favours an Indo-European homeland in the eastern part of Asia Minor, also expresses doubts whether there were significant loans between the north and south Caucasian languages and proto-Indo-European and whether these language groups were therefore immediately adjacent to each other (Sheveroskin, 1987, 227). Quite different from all this Nichols argues that proto-Indo-European could not have been situated between Mesopotamia and the Black Sea coast or between Mesopotamia and the eastern Caucasian foothills and the Caspian coastal plain (Nichols, 1997, 124). According to Nichols, the Semitic loans in the proto-language show signs not of direct borrowing but of filtration through an intermediary. Nichols accordingly situates proto-Indo-European still further to the north-east, in Bactria–Sogdiana, from where it could spread across the steppe.

Situating the Indo-European Language

The large degree of cognatic relationship between European dialects and the dialects of South Asia and Iran also needs explanation. Since such a relationship can emerge only after a long period of physical contiguity and acculturation, the role of a demographic movement from one continent to another cannot be ruled out, notwithstanding the assertion that physical contact is not necessary for language change (Barth, 1972). The role of environment in the history of the Indo-European language family has recently found primacy (Adams, 1998). However, such demographic movements can be established only on the basis of hard historical evidence, like skeletal records of Asiatic people in Europe or of European communities in Asia. The idea of a European origin of Indo-Europeans and/or Indo-European languages remains highly specious in the absence of any explanation of why and when the speakers of Indic and Iranian dialects headed for Europe and, if they did, what is the testimony of their arrival in the physical biology of the white continent. Since Mediterraneans are common to both

Europe and Asia, particularly South Asia, one would expect some evidence of the proto-Austroloids who constitute the bulk of the South Asian population in the skeletal records of Europe. But so far, no proto-Astroloids have been reported from Europe.

Compared to this, ethnic Europeans are known to have migrated to different parts of Asia right from the time of the Neanderthals (Sankalia, 1974, 205) mainly under the heat of inhospitable geo-climatic conditions. The presence of Alpines or proto-Nordics in the physical biology of South Asia (Guha, 1935; Chatterjee and Kumar, 1963; Kumar, 1973) probably after 4500 BC (Kennedy, 1995) shows that similar trends continued during the early Holocene Age as well. This might suggest that migration of ethnic Europeans (not the imaginary Indo-Europeans) must have been an event of the early Holocene Age. The likelihood of such an event or a series of such events is evident from a comparison of geo-climatic conditions in Europe and Asia, the former reeling under an extreme dry-cold regime which nearly destroyed the habitat economy in large parts of the continent (Guiot *et al.*, 1993, 146; Harrison *et al.*, 1993, 148; Bond *et al.*, 1997) and the latter experiencing a warmer and comparatively humid conditions during the same period (Clarke and Fontes, 1990; Swain *et al.*, 1983, 15; Harrison *et al.*, 1996, 138). Migration to certain parts of the Northern Mediterranean region, which too enjoyed a favourable environment during the early Holocene Age, is also not unlikely. Long periods of contact between ethnic European dialects and the dialects of the Indo-Iranian subcontinent during the post-early-Holocene phase may have given rise to the 'Centum' division which assimilated many of the Indo-Iranian linguistic features. Estimates of the linguistic chronology of the Indo-European languages suggest that much of their common vocabulary has a more recent origin, about 7,000 years ago (Swadesh, 1972). The physical palaeobiology of Asia, which shows that after 4500 BC there has been no change in the racial demography of West Asia, Iran, Central Asia and South Asia (Hemphill *et al.*, 1991; Hemphill *et al.*, 1991b), also seems to confirm the fifth millennium BC as the likely date for the evolution of the Indo-European language family. However, this was only the preliminary stage of language contact followed by several such episodes of migration not only from Europe to Asia but also *vice versa* during the fourth, third and second millennium BC. During the fourth millennium BC, for instance, there could have been an episode of diasporic return to Europe following the onset of mid-Holocene hyper-arid conditions in vast tracks of Asia with a corresponding degree of return to warm and wet conditions in Europe. This may have coincided with the arrival of the Centum dialect in Europe, where a new phase of bilingualism between the older ethnic dialects and the newly arrived Centum dialect got underway.

A distinction also needs to be made between Indo-European peoples and Indo-European languages. In Europe as well as in South Asia and Iran, there are groups of people who do not relate to any branches of the Indo-European language family, like the Basque, the Ligurian, the Iberian and the now extinct Etruscan in Europe and numerous aboriginal dialects in South Asia and Iran. In the former case, availability of habitable niches may have prevented the speakers of the concerned languages from migrating to Asia. In the latter case, it could be the lack of cultural interaction between the speakers of aboriginal dialects and the speakers of Indic and Iranian branches of the Indo-European family. This may justify the limitations of demographic movements and consequent bilingual processes both in time and space. The presence of Tocharian, a distinct Centum dialect in inner Asia, shows that several Centum dialects, which fructified in Asia, did not go back to Europe.

Destination Asia: The Younger Dryas in Europe

The Younger Dryas cold event (about 10,800-9,400 BC), which turned much of Europe into cold semi-desert conditions (Huntley and Birks 1983; Starkel, 1991; Landmann *et al.,* 1996; Rossignol-Strick and Planchais 1992; Velichko 1993), apparently through a series of rapid stepwise cooling events, may have been a major catalyst in the dispersal of ethnic European populations of hunter-gatherers towards warmer and more humid southern latitudes. In northern and central Europe, the record is perhaps detailed enough to suggest a complete or almost complete de-population during the Younger Dryas. In Scandinavia, the forests were replaced by glacial tundra, the habitat of the plant dryas (octopetala). In the UK, coleopteran (fossil beetle) evidence suggests that the mean annual temperature dropped to approximately -5 °C (Atkinson *et al.*, 1987), and periglacial conditions prevailed in lowland areas, while icefields and glaciers formed in upland areas (Sissons, 1979). However, in the Levant, conditions seem to have remained relatively moist (Rossignol-Strick, 1995), with relatively strong signs of continuity in human settlement, the Natufian (Henry, 1989). But even in this area, for instance in the Jordan Valley, aridity and a large decrease in food plants are accompanied by more restricted human populations clustered around relatively moist 'oases' (Wright, 1993). In many areas of Greece and across Turkey, the Younger Dryas period was even more arid than the most extreme part of the last glacial, with semi-deserts predominant (Rossignol-Strick, 1995). Conditions across most of the rest of Europe are variously thought to have resembled open dry forest steppe or possibly (at some stages) semi-desert (Starkel 1991). Another cold event, which occurred around 8200 cal. y. a and was half way as severe as the Younger Dryas (Adams *et al.*, 1998), lasted 200 years and may also have induced widespread population dispersal from Europe. However, the one-and-a-half millennium of the Younger Dryas (10,800–9,400 BC), which almost depopulated the whole of Europe, appears to have been a decisive phase in hominid history at the turn of the last Glacial Age. The continents which escaped the disaster with marginal events, like glaciations or increased snow in mountain ranges around the world, more dust in the atmosphere originating from deserts in Asia and drought in the Levant, were surely Asia and Africa. Migrations to Africa may have been hindered by a longish spell of drought in the Levant. But migration to different parts of Asia, particularly the more southerly latitudes, provided the only viable option for the large mass of hunting-gathering ethnic Europeans.

The Early Holocene in Asia and Europe

Climatic variations and the corresponding changes in habitat conditions can also be evidenced from the early Holocene tree-line history of northern Eurasia. The early Holocene history of tree-line in northern Eurasia shows longitudinal trends as one proceeds from west to east. In the Kola Peninsula (68°43′N, 35°19′E) of Russia, which forms part of the north European climatic regime, a tree line of *pinus slyvestris* was established around 6680 yr BP and continued till 3880 yr BP. The timing of the advance and retreat of the treeline here is consistent with evidence from radiocarbon-dated wood found in adjacent Finno-Scandinia (MacDonald *et al.*, 2000, 302). Compared to this, Betula trees were established in the far north-east of Russia between 11,000 to 10,000 yr BP and were widely distributed beyond limits across Eurasia by 9000 to 8000 yr BP. The radiocarbon dates of macro fossils from the Pechora river sites (67°58′N, 51°35′E), the Taymyr Peninsula sites (70°22′N, 87°33′E), and the Lena river sites (71°52′N, 27°04′E) fall between 9000 to 8000 yr BP. From Pechora and Taymyr sites, samples of both Larix and Picea were reported while from the Lena river sites only Larix wood was identified (MacDonald *et al.*, 2000, 302). The retreat of the tree line in all these sites is dated uniformly between 4000 and 3000 yr BP. Consistent with tree line development in Asiatic Northern Russia, the annual mean summer temperature in this region was 2.5°C to 7.0°C warmer than modern.

Apart from Asiatic Northern Russia, much of the continent and Africa experienced warm and humid climatic conditions with high water levels in lakes relating fairly well to a favourable hydrological regime between 8000 and 3000 BC (Swain *et al*, 1983, 1). A wet early Holocene has been well documented in the Middle East as well. In northern Oman, which lies centrally on the North Equatorial Desert Belt, early Holocene pluvial conditions were established by about 10500 yr BC and persisted until as recently as 4100 yr BC (Clarke and Fontes, 1990). In Rajasthan, lakes were not only larger in size but even the water level varied from 6 to 21 meters with occasional overflows during the early Holocene (Swain *et al.*,

1983, 15). In Central Asia, the early Holocene shows a gradual shift to conditions wetter than the present, associated with the expanded Asian monsoon, and in the Mediterranean in response to local monsoon-type circulations (Harrison *et al*, 1996, 138).

Compared to these wet and warm conditions in neighbouring Africa and Asia, almost the whole of Europe was reeling under extreme cold-dry conditions. The continent is said to have been 2°C colder at 7000 yr BC than at 4000 yr BC, and much cooler up to 10°C, than the present along the western seaboard'. It was 'drier overall at 7000 year BC than at 4000 year BC, except for a region of higher than present precipitation in western France' (Guiot *et al*, 1993, 146). Conditions were particularly inhospitable in northern and north-eastern Europe. At the beginning of the early Holocene Age (9500 BC/7500 BC), the lakes show conditions similar to or drier than present in a broad band across southern Britain and southern Scandinavia and into the Eastern Baltic, and wetter conditions along the west coast, in Central Europe and in the northern Mediterranean region (Harrison *et al*, 1993, 148). Although wetter conditions returned to northern Europe by 4000 yr BC, the region continued to experience climatic deterioration at regular intervals. According to one study, three major episodes of climatic deterioration have been recognized in 3300 BC, 1300 BC and AD 1200–1700 in the Holocene history of the forest Alpine tundra ecotone in the Scands mountains (Magni, 1993, 7). Within and overall dry and cold conditions, there were sudden downturns in both aridity and chill every 1,500 years throughout the early and mid-Holocene epochs (Bond *et al*, 1997). These extreme dry and cold conditions simulating a mini Ice Age lasted for a century or two before returning to normal. The first few episodes which took place between 8000 BC and 4000 BC may have witnessed, like during the Younger Dryas, large-scale movement of ethnic Europeans towards warmer southern latitudes and their eventual settlement in different parts of Asia.

Since migrations do not mean complete de-population of original habitations, a distinction needs to be made between ethnic Europeans who spoke different local dialects and continued to inhabit the continent during the early Holocene Age, and their linguistic fraternity who migrated during the same period and settled down in a broad, culturally interactive zone of South Asia, Iran and South Central Asia. The contacts between ethnic European dialects and dialects spoken in this cultural subcontinent influenced the formation of a European relative of the Indo-Iranian dialect family, known as the Indo-European. The proto-forms of the 'Centum' and 'Śatem' divisions may have fructified by the close of the fifth millennium BC, the former assimilating a large number of Indic and Iranian linguistic features and discarding some others.

The Tentative Dialect Scenario

The languages that participated in the process appear to have been protoforms of Old Vedic, Zend, Prakrit, Munda, Dravidian, Elamite and perhaps Sino-Tibetan to a lesser degree. The role of one or more 'X' languages in this interaction cannot also be ruled out. The influence of a 'Zagrosian family of languages linking Elamite and Dravidian on the Iranian Plateau' (McAlpine, 1974) in the development of an Indo-European proto language is also in the reckoning. The importance of Dravidian in creating an Indic lexical base in European dialects of the pre-Indo-European stage is well suggested by the presence of nearly 500 Dravidian lexical items, both roots and radicals in different European dialects of the present day (Keerthi Kumar, 1999). Since Dravidian dialects are said to contain nearly 50 to 60 per cent of Sanskrit vocables, the latter may have found their way into European dialect through Dravidian. Such a possibility becomes stronger in view of the determination of a cognatic relationship between Dravidian and Uralic (Marlow, 1974). This shows that the Dravidian speech area extended beyond Iran into Eastern and South-eastern Europe.

The substantial presence of Prakrit, Dravidian and Munda substrates in the Old Vedic dialect, the either way convertibility of Prakrit and Old Vedic, Old Vedic and Old Avestan, the sharing of a common vocabulary by Old Vedic/Sanskrit and

Dravidian, the existence of a large number of Dravidian vocables in European dialects may provide some idea of the complex historical processes which resulted in the formation and subsequent devolution of a broad Eurasian language family in several stages which cannot be determined with any amount of precision at the present stage of our knowledge. Sir William Jones in his comparison of the Zend with the Vedic Sanskrit observed 'that six or seven words in ten are pure Sanskrit, and even some of their inflexions formed by the rules of Vyākaraṇa, as Yuṣmākam, the genitive plural of Yuṣmad'—that the language of the Zend was at least a dialect of the Sanskrit approaching perhaps as nearly to it as the Prakrit (Jones, 1790). As interactions between ethnic Europeans and Asians intensified, phonological and lexical features on either side changed places and ultimately the older proto-Asian dialect acquired the character of an Indo-European proto language. Perhaps the 'Śatem and Centum' divisions had already taken shape in Asia during the fifth millennium BC though the latter was still in a sprouting stage. The Centum speakers, who returned and settled in different parts of Europe and entered a new phase of bilingualism probably after 4000 BC with ethnic Europeans already living in these separate areas gave rise in the course of time to the different European relatives of the Indo-European family. The Finno-Ugric people, whose dialect contains a substantial amount of Indo-Iranian (Burrow, 1970, 23) or Indo-Aryan (Misra, 1992, 16) loans may have been one of the European groups which returned after a brief sojourn in Asia probably somewhere near the Caspian Sea. However, these developments were not as simple or unilinear, as suggested here and may have taken a millennial scale of time to take their present shape.

Destination South-Eastern Europe

With the return of wetter conditions and higher lake levels in northern Europe by 4000 BC (Guiot *et al*, 1993,146; Harrison *et al*, 1996, 152), movements from this region may have stopped altogether and the return of the diaspora settled in Asia may have started around this time. There would not have been much incentive for migration to Asia after 4000 BC which marked the onset of mid-Holocene hyper-aridity characterized by reduced precipitation, receding lake levels, transgressive deserts and expanding salt ranges in large parts of Iran, north-western South Asia and Central Asia.

These conditions intensified after 3000 BC and reached a flash-point around 1500 BC when the south-west monsoon which used to bring summer rains to large parts of South Asia including the Greater Indus Valley disappeared from the region (Naidu, 1998, 69). But migrations from Central and Western Europe may have continued as these regions were still experiencing hyper-arid conditions even after 4000 BC. The migrants could either be heading towards a wetter northern Europe or towards northern shores of the Mediterranean where a habitable micro-environment existed throughout the early- and mid-Holocene epochs. This micro-environment was characterized by high water tables in the lakes, occurrence of steppe-type vegetation and evergreen and warm mixed forest throughout the early and mid-Holocene epochs (Harrison *et. al.*, 1996, 151). However, these conditions resulting from a local monsoon type circulation were largely confined to more extensive land areas of the Iberian and Balkan peninsulas (Giraudi, 1989).

Disaster was also stalking the people of northern Eurasia, where the tree line established between 9000 and 7000 BC started retreating by 2000 BC and completely disappeared by 1000 BC. The retreat of the tree line coincided with decreasing summer insolation, cooling of Arctic waters, possible expansion of sea ice, and neo-glaciation. Declining summer insolation would have decreased solar engery and temperatures during the growing season at tree line (Kutzbach *et al*, 1993). Cooler surface waters in the Norwegian, Greenland and Barents seas would have promoted cooler conditions in northern Eurasia. In turn, the summer persistence of sea ice would lead to cooler air temperatures. The southward progression of the tundra would have resulted in an increase in albedo and displacement of the Arctic front, providing positive feedbacks which enhanced cooling (Foley *et al*, 1994; Tempo, 1996; Ganopolski *et al*, 1998). Afflicted people from these areas may have been heading for greener pastures in the North Pontic region and its immediate eastern and southern neighbourhoods.

Adverse geo-climatic conditions in Asia after 4000 BC also induced ethnic South Asians and Iranians to look for greener pastures in eastern and south-eastern Europe. The people, who may have earlier practised intensive agriculture and even participated in the continental networking of trade and urban places during the Early Bronze Age, now became fully dependent on pastoral activities and spoils of war. The horse, which may have been domesticated in Iran by this time, proved very useful as an instrument of war for the Sagis on the move. The movement of Sagis or Śaka Iranians into southeastern Europe took place in several stages, the first starting about mid-second millennium BC and the last one coming around 1000 BC (Sulimirski, 1985, 152). An Iranian community, which combined herding with a little farming, made use of bronze weapons and chariots and practised diverse types of funeral, is said to be represented by Pit Grave Culture at Sintasta in the Cheliabinsk region on the eastern flank of the central Urals around 1500 BC (Genning, 1979; Boyce, 1989, 64). Considering, however, the similarities of the Śaka Iranian Srub Culture with the Catacomb, Timber-grave and Andronovo cultures, a much earlier date, probably early second millennium BC would be more appropriate for the beginnings of Śaka exodus from Iran. The presence of Indo-Aryan chiefs and a large number of Vedic words in West Asian inscriptions from the early seventeenth century BC also suggest earlier waves of migration from the Indo-Iranian subcontinent towards West Asia and south-eastern Europe.

However, the humid conditions prevailing in the Eurasian steppes during the second millennium BC were interrupted by a period of severe drought towards the close of the millennium (Lamb, 1982; Boyce, 1989, 64) when there was a reverse movement from the Near East and the Eurasian steppes towards Iran. This in turn intensified hegemonic conflicts for fast-depleting resources and consequent population shifts. During this period, the Śaka Iranians, who had earlier colonized the steppes once again started dispersing, many of them towards their original homeland to the south of the steppes. Some of the ethnic Europeans settled in this region were also looking for new homes. One such group may have been the Phrygians who trooped into Armenia, the traditional homeland of the Hurrian peoples. In their new home, which was already under the dialectal and ideological influence of the Daivas and the Mazdians, the Phrygians may have undergone some sort of cultural transformation. A few centuries earlier, the Hurrians of Armenia themselves had moved out of the country to adopt Syria as their new home. These cross-currents of shifting populations accelerated the process of language displacement, superimposition and adoption. This may also explain the substantial presence of East Iranian vocables in the ancient European dialects (Gamkrelidze and Ivanov, 1983, 77).

In the steppes, settlements to the north and east of Kiev reveal an extraordinary increase of domesticated and wild animal bones including stag and elk (Sulimirski, 1985, 150). Nearly ninety percent of the tools at these sites were made from antlers of stags and elk (Gimbutas 1956, 106). Bones of beavers discovered in the kitchen refuse of prehistoric settlements in this area suggest that these animals lived in the valleys of the lower Dneiper and lower southern Bug, whereas at present the southernmost existing colony of these animals is on the Tetrev, north of Kiev. Similarly, 'bones of elk were found in a series of prehistoric settlements in the south of the Ukraine and even in the debris of the ancient Greek city of Olbia. At present, the southernmost region in which these animals live is the forests of the Pripet Marshes, some 500 kms north of Olbia (Sulimirski, 1985, 150).

The linguistic study of the Ukrainian toponymy and of the toponyms and personal names that appear in ancient inscriptions in the debris of the Greek North Pontic colonies, suggest that besides the Greeks and Thracians, Iranians also inhabited these colonies. The Greeks and the Thracians were the natives of the region whereas the Iranians were newcomers, the earliest of whom probably arrived during the second half of the second millennium BC (Sulimirski, 1985, 152). The

Scythians who were a diverse people of Iranian origin settled in a vast area in different parts of south-eastern Europe. Linguistic evidence of the presence of the Iranian speakers surfaces in the form of Sakasena and Kambisena, the two Iranian language areas located in Eastern Transcaucasus (Misra, 1992, 46). The route taken by these groups may have been along the western source of the Caspian Sea which was also used by later groups of Iranian-speaking peoples (Aliyev *et al*, 1981) and subsequently by the Alans.

The more important of the Śaka Iranians or Scythians were the Skolotoi or the Royal Scyths, who were nomads inhabiting the steppes east of the Dnieper up to the Don and the Crimean steppe (Sulimirski, 1985,150). Another group of steppe-dwelling nomadic Scyths occupied the country extending west of the Dnieper bend to the Ingul, a tributary of the lower southern Bug. A third group of pastoral Scythians who lived west of this region comprised Alazones or Alizones who were in possession of the steppe up to the Dniester. The first part of their name Ala or Ali would be a regular development within Scythian phonology of the term Ārya (in the sense of 'Iranian'), but some scholars are of the opinion that the Alazones were of mixed blood, Iranian and Thracian (Sulimirski, 1985, 152). Another important group was the Callipidae or the 'Greek Scythians', who occupied the wide strip of land along the sea coast west of the estuary of the southern Bug, extending up to the regions of Odessa, or perhaps even beyond it up to the estuary of the Dniester. Finally, a group of Scythian agriculturists lived in the valley of the lower Dnieper. The Scyths were not the only Iranians in the North Pontic region. The Melanchlaeni and the Androphagy, who may be regarded as Iranian or of mixed Iranian and native stock, lived in a region extending over the Ukrainian forest steppe zone east of the middle Dnieper, north of the country of 'Royal Scyths' (Sulimirski, 1985,153). The Sauromatians, the Sairma of the *Avesta* who represented the eastern neighbours of the Royal Scyths were also Iranians living in the region extending over the steppe east of the Don and the Volga.

Like the Iranians, who were driven to the North Pontic region by the heat of geo-climatic devastations in Iran, peoples from northern and north-eastern Europe were also forced to leave their homes under extreme dry-cold conditions during the second half of the second millennium BC. As already noted, northern and north-eastern Europe experienced a severe climatic deterioration around 1300 BC (Magni, 1993, 7), which may have driven the Balts and Finno-Ugric peoples towards the steppes. The presence of these peoples in the North Pontic region during the late second and early first millennium BC is well supported by the toponymy and hydronomy of this region. An important Baltic-speaking people who inhabited modern Byelorussia north of ancient Scythia were the Neuri. East of the Neuri there lived a great variety of Finno-Ugrian tribes in the forest zone of eastern Europe up to the Urals, and probably beyond (Sulimirski, 1985,153). According to Herodotus, the Budini were one of these Finno-Ugrian tribes. Towards the south, the Finno-Ugrians were represented by the Maeotians and Taurians, each of which had several subdivisions as attested by archaeological remains. The Maeotians lived on the eastern coast of the Sea of Azov whereas the Taurians lived around the Crimean Mountain.

Environment continued to influence demographic dispersal and dialect development through cultural interaction. Drier conditions, which affected nearly the whole of Europe during the early and mid-Holocene epoch seemed to be advancing towards the northern Mediterranean during the last quarter of the second millennium BC. The limited evidence from Italy suggests that conditions were drier during the early to mid-Holocene (Giraudi, 1989). Conditions were further aggravated in this region by a series of volcanic eruptions on Mount Etna in Sicily. With the steppes also under a severe drought about the same time (Lamb, 1982), a series of migrations to different destinations began to influence demographic and linguistic structures in large parts of south-eastern Europe, Iran, the Near East and the southern Mediterranean, particularly Libya and Egypt. More prominent among the migrants were the Etruscans, the Sicilians, the Sardinians and others. Adverse conditions also forced people to migrate from Asia Minor and the Aegean islands to the Egyptian delta across the

Mediterranean. Starvation stalked people in the Hittite empire and survival was possible only on the basis of the help provided by the Egyptian king. These conditions induced enterprising warriors from outside to invade the country and destroy the 800 year old Hittite empire.

These outsiders were Illyrians, who were fighting with mounted warriors and weapons of iron. The Anatolians with their defending charioteers and inferior bronze weapons lost ground and were driven out. The Illyrians eventually settled in Slovenia in northern Yugoslavia. At about the same time the Phrygian and Mycenaean people from Thrace settled in Central Anatolia west of the Helys. The Armenian people, whose language is related to the Thraco-Phrygians branch of the Indo-European family, invaded the Armenian plateau from the west. In the fifth century BC Herodotus described the Armenians as a people from Phrygia whose speech resembled Phrygian. With the coming of the Phrygians, a new branch of the Centum division began to take shape in the highland country of Armenia. On their arrival, the Phrygians interacted with the Hurrians, who were already settled in the region and represented an early form of the Indo-Iranian dialect. This bilingualism became intensified as the province became part of median kingdom sometime during the sixth century BC. In this formative period the Armenians appear to have absorbed Hurrian, Hittite and Phrygian elements in their religious belief (Papajian, 1985, 439). The presence of 686 Iranian loan words and 217 Iranian personal names underlines the influence of the Indo-Iranian language on the development of the Armenian dialect.

The twin processes of cultural fusion and fission began with the coming of ethnic Europeans to the neighbouring regions of Iran, Central Asia and South Asia and their interaction with proto-Vedic and proto-Iranian dialects to develop a proto-form of the Indo-European languages about the fifth millennium BC. The process became much more intense with the subsequent coming together and dispersal of peoples at different times and in different regions for altogether different reasons. The more important of these regions were Central Asia, South-eastern

Europe and West Asia. These trends in the annals of Indo-European languages cannot, however, be ascertained with any amount of precision in terms of firm historical dates. In this interaction, Central Asia, particularly South Central Asia, functioned like a cultural conduit through which ideas and influences passed from South Asians and Iranians to immigrant Europeans and *vice versa*. Those who postulate contacts between groups from the Eurasian steppes and those from the north-western parts of South Asia, must not therefore overlook the intermediary or filtering role played by the peoples of southern Central Asia (Jarrige, 1984, 63).

The centrality of the contiguous regions of Iran, South Asia and Central Asia in the coming together of different ethnic European, Indic and Iranic dialects, their fusion, fission and diffusion may fall in line with a recent study which considers the Indo-Iranian subcontinent particularly Bactria and Sogdiana as the cradle of Indo-European language family and its gradual dispersal towards west and north west. The work suggests that the development of several European dialects was complete by the third or second millennium BC. These included Italic, Celtic, and perhaps Germanic in the environs of Central Europe (and presumably Balto-Slavic as well), and the 'proto-forms of Greek, Illyrian, Anatolian and Armenian stretching from northwest Mesopotamia to the southern Balkans' (Nichols, 1997, 134).

Chapter 3

The Problem of the Origin of Vedic Culture

Old Ideas

For many long years, scholars have shown considerable reticence in working out a firm historical context for the earliest Vedic speakers of north-western South Asia. The focus has largely been on the migration of Vedic-speaking communities supposedly representing a new racial element from outside the Indo-Pak subcontinent, notwithstanding the inability of philologists 'to identify any compelling racial traits in the *Ṛgveda*' (Bryant, 2002, 63). Neither did the absence of convincing data prevent Indo-Europeanists from hyping the idea of an outside origin of Vedic culture of South Asia. Muir, an ardent supporter of this theory, could not muster any textual evidence in support of what he fondly believed. Instead, he makes a 'candid admission' that 'none of the Sanskrit books, not even the most ancient, contains any distinct reference or allusion to the foreign origin of the Indians' (Muir, 1860, 322). However, attempts to locate this 'outside' home on the basis of linguistic palaeo-ontology and archaeology have been largely inconclusive, with scholars challenging the findings of one another, each one proposing a separate homeland either in Europe or in Asia. These quests of an Indo-European homeland have frequently been unsettled by severe criticisms in the Western intellectual circle itself.

The infructuous nature of research on the Indo-European homeland has been succinctly summed up in a work of the late 1950s (Hankins, 1948, 265), which draws attention to 'The obvious impossibility of actually locating the Aryan homeland, the even more remote possibility of ever learning conclusively the traits of the mythical 'Original Aryans', the increasing realization that all the historical peoples were much mixed in the blood and that the role of a particular race in a great mélange of races, though easy to exaggerate, is impossible to determine'. The whole exercise thus turns out to be a 'ridiculous and humiliating spectacle of eminent scholars subordinating their interests in truth to the inflation of racial and national pride'. 'All these and many other reasons led scholars to declare either that the Aryan doctrine was a figment of the professional imagination or that it was incapable of clarification because the crucial evidence was lost, apparently forever' (Hankins, 1948, 265). Such words of caution and sagacity could not, however, prevail much on the intellectual mind which displayed renewed interest in the research of an Indo-European Homeland during the post-war period with Marija Gimbutas almost spearheading the quest on the basis of the Kurgan Culture and steppe homeland of the Indo-Europeans. But another fifty years of intensive research, though much useful by way of addition of new knowledge, leaves the homeland problem where it was 50 years or even 200 years ago.

Current Thinking

Linguistic palaeo-ontology, which accounts for the bulk of homeland theories during the last 200 years, has recently come under the scanner. It has been argued that with this method anything can be proved as proto-Indo-European, though none can be proved as typically proto-Indo-European. The radical error in this approach lies in the fact that any cultural markers, which are said to form part of a particular homeland reconstruction, may also have existed in other language families (Schmitt, 1974, 283). Renfrew who also criticizes the use of linguistic palaeo-ontological data to corroborate archaeological evidence in a chosen area, as Gimbutas tried to do in relation to the Kurgan culture and the steppe homeland of the Indo-Europeans (Gimbutas, 1966, 79), feels that this method can accommodate almost any homeland theory and that since the method itself is suspect the results following its application are also suspect (Renfrew, 1987, 86). Viewed as a discourse relating to interpretative logic and ideology, 'the problem therefore lies in the head of Indo-Europeanists' (Demoule, 1980) and for that reason the obsession with Indo-Europeanism is unlikely to relent despite serious studies rectifying the 'absurd theories' relating to invasion or migration of Indo-Aryan-speaking Vedic communities (Kenoyer, 1998, 74) and the specialists 'pointing out misinterpretation of basic facts, inappropriate models and an uncritical reading of Vedic texts' (Jarrige, 1984; Shaffer, 1993). Though the findings of the latest studies take their own time to prevail over popular perceptions, ideological and even sectarian interests frequently intervene between the two to the extent of preventing minimum necessary updating. This may explain why the scientific and well reasoned arguments in the new genre of writings have been least noticed in the intellectual circle, let alone 'rooting out misinterpretations in popular literature' (Brown, 1994).

With the 'homeland' remaining as elusive as ever, the possibility of Indo-European migration from a central area recedes into the background with the focus shifting to ground realities of cultural processes as documented in archaeological records of north-western South Asia and the adjoining borderlands. Understandably, during the last one and half decades there has been a growing disapproval of the migration idea and culture supplanting with the emphasis shifting to a process of radical social mutations and cultural reorganization, which is said to account for the origin of Vedic culture in north-western South Asia within the parameters of the Harappan civilization. The approach is exclusive to a theoretical construct, which does not recognize any discontinuity or abrupt end in a civilizational process which is considered to be a historical continuum with major or minor paradigm shifts in the cultural experience of a people. Scholars specializing in Harappan archaeology have noticed 'significant continuities in subsistence activities, technologies, economic networks, urban organization and possibly socio-ritual as well as political structures' (Kenoyer, 1998, 18) in north-western South Asia. If cultural continuities are any indication, the late Harappan phase never came to an end. It only merged into the mainstream of Indian cultural developments (Chakrabarti, 2000, 277). Depending on the types of cultures encountered both within the Greater Indus Valley and outside of it, the Indus cultural traditions took very different forms in different regions to the extent of appearing as strangers to one another.

From the demographic angle also, 'there is no evidence of new populations entering into the subcontinent and replacing the indigenous people of the Indus valley although the archaeological data do not preclude the possibility of micro-evolutionary shifts in prehistoric populations due to small enclaves of people entering South Asia from the neighbourhood areas' (Kennedy, 1995, 60). The prehistoric human remains recovered thus far from the Indian subcontinent are said to be phenotypically identifiable as ancient South Asians whose biological continuity with living peoples of India, Pakistan, Sri Lanka and the Border Regions are well established across time and space (Kennedy, 1995, 60). Studies on skeletal biology even rule out the possibility of racial intrusions not only in north-western South Asia but also Iran, Iraq and Central Asia between 4500 BC and 800 BC (Hemphill *et al*, 1991). Given this latest archaeological scenario in South Asia and South-Central Asia, it is unlikely that the dream of generations of scholars to map out the movement of Indo-Aryans from the Eurasian steppes to South Asia will ever materialize (Jarrige, 1984, 63).

A reexamination of textual materials also rules out, as in the past, the possibility of a Vedic homeland outside South Asia or migration from that homeland. According to one study (Erdosy, 1989, 40-41), 'There is no indication in the *Ṛgveda* of the Aryan's memory of any ancestral home and by extension of migrations. As a study of place names in the *Ṛgveda* reveals, the Sapta Sindhu or the land of seven rivers was indisputably the universe of the Aryas, and its veneration leaves little doubt about its status as their homeland. That Sapta Sindhu signified not only seven rivers, but also a territory with strong emotive associations is shown by such hymns as 10.49, in which Indra boasts of having taken the seven rivers as his own domain' (7.67.8; 8.24.27 for further examples).

The latest studies in history, archaeology, and social linguistics should also clarify a few suppositions high on the wish list of migrationists. First, the steppe origin of chariot aristocracy and mounted warriors during the mid-second millennium BC seems to be a non-starter. A large number of chariot petroglyphs belonging to the late third and early second millennium BC, largely drawn by oxen or bullocks and occasionally by horses, have been reported from vast highland tracts of Asia, from Siberia in the north to Kirghizia and upper Indus in the south and from Tajikistan and Kazakhstan in the west to inner Mongolia and the Xinjiang province of China in the east (Frankfort, 1989, 100) make it amply clear that the chariot aristocracy was well entrenched in almost the whole of Asia from the late third millennium BC. According to one opinion, horse-drawn chariots and chariotry are said to have been developed in the Near East early in the second millennium BC by diverse peoples there, including the Indo-Aryan aristocrats of Mitanni (Boyce, 1989, 64). In the steppes, the earliest evidence of chariot is dated around 1500 BC on the basis of the Sintasta Grave in the Cheliabinsk region on the eastern flank of the Central Urals (Boyce, 1989, 64). But the Sintasta Grave has been attributed to a heterogeneous Iranian community (Boyce, 1989, 64), which may have left Iran in the wake of geo-climatic disorders during the Middle Bronze Age. As for mounted warriors, the earliest evidence from Europe is said to be not until 1000 BC (Renfrew, 1999, 268). Compared to this, the discovery of terracotta figurines of horse riders from the early second millennium context of the Pirak valley (Baluchistan) relates to a date much earlier than the mid-second millennium BC in the European steppe.

Second, the steppe origin of the practice of cremation suggested on the basis of the seventeenth century BC steppe cemetery at Sintasta (Genning, 1979) and other cremation related contexts in 'southern Tajikistan, especially at Tulkhar (Kohl, 1984), Dashly-III in southern Bactria and Zaman Baba in northern Bactria (Klejn, 1984), all belonging to the first half of the second millennium BC also becomes inconsequential in view of the fact that full cremations are already well documented in the Harappan archaeological record of early and mature phases, like Tarkhanewala Dera in the Ganganagar district of Rajasthan and Mehi in the western Harappan province of Baluchistan. Even at Sintasta there is a diversity of funerary practice, and the culture itself attributed to heterogeneous Iranian community (Boyce, 1989, 64). Diffusion of the practice, if at all, should then take off from north-western South Asia and move towards the north-west, the east and the south-east, losing or gaining in importance according to the local conditions. Cremation was not even an exclusive marker of Ārya who practised besides cremation full burials, post-cremation burials and post-exposure burials, all of which have been described at length in the tenth book of the *Ṛgveda* (10.14-16; 10.18). Whether or not the Ārya of the *Ṛgveda* had anything to do with the Harappans, all these modes of disposal of the dead are evidenced in the Harappan archaeological context of the third millennium BC.

Further, contrary to the common perception of a homogeneous and monolithic ethnolinguistic community, the Ārya of the *Ṛgveda* represented a loose association of diverse and disparate ethnocultural groups at the same or different levels of social formation, interactive or unrelated, each with a separate identity but all put together under a common religious umbrella. Though the point was made more than a decade ago (Nandi, 1993), it seems to have been a little too unconventional to shake up path dependency in this specific area of study. The plurality of the Ārya, however, seems well recognized in certain informed writings. According to one opinion, the term 'Ārya' represented a broad religious ideology, which could accommodate anyone who subscribed to it (Erdosy, 1989,41). However, Erdosy does not explain why the ideology should have originated where and when it did. Another scholar holds that as a sociological expression, the term 'Aryan' denotes all those who took part in the concerned sacrifices and festivals (Kuiper, 1991, 96). There are clear indications that the Vedic speakers of the *Ṛgveda* Sanskrit knew, and interacted with, Dravidian and Munda speakers (Kuiper, 1948, 1955, 1962). There may have been other ethnic or linguistic groups subscribing to the ideology but not always identifiable.

The traditional time frames assigned to the *Ṛgveda* (1500 BC–1000 BC) and the *Avesta* (1400 BC–900 BC), appear to have been unduly influenced by the discovery of the Boghuz Koi treaty of 1380 BC, which mentions the names of four Vedic gods as witnesses to an agreement reached between the Hittite ruler of Anatolia and a Mitannian ruler of Syria besides a Mitanian manual of chariot racing which refers to Sanskrit numerals like Panza (*pañca*) and Prakrit numerals like *satta* (Vedic *sapta*). By this token, the appearance of old Vedic vocables in numerous Syro-Palestinian inscriptions of the seventeenth century BC and the mention of two Vedic gods, Sūrya and Maruts in a Kassite inscription of the eighteenth century BC should push the date of earliest *Ṛgveda* compositions to the eighteenth and nineteenth centuries BC respectively. Although firmly dated historical records can be a good basis for ascertaining the history of a language, the main problem with this approach is the naive supposition that such firmly dated historical records synchronize with the origin of a language or the beginnings of literary creations in that language. Literary creations can come about only after the concerned language has been in popular circulation for quite some time. In other words, if the earliest compositions of the *Ṛgveda* are assigned to the beginning of the second millennium BC, the old Vedic language will precede these compositions at least by a couple of centuries. A linguistic analysis of loan words in the *Ṛgveda* also confirms that the South Asian linguistic area seems to date back longer than we usually care to admit (Kuiper, 1967). Recent estimates of Vedic chronology (Thapar, 1981, 295; Misra, 1992, 5; Witzel, 1999) appear to concur that the authors of earliest Vedic hymns were already firmly entrenched on the Indo-Iranian subcontinent by 2000 BC. The origin of Vedic culture has therefore to be traced in the area where the earliest Vedic hymns were composed and the makers of this culture to be found within the Harappan demographic scenario during the Middle Bronze Age.

Middle Bronze Age and the *Ṛgveda*

The Middle Bronze Age occupies a nodal point in the history of north-western South Asia, Afghanistan, Iran and South-

Central Asia. This vast territory was inhabited by ethno-linguistic communities with diverse material cultures but strong biological and cultural affinities. The two most important developments of the Middle Bronze Age in this area were persistent and widespread geo-climatic disorders which struck the region from the close of the third millennium BC and disintegration of urban and proto-urban civilization over this vast area from about the same time. The urban decay also triggered an internal dynamic, which fructified in the shape of new cultural traditions and social reorganization. Many of the old customs and ideas still continued and the pursuit of gainful economic activities surfaced with new dimensions. Older dialects, which occupied a marginal space during the urban phenomenon, surged forward and new literary forms were articulated to give expression to the changing experiences of life. The destabilizing influence of the widespread geo-climatic disorders and their social fallout can already be deciphered from the archaeological remains of the region. However, archaeology can provide only the visuals of a disaster and may even conceal much that would have filled many shortcomings in a loose baggage of information. A textual record, which is well within the chronological and geographical parameters of the Harappan civilization, assumes great significance from this angle.

Not much effort is needed to understand that the hymns of the *Ṛgveda* give considerable importance to catastrophic events in nature and society, the traumatic experiences of people on this account and a package of divine deliverance through a system of prayers in honour of different divinities representing the forces of nature. The reactions and responses to these devastations varied from people to people. Some accepted the misfortune in silence and continued to suffer in their homeland. Others preferred to move away from the scene of disaster and begin life afresh, the quality of life being determined by new habitat conditions. There were still others who were not merely willing to overcome the crisis but even to lift the morale of hapless compatriots around. The religious leaders of the community, who claimed to intercede between the human mind and the divine power, appeared to have played a proactive role in rejuvenating the despondent mind fields with the promise of a divine deliverance and a religious ideology to that effect. Depending on the skills of rote and communication, some were able to preserve and transmit the oral compositions while others virtually lost track of a literary heritage. The skills of preservation and transmission were particularly effective in liturgical circles for reasons of preserving and propagating the newly developed ideology. Two of these dominant liturgical groups were evidently the speakers of the Old Vedic dialect and the speakers of the old Avestan dialect, the former preceding the latter by a few centuries. In the *Avesta*, social upheavals occupy a major space and environmental disorders, especially hydrological catastrophes are alluded to occasionally. This may suggest that Avestan poets, unlike the Ṛgvedic bards, lived in an age when natural calamities had relented to some extent, but the resulting social upheavals continued unabated. This also falls in place since Avestan ideas represent a subsequent breakaway ideology of the *Ṛgveda* so much so that many of the important Ṛgvedic divinities like Indra, Sarva and Nāsatyas were reduced to the position of demons in the Gathic document (*Vendîdâd, X, 9 and X1X, 43)*. The Avestan word for 'demon', *deuu* or *daiva* goes back to deva, which means god in the Vedic language, while the Avestan word for god is *Bega* which is said to be related to the Old Slavic *Bogu* meaning 'god' (Parpola, 1995, 111).

If the *Ṛgveda* is situated within or in the vicinity of the time of Harappan disaster, then the information would be the personal experiences of earliest bardic composers. But, if the hymns are assigned to a period later than the time of the Harappan disaster, the same information can pass as memories of disaster experienced by the earliest bardic composers. The latter possibility seems unlikely in view of the upward revision of the Ṛgvedic chronology on the basis of ethno-linguistic information in the text and the eyewitness nature of catastrophic events and their debilitating effects on the people, so graphically recorded in the *Ṛgveda* hymns. According to one study, the earliest hymns of the *Ṛgveda* can be assigned to the period 1900-

1700 BC and the latest ones to 1200 BC (Witzel, 1999). Accepting the internal relationship between the poets and kings as decisive, and coupling these individuals and the tribes with which they are connected with the geographical horizons of the texts that feature them (Witzel, 1995, 312), Witzel emphasizes an outside origin of the Aryans, entering South Asia, tribe after tribe, clan after clan and provides an ingenious explanation for why no evidence of 'Aryan blood' or 'Aryan skeleton' has survived in South Asia (Witzel, 1995, 113). The upper limit of the *Ṛgveda* in this reckoning is still very much on the lower side. Besides, the estimate is based on the assumed presence of certain ethnolinguistic groups in certain areas at certain periods of time though no historical verification is forthcoming for any of these suppositions. As for the Harappan chronology, the period of late Harappan urban places extends to 1500 BC and even afterwards (Shaffer, 1995, 138). Added to this is the concept of rural towns, the likes of which continued through the second millennium BC. At Pirak, some twenty kms east of Mehargarh and Nousharo, a proto-urban settlement covering 9 ha and rising 12 m above the surrounding plain is said to have existed between 1700 BC and 700 BC (Jarrige, 1984, 44). This might suggest that there is no chronological gap between the decaying stages of the Harappan civilization and the earliest compositions of the *Ṛgveda,* and that for nearly half a millennium (2000–1500 BC) or more Ṛgvedic communities and the Harappan people were not only compatriots but even participants in the same historical processes.

Correlation between the early Vedic culture and the Harappan civilization has been stressed by different scholars, sometimes on the basis of the correspondence of social data in the *Ṛgveda* and Harappan archaeology (Sastri, 1965) and sometimes on the basis of semi-historical Epic tradition (Gupta and Ramchandran, 1976). However, these ideas have not been effective because of imprecise data recovery and inappropriate synchronization in the first case and the attempted synchronization of diachronic textual materials in the latter case. The attribution of the origin of Harappan culture to the Indo-Europeans (Allchin and Allchin, 1968, 144) may even suggest that the old Vedic dialect or a proto-form of it and its speakers were present in the Greater Indus Valley several centuries before the beginning of the Middle Bronze Age. But there is no explanation of why and how the Indo-Europeans happened to be in the area when they did.

The recent suggestion that the Harappan inscriptions represent a sign system without encoding any spoken words, that it was meant to fulfil limited political, economic and religious functions and was universally understood in a multilingual space (Farmer et al., 2004, 47), would mean that the basis of communication in the Harappan civilization was not the scripted word, but the spoken word of which many versions were in circulation. Some of these dialects may have comprised a literary and a colloquial segment. This would also mean that different forms of knowledge and day-to-day experiences of life were communicated by word of mouth in the form of short and long compositions, both in prose and poetry. Since such linguistic skills were homespun and hereditary, every person irrespective of his vocation was capable of articulating or expanding the inherited information depending on the changing ways of life. However, in the liturgical circle, the same language would take a different form because of a strict metrical regimen and a stricter mode of chanting. The language of the *Ṛgveda,* as represented in the existing Śākalya text, was thus not just another spoken dialect; rather, it was a dialect specially articulated by the priests and poets for exclusive liturgical functions. This presupposes the existence of a vernacular Vedic dialect which preceded the Mantra dialect by several centuries and was used in the families of poets and priests. 'Not insignificantly, some colloquial forms of speech, such as that used by wives of the gods, show various levels even in the *Ṛgveda*' (Hoffman, 1975, 7). Considering that the earliest hymns of the *Ṛgveda* were already underway about the beginning of the second millennium BC, the vernacular Vedic dialect can easily go back to the end of the third millennium BC or even earlier.

The vernacular Vedic dialect appears to have stood halfway between the Mantra dialect and various spoken dialects like Prakrit, Dravidian and Munda. According to one opinion, the Vedic speakers knew and interacted with Dravidian and Munda speakers (Kuiper, 1948, 1955, 1962, 1991). Like Kuiper, his disciple Michael Witzel also concentrates on the Dravidian and Munda substrates in the *Ṛgveda* (Witzel, 1999). However, there are other scholars who have taken good care of the Prakrit element in the Śakālya text (Deshpande, 1993). The vernacular Vedic, which was confined to conversation among the members of priestly families, accumulated substantial substrate influences from these spoken dialects in the course of interactions and communications between the members of the priestly families and the society at large. Since all the relatives were not immediately concerned with the liturgy, their familiarity with the Mantra dialect was not even peripheral. But in view of their concerns with the larger society, they were fairly conversant with the spoken dialects. Many of the lesser members of these families may have grown up with one or the other of these non-Vedic spoken dialects as their first language.

As the Mantra dialect and the accompanying liturgy grew in importance and covered new territory and the priestly craft became a lucrative enterprise, it may have motivated some of these half-learners to try their hand at the Mantra compositions and carve out a fortune in the political circles. Perhaps the substrate influences, whether in the Mantra dialect or in the vernacular Vedic dialect, were considered a normal feature and there was no conscious attempt to prevent these influences. This can be evidenced from the fact that the substrates are not confined to the old Vedic language; rather, they continued to occur in good measure in the middle Vedic language as well. The substrate elements may also have entered the Mantra dialect by way of compositions undertaken by Prakrit or Dravidian-speaking poets with inadequate training in the Mantra dialect.

Viewed in the background of widespread geo-climatic disorders, the *Ṛgveda* may pass as the bardic documentation of a decaying civilization characterized by degenerate urban places, political instability, regressive trade, declining peasant production, growing scarcity and starvation deaths, all culminating in violent civil disturbances and the scramble to capture existing resource centres. These devastations may have triggered radical cultural mutations in the Greater Indus Valley and the beginnings of new cultural paradigms. This may lend well to the idea that the 'Vedic literature reflects then, not a foreign human invasion, but a radical alteration in the social, political, and economic organizations of the indigenous culture, that a dominant social group is depicted as a conquering invader in this social reorganization may reflect a cultural rationalization, or justification for the ascendancy of one social group over others' (Shaffer, 1983, 86). In a restructuring of social relations, this ascendant social group developed a mechanism of stratification which divided the whole community into a superior Āryavarṇa and an inferior Dāsvarṇa, the former claiming more power and prestige at the cost of the latter. Later, towards the end of the Late Bronze Age, the superiority of mental work over physical labour became idealized with the Brāhmaṇa priestly class claiming the top spot and the Kṣatriyas, Vaiśyas and Śūdras following in the descending order. Alongside, the liturgy, which began with articulate spoken words as oblation to gods (*kavya-havya*), soon incorporated the practice of offering food and beverage to fire probably with a view to preventing the non-priestly classes from accumulating resources in excess of their requirement and use this economic power to enhance the authority of the priests.

The early practitioners of the prayer liturgy tried to impress upon the people that spirituality and moral behaviour were the need of the hour and that transgressions of the laws of nature amounted to sinful acts of a deadly nature and invited divine wrath in the form of social and natural calamities. The worship of the forces of nature represented by powerful divinities would only be a short step from such a perception of linkage between human beings and nature. Possibly, all this relates to an attempted renewal and reinvigoration of human efforts to overcome trauma and integrate as many ethnic groups as possible under the overarching influence of a new religious ideology and supra-local identity.

From the archaeological point of view, the latter half of the Middle Bronze Age presents a mixed scenario of urban degeneration with some of the fortified structures still serviceable but others deserted or dilapidated. A fortified building is almost always a centre for accumulating social goods and therefore needs special protection against outside attacks. This already illustrates the contradictions inherent in the process of accumulation and the possibility of attacks by those people who are deprived of a share of the social goods. With the urban networking falling apart during the opening centuries of the second millennium BC and the regression of hydraulic state managing large irrigation dams, the level of peasant surpluses declined and conflicts for forcible capture of resources in the fortified structures (*pur*) and diversion of drainage through dam bursts (*vṛtrahatyā*) may have become a common feature of the social landscape during the first half of the second millennium BC. Such a scenario falls in line with bardic descriptions of fortifications and enclosed settlements, some thriving and some others ruined and deserted, and the bardic desire to occupy the former and even undertake fights for this purpose. The chiefs and warriors, whose exploits in the course of such missions are eulogized by the poets, may have been the owners of certain resource centres fallen on bad days. Even otherwise, every political authority takes advantage of an anarchic situation and tries to establish its hegemony over as large an area as possible.

Looking for other areas of correspondence between textual and archaeological information, attention may focus on bardic preoccupation with natural calamities like floods, droughts, earthquakes and epidemics and the destabilizing effects of these events in the form of hunger, scarcity and civil war, all of which are corroborated in varying degrees by archaeological investigations. As for the natural calamities, nearly 5 per cent of the compositions deal with one or the other of natural disasters and the whole text is devoted to prayers to gods for deliverance from misfortune and the conservation of life and resources. In the characteristic bardic tradition, these events frequently appear as the doing of one demon or the other, Ahi and Vala representing low precipitation, Śuṣna signifying desiccation and desertification and Vṛtra referring to dams which deprived many distant peasant localities of a viable source of drainage. The plurality of social formations detailed by bardic composers in different portions of the text may compare with divergent archaeological cultures representing hunting-gathering societies, nomadic pastoralists, sedentary stockbreeders, well-developed peasant societies and marginal urban communities, all existing side by side and interacting. The ethno-cultural diversity outlined in the text and encountered in the archaeological excavations lends well to the correspondence of diverse funerary behaviour outlined in the text and those found in Harappan archaeological contexts during the third millennium BC. The more important of these practices were, as already noted, full cremations, full burials, post-cremation burials and post-exposure burials.

Scattered textual information on regressive trade and marginal craft workings may relate to a likely late Harappan scenario. Occasional inputs relating to long-distance exchange of goods, both overland and overseas, also fall in line with the regressive overland and maritime trade pursued by the Harappans throughout the first half of the second millennium BC. In terms of business terminology, the *Ṛgveda* incorporates almost all the vocables which signify different aspects of the exchange process, like sale, purchase, lease, mortgage, taking of loans, repayment of loans, money transactions and barter. Terms denoting a professional trader (*vaṇik*) and a class of professional usurers (*paṇi*) besides the value of a commodity or price (*śulka*) are mentioned. Copious details of riverine and maritime trade and the commodities exchanged are also given. The commodities exchanged appear to have included all the products of animal farm and the agricultural farm (*gavyam-yavyam*), the various products of the forests besides gems and pearls (*ratna*) obtained from the high seas. However, because of the regressive nature of the exchange system, some of the words provide slightly different meanings in certain contexts. Two good examples are *niṣka* and *śulka*. In one example, the former means a metallic coin perhaps a gold coin and in the other, a gold necklace. The term *śulka* means price at one place and a wager in another. In traditional societies, coins of precious metals like gold, silver and copper are often used as ornaments or talisman, especially when there was no commercial use of these objects.

Put together, these stray bits of textual information may suffice to correlate with the decadent stages of trade and craft production in the Greater Indus Valley after 2000 BC. Archaeologists have noticed marginal but significant continuities in the fields of external trade and craft production during the late Harappan phase. Finds of Indus seals in the Kassite contexts at Nippur and in Failaka and the occurrence of a seal with a whorl motif at Bet Dwaraka are good indicators of the marginal nature of external trade during the late Harappan phase. Craft production was also regressive and less organized though at certain centres the Harappan manufacturing tradition appeared to have continued like bead making at Dher Majra near Ropar and shell working in the Jamnagar region of Bet Dwaraka (Lahiri, 1992, 129).

However, in a religious document such information is always incidental and disorganized and, as in the present case, frequently a baggage of unrelated data far removed in time and space. This would suffice to warrant that collection of information has to be thematic irrespective of hymns or stanzas in which this information may appear. A pathological preference for communicating with the help of similes and metaphors, many of which are out of place, further distances the reader from the actual social realities of the same or different times. Finally, myths play an important role in the mode of bardic communication. Since myths reflect the coding of social information and an attempt to explain relationships between phenomena which are both cultural and natural, these need careful decoding and contextualization to get the full benefit of the data recovered. Such decoding becomes significant in view of the fact that 'myths are ways of explaining paradoxes, the paradoxes of social order within extra social chaos, of the relationship of authority to power and the like' (Middleton, 1967).

The Indo-Iranian Homeland

The term Indo-Iranian Homeland relates to a large surface area covering north-western South Asia, Afghanistan, Eastern Iran and the adjoining parts of South Central Asia with strong biological and cultural affinities from the beginning of pre-historic time. These relations are broadly corroborated by archaeological findings notwithstanding diverse assemblages of material culture in different parts of this area. For a textual confirmation of these affinities one may refer to the *Ṛgveda* (Müller, 1890-92/1966) and the *Avesta* (Darmesteter, 1887/1992; Mills, 1887/1988) both of which outline the Indo-Iranian subcontinent as a common homeland during the Middle Bronze Age and afterwards. The whole area is fairly well outlined in the *Ṛgveda* and the *Vendîdâd* and the portions which document this geographical information are of the same date. On the basis of correspondence between textual and archaeological evidence, the earliest compositions of the *Ṛgveda* can be dated back to the late third and early second millennium BC when the Indo-Iranian subcontinent in general and north-western South Asia in particular were under the destabilizing effects of diverse geo-climatic disorders. The *Vendîdâd*, which is a compilation of religious laws and of mythical tales (Darmesteter, 1887/1992), is said to be younger than the Gāthic text on linguistic grounds but contains certain portions which seem to be much earlier than the Gāthic compositions. These portions have no direct connection with the general object of the Fargards, and are remnants of an old epic and cosmogonic literature. For instance, Fargard II, which speaks of Yima as the founder of civilization, appears to be a myth. The second part of this Fargard refers to Ahura Mazda's advice to Yima to prepare a Varah and keep the seeds of every kind of animal and plant so that civilization could be recreated when the world, lasting a long year of twelve millennia, came to an end as a result of dire winter. The tale reminds the readers of the Biblical narrative of the great deluge and the legendary Noah's ark which was prepared before the deluge and loaded with one representative of every species of life and in which Abraham and his elk escaped to a safer land. Compare this with Fargard I of the *Vendîdâd,* which relates to well-defined geographical regions in Eastern Iran, Afghanistan and north-western South Asia and envisages a space of time which intervened between the creation of these lands by the Ahura Mazda and their subsequent destruction by Angra Mainyu, clearly has a firm historical background and does not belong to the category of creation myths. Probably, this is a mythical characterization of various urban and proto-urban settlements on the Indo-Iranian subcontinent which flourished during the Early Bronze Age (2900–2300 BC) and began to decay and disintegrate from the beginning of the Middle Bronze Age (2300–1700 BC).

Judging by the geographical information furnished in the *Ṛgveda*, the homeland of the Āryas of the *Ṛgveda* stretched from Haryana in the east to Afghanistan in the west and from the vale of Kashmir in the north to Kutch, Sindh and Baluchistan in the south. Except for the vale of Kashmir and certain parts of Afghanistan, this area was also the home of the Greater Indus Valley civilization.

The *Vendîdâd* (Fargard I), which on linguistic grounds is assigned to a date much later than that of the Gāthic portion of the *Avesta,* relates to themes which would be appropriate to a time which witnessed widespread destabilizing of urban and proto-urban settlements on the Indo-Iranian subcontinent and, accordingly, may easily go back to the beginning of the Middle Bronze Age in this whole area. In the *Vendîdâd* (Fargard I), Ahura Mazda is said to have created sixteen excellent regions for the habitation of the Ārya or Airya people which roughly corresponds to the area delineated by the *Ṛgveda* bards. The enumeration starts from the north with Gava (Sogdiana), Baxdi (Bactria), Mouru (Marziana) and Nicaya, which lay between Baxdi and Mouru. Taken together, these four regions constituted the northern extremity of the Aryan homeland according to the *Avesta.* Similarly, the western extremity of the Aryan provinces was marked by the valleys of Haroiva (Ṛgvedic Sarayu, old Persian Haroiva and modern Harirud), Haraiti (Ṛgvedic Sarasvatī, old Persian Haraiti, modern Argandab) and Haitumant (modern Helmand), all of which together account for the entire stretch of the Irano-Afghan frontier. On the eastern site, the *Vendîdâd* refers to Vaekreta, Varena, Haptahindu and Ranha. Ranha has not been satisfactorily identified, but Vaekreta refers to Gāndhāra, Varena to Buner and Haptahindu corresponds to Saptasindhu or the land of seven rivers. Together these three provinces accounted for the whole of the Indo-Pak subcontinent. The remaining five provinces of the Aryans lay in the central and southern parts of Afghanistan. The most important of these, Airyena Vaējah with its almost year-long winter is said to have been situated in the high altitudes of Central Afghanistan ranging from the Hindu Kush on the west to the Pamirs in the east (Gnoli, 1989A, 44).

This is the precise area of Afghanistan with its borderlands which can be easily figured out from the hydronyms and ethnonyms mentioned in the *Ṛgveda.* The references to hydronyms such as Kubha (Kabul), Krumu (Kurram), Gomatī (Gomal), Sarayu (Harirud), Saraswati (Avestan Haraiti, present day Argandab) and ethnonyms such as Bhalanas (the people inhabiting the Bolan valley), Śivas (Siboi of the Greeks, modern Śibi about 100 km south-east of the Bolan Pass) and Paktha (Pakhtoons of eastern Afghanistan) would suggest that Baluchistan and the whole of central and southern Afghanistan were part of the Aryan homeland in the *Ṛgveda*. The central Afghan highlands, which contain Airyena vaējah of the *Avesta* was also home to the Soma plant. Mount Mujavanta of the *Ṛgveda,* Muja of the Ferverdîn Yast (Yt. XIX.125.127), was the region where the Soma plant grew and was guarded by a dark-skinned people inhabiting the valley of the river Anśumatī. It is interesting to note that these hydronyms and ethnonyms are not passing allusions in the text. Rather, these areas and peoples are connected with the gift-collection missions of bardic composers and violent conflicts between chiefs for hegemonic supremacy in the concerned area.

Perhaps the geographical familiarity of Ṛgvedic bards went beyond the western frontiers of Afghanistan well into Iranian lands where they interacted with Iranian chiefs and peoples. This is fairly evident from bardic allusions to Iranian chiefs, poets and landscapes. One of the Iranian chiefs, called Persian

Tirindir (*parśu tirindir*, 8.6.46), patronized bards of Kāṇva descent, probably from the Swat valley. The other chief was Iṣṭāśva (Visṭāspa) who, possibly under the influence of a dissenting priestly group spurned a poet of Angirā descent (1.122.13). Among the bards of Iranian origin who served South Asian chiefs, mention may be made of Vadhṛyāśva, the chief priest of Divodāsa (6.61.1), and Śyāvāśva, who received patronage from several chiefs in Afghanistan, Pakistan and India (5.53.9; 5.61.6,9-10,18-19). The highlighting of camels and camel carts for transport of donated goods across desert tracks and the importance of camels in negotiating these areas may also relate to vast expanses of arid region in Afghanistan, Baluchistan and eastern Iran. Torture meted out by Persian detractors (*parśavaḥ*, 1.105.7; 10.33.2) to South Asian Soma oblators migrating to Iran also falls in line. If South Asian and Iranian bards swapped homelands in connection with gift collection missions, chiefs and military adventurists from Iran and north-western South Asia trailed their enemies on either side of the Indo-Iranian subcontinent. The battle of Hariyūppiyā, for instance, saw a Parthian chief (*pārthava*) engaging in fighting and, the battle over, making liberal gifts to associated bards (6.27.8).

Curiously, there is no dearth of scholars who would like to wish away all this information and confine the South Asian and Iranian peoples in geographical and cultural isolation. Consider the statement that 'the *Zend Avesta* is aware of areas outside the Iranian plateau while the *Ṛgveda* is ignorant of anything west of the Indus basin' (Erdosy, 1989, 42). In a similar vein is the attempt to restrict the Vedic homeland to a much narrower geographical area by equating the term 'Saptasindhu' with Punjab (Witzel,1995,323). The term Punjab (Sanskrit *pañca apa*) literally means the land of five rivers. No such term is found either in the *Avesta* or in the *Ṛgveda.* The term which is more common, is 'Haptahindu' in the *Avesta* and Saptasindhu or 'saptasindhavah' in the *Ṛgveda*. 'Saptasindhu' means seven rivers or the lands encompassed by seven rivers and not five rivers. The western-most river of this geographical area was evidently the Indus or the Sindhu and the eastern-most river was the Saraswati or the Hakra Ghaggar of the present day.

However, there is a basic difference in the presentation of geographical data in the two texts. The Avestan account recorded in *Vendîdâd* Chapter 1 refers to river valleys as the settlements of the Aryan people. But it also names particular regions not necessarily associated with rivers. Compared to this, place names in the *Ṛgveda* are extremely difficult to come by except in a few examples like Gāndhāra (1.126) and Hariyūppiyā (6.27). In the former case, reference is made to the ewe of the Gāndhāra people. In the other example, reference is made to the elimination of infidels on the eastern side of the settlement called Hariyūppiyā. The *Avesta,* which belonged to a country of landlocked rivers and lakes, does not evidently refer to the high seas or maritime journeys. The only sea known to the *Avesta* was Vouru Kasha, which seems to represent the Helmand Sea watered by the Helmand river and its tributaries. Compared to this the descriptions of high seas and maritime journeys are a normal feature in the *Ṛgveda.* Further, the *Vendîdâd* description of sixteen excellent settlements created by Ahura Mazda and their eventual destruction by Angra Mainyu encapsulates two different chrono-zones, one relating to a time of flourishing settlements, probably the mature phase of urban and proto-urban settlements on the Indo-Iranian subcontinent and the other relating to the destruction and depopulation of these settlements, probably during the Middle Bronze Age and afterwards. There is not much evidence of widespread destruction of settlements in the *Ṛgveda* though the text frequently refers to different types of geo-climatic devastations.

The two texts also differ in relation to the use of the term Ārya as ethnic, linguistic or geographical qualifier. Although the term Ārya is frequently used to identify a new genre of people probably drawn from across diverse ethnic communities and profoundly confiding in a system of nature worship, the concept of an Aryan land is unknown to the *Ṛgveda.* From the linguistic angle, non-Vedic dialects and even perverted Vedic dialects are denounced as corrupt or hostile (*mṛdhravāca*) and unproductive (*vadhṛvāca*); the term Ārya is never used as a qualifier of the Vedic dialect though it may have been understood as such. On the other hand, the *Vendîdâd*, which was later than not only the earliest compositions of the *Ṛgveda*, but also the old *Avesta*, considers the Āryas as an exclusive group who inhabited sixteen excellent regions meant for them. The period following the *Vendîdâd* shows further devolution of the term, which represented a country, a language and even an ethnic group, just as it happened in India during the post-Vedic phase.

For a reconstruction of Ṛgvedic geography, one may also refer to certain topographical features, like uncharacteristic shifts in the course of a river or certain practices exclusive to peoples in certain mountainous regions. For instance, the expression *sodañcam sindhum* (2.15.6) relates to the river Indus flowing due north. Throughout its entire course, it is only at one place, near Skardu in Baltistan Kashmir, that the river flows due north for quite a distance before turning on itself for the same distance and turning west and south-west to take its normal course up to the sea. This uncharacteristic shift was thought to be the work of great physical strength and was accordingly attributed to Indra, suggesting thereby the presence of certain groups of Vedic speakers in this area (Nandi, 2001). Similarly, the term *udavraja*, which figures in association with Śambara in a lone passage of the text (6.47.21), literally means floating pastures or fields. In the vale of Kashmir, there is a tradition of preparing small floating fields by sprinkling a little earth on rafters and raising a reasonably good harvest with the help of fertile waters in the lakes and rivers. The association of Śambara with *udavraja* is also significant inasmuch as it was in the mountainous hideouts, possibly the Karewa pit dwellings that Indra besieged his arch enemy for forty long years before tracking him down and burning his settlements. (Nandi, 2001).

A recent study (Witzel, 1995b), which tries to reconstruct Ṛgvedic geography and provide the information in a tabulated form, seems to depend a little too heavily on unintelligible passages to suggest fresh geographical entities besides ignoring some of the known identifications, as in the case of Gāndharā in the first book. Some of the 'suggested identifications' are *pastya* or *pastyā*, *urjayanti* and *kṛtva*. There is some mix-up between the neuter *pastya*, meaning a stall or stable and the feminine *pastyā*, meaning a homestead, dwelling, household (9.65.23). In other contexts, *pastyā* means the two halves of the Soma press (10.96.10) and also the goddess of domestic affairs (4.55.3; 8.27.5). If anything, the expression *pastye sadane* in 8.27.5 may simply mean, 'in the stall', 'in the stable' or 'in the cattle farmhouse', the idea of a settlement being nowhere implicit. Similarly, in the case of feminine *pastyā*, which appears in connection with the locative *arjikeṣu* and *kṛtvaṣu*, the expression *pastyānām madhye* may simply mean 'in the central place of the household' (9.65.23). Once again, the idea of a settled territory is missing. Another term, *ūrjayanti* (2.13.8), which is taken to mean a region in Afghanistan, is all the more arbitary. The expression *ūrjayantā Aparivisṭamāsya* simply means that Indra uncovered the face of his thunderbolt to eliminate Narmara or the son of Nṛmara. The two alternative interpretations given by Sāyaṇa also leave no doubt about the obscure nature of this passage, which Griffith (Griffith, 1973, 138) already describes as unintelligible. According to Grassman, *ūrjayanti* means the sun. Whether the passage is unintelligible or not, there is certainly no basis for associating it with Afghanistan. The study mentions three other terms, viz. *kuṣava, vibāli* and *udavraja*. The first two may or may not mean a river, but the last one, as already shown above, has escaped the attention it deserved.

Horses, Riders and Chariots

The presence of *equus caballus* within a certain community calls for determining the possible uses to which the animal may have been put. There are examples in which people learnt to domesticate the horse, but used it for diet and ritual purposes as in the case of European steppe people during 5000 BC. There are other examples in which the horse was regularly bitted and ridden, probably to hunt wild horses as at Botai, east of the Urals between 3500 BC and 3000 BC (Derevyanko and Dorj, 1992/1999; Anthony and Brown, 2000).

Bit and Bit Wear

The importance of horse and horse riding at this Kazak site is evident from the fact that 90 per cent of the animal bones recovered from this site are horse bones. The most important evidence of the bridling or bitting of horses is bit wear in the form of a significant bevel or slope on the front or mesial corner of the lower second premolars (Anthony and Brown, 2000). The bridling is caused as the bridled or bitted horse chews up the bit in the course of riding, which increases the bevel or slope in the lower second premolars either on one side or both, depending on the manner in which the rider controls the horse. Bits could be made from organic materials, like hemp rope, horsehair rope, leather and bone, besides metal. The metal bit causes the maximum damage to the dental pathology of the equid. Among the organic bits, it is the hemp rope and the bone that cause maximum increases in the bevelling of lower-second premolars of horses, whereas bits made of leather and horsehair rope almost do not affect the dental pathology of the animal.

In the Harappan context, there is no dearth of equid bones throughout the Greater Indus Valley, but there are no representations of horse riders on the Harappan glyptic art. No studies of equid dental pathology from the area are yet forthcoming to indicate whether the animal—horse or onager—was controlled by the rider with the help of bits of some sort. In case the bits were made from horsehair rope, leather or some similar soft material, the possibility of increased bevelling in the lower second premolars of the equid would be difficult to ascertain. Bits can be altogether out of the reckoning in the event of the rider controlling the equid with the reins passing through the nostrils of the animal. This is precisely what appears in one passage of the *Ṛgveda* (5.61.2), which refers to *naso yama* or the rope passing through the nostril of the horse. The *naso yama* is understood by Sāyaṇ as the part of the reins that passes through the nostrils of the horse and prevents it from running away. The passage also refers to *abhiṣu* or the whip, which actually was the part of the reins held by the rider and used to strike the animal on its neck whenever required.

Probably, the saddle was also in use, as can be seen from the expression *pṛṣṭhe sada* (5.61.2). This must have been a thick sitting pad with nooses of rope hanging on either side for holding fast the feet of the rider. The image of the rider, that emerges from this description would be of a person who held the reins with one hand and some weapon in the other. To goad the horse to move on, the rider would strike the thigh of the horse with his feet (*jaghane coda*, 5.61.3). The expression is formed by compounding the locative singular *jaghane* with a derivative of √*cud*, meaning to motivate, to impel, to force, to activate, to send, etc.

The Equid Family in the Greater Indus Valley

As for the horse, the bones of the animal or the absence of it has long been a bone of contention between archaeologists and historians subscribing to divergent opinions. The representation of the animal in the Harappan glyptic art and the discovery of equid bones from different parts of the Greater Indus Valley are both focal points of a raging debate as to whether these refer to the horse (*equus caballus*), the onegar (*equus hemionus*) or the ass (*equus assinus*). There is no doubt that the onager and the ass were domesticated by the Harappans from very early times, whereas the domestication of the horse was confined to certain regions like Gujarat, which is said to be a natural habitat of the equid family. A good survey of equid bones in the Harappan context is worth reproducing here (Possehl, 1999, 186). 'There are claims for the presence of the horse (equus caballus) at Harappa (Prasad, 1936; Nath, 1959), Ropar (Nath, 1968), Mohenjo-daro (Sewell and Guha, 1931) and Kalibangan (Sharma, 1990). Horse remains have been reported from Bronze Age sites in Gujarat and are reported from Surkotada in Kutch (Sharma, 1990; Bokonyi, 1997), Lothal (Nath and Rao, 1985), Malvan (Sharma, 1990) and Kanewal (Sahni, 1920-21)'.

The bones of *equus hemionus* have been found at Rojdi (Stack-Kane, 1989) and Surkotada (Sharma, 1990). A 'domestic ass' has been identified in a preliminary report for Kalibangan (IAR, 1964-65), which may be *equus hemionus*. B.S. Guha and B.K. Chatterjee (Guha and Chatterjee, 1946, 316) identified the ass (*equus assinus*) and the horse (*equus caballus*) at Rana Ghundai in northern Baluchistan. It is now thought by some that only the onager (*equus hemionus*) was present there (Richard Meadow, personal communication to Possehl, 1999). In a slightly later context, the horse and ass have been identified at Pirak, a site of the early second millennium BC, very close to Mehrgarh and Nausharo (Meadow, 1979). There are also terracotta figurines of an equid which is a reasonably convincing rendering of *equus caballus* (Enault, 1979).

The Proxy Horse

"The onager (*equus hemionus*) and horse (*equus caballus*) are closely related and their osteological remains are not easily distinguishable" (Possehl, 1999, 186). Differences are present, but it requires skill and good comparative material to determine them. The evidence from terracotta figurines is even more difficult to use in distinguishing the ass from the horse (Possehl, 1999, 186). Because the onager is native to the Greater Indus Region, there is a reasonable certainty that some, perhaps all, of the bones and teeth found so far at archaeological sites of the Indus Age are from this animal".

Some observation of the *equid hemionus* and its correlation with literary information would at once show that in the third millennium context of north-western South Asia, the presence or absence of *equus caballus* is of little consequence. The onager, which provides plentiful good meat (Possehl, 1999, 188; Roberts, 1977, 161), functions efficiently as a pack animal or draft animal and runs even faster than the horse (Elphinstone, 1819, 10), could very well represent the horse in north-western South Asia during the third millennium BC. In the earliest literary records, it is the distinctive reddish-brown colour, that is frequently associated with a fast-moving animal called *aśva* and even led to the coining of a new term *śoṇa* for the animal.

The *Ṛgveda*, which is the earliest literary record of north-western South Asia, has several terms meaning a horse. The more important of these are *aśva, tura, haya, hari, arvat* and *vājī*. Of these, the term *āśva* occurs 368 times in the text including a hundred compounds. The term may be derived from *aśu* meaning to reach, visit, arrive, but more appropriately from *aśva*, which is also derived from *āśu*, but means fast, quick. Āśu figures eighty-six times in the *Ṛgveda* in the sense of quick or fast, but in several passages it means the horse itself. This is in line with the derivation of *aśva*, which is a nominative plural of *aśu*. With a little shortening of the initial vowel *āśva* would become *aśva*. Tura meaning quick, powerful, prompt, appears 49 times in the *Ṛgveda* and on several occasions in the sense of a horse. Haya from √*hi*, meaning send forth, stimulate, is much less recurrent in the text appearing in five passages in the sense of a horse. Hari, which signifies several colours, like brown, yellow, tawny, pale, and appears nearly 150 times in the text, also means a horse in a few passages. Arvat meaning running, hastening, a courser, appears eighty-five times, mostly in the sense of a horse. Vājī is nominative singular of the term *vāja*, which means several completely different things like energy or strength, a contest or battle, booty, gain or reward and a swift horse, appears nearly 200 times in the text. It may have been applied to the horse since the animal was a symbol of strength and was instrumental in fighting a battle or capturing booty. This vocabulary of horse underlines that the animal was the symbol of strength, promptness and quickness.

Archaeology of the Wheeled Cart

As for the cart, there can be no doubt that the Harappan people used it like all other contemporary communities in Iran, Central Asia and West Asia. In the desert region, the principal draft animal was the camel, but in the river plains, the carts were drawn by either the bullock or members of the equid family—the horse, the onager or the ass. Bullocks came in handy for transport of large quantities of goods, whereas the horse or the onager was used for lighter and swifter carts. Like the bullock, the ass may also have been used for heavy transport duty. Clearly, the carts used by the Harappans were of two categories, the slow-moving carts meant for heavy transport operations and the lighter ones meant for passenger traffic. The earliest examples of toycart wheels found at Mohenjodaro, Harappa, Kalibangan and Lothal show that these were of two major types, solid and spoked (Ghosh, 1989, 337). Solid wheels were of three types, some without a hub, some with a single-hub and some with a double-hub. The solid wheel was very heavy and sturdy and was made of three to twelve pieces (Ghosh, 1989). It was easy to make and was very useful and efficient for transportation of goods but could not be used when speed and manoeuvre were required. Since it was difficult to maintain the balance with a solid wheel without a hub, the single hub was introduced in order to control the undulating movement of the wheel. Finally, the double-hubbed wheel was invented because it was more convenient and practical than either of the other types.

However, the observation that the spoked wheel came into existence in order to reduce the weight of the wheel and make it more suitable for speed (Ghosh, 1989) or that the Indus people used carts with solid wheels tied to the axle and turning round along with the axle (Dani and Thapar, 1992/1999, 301) does not quite agree with the presence of spoked wheels in pre-Harappan or early Harappan cultures. A painted sherd depicting a canopied cart with spoked wheels has been reported from the pre-Harappan or early Harappan sequence at Banawali, situated on the Sarasvatī in district Hissar, almost midway between Kalibangan and Rakhigarhi, about eighty kms from the latter (Shaffer and Thapar, 1992/1999). Since spoked wheels are much lighter and technologically advanced, it is unlikely that its use would be discontinued by succeeding generations of mature Harappan people. In all likelihood, solid wheels with or without hubs, were used for heavy transport, whereas the lighter and swifter spoked wheel carts with a canopy overhead were meant for passenger traffic in major cities. It is also likely that solid wheels without a hub, a solid wheel with a single or double hub and spoked wheels continued side by side depending on the crudity or sophistication of social contexts, like the interior countryside and the mega cities or the nature of the work assigned to each of these types. In traditional societies, older technologies are never completely replaced by advanced models, as in the case of the prehistoric saddle and quern which still prevail in numerous South Asian households not only in villages, but also in the towns. Similarly, a prototype of the Harappan solid wheel tied to the axle and turning round along with the axle can still be seen plying in the villages of Sind (Dani and Thapar, 1992/1999).

The Harappan evidence of two-wheeled light carts from the early and mature phases should suffice to discourage the idea that such a light vehicle was the innovation of a supposed Aryan aristocracy who swarmed across different parts of Europe and Asia during the mid second millenimum BC and afterwards. It is also not correct to hold that the so called Aryans were the first people to use the domestic horse for drawing these light carts. A good study of chariot petroglyphs reported from widely separated regions like upper Indus, Central Asia, Siberia, the P.R. of Mongolia, Altai, Inner Mongolia, Kazakhstan, Kirghizia, Tajikistan, Xinjiang and other places (Frankfort, 1992, 100) would suffice to show that the use of chariot was not a monopoly of the so called Aryan aristocracy. However, the obsession with the supposed linkage between Aryans and horse-drawn chariots frequently leads scholars to conclude that these petroglyphs represent the horse-drawn chariots of the Vedic Aryans on the road to India (Piggott, 1983; Kuz'mina, 1986). Closer examination shows that most of the drawings represent either oxen-chariots or bullock-chariots and only a few suggest horse-drawn chariots. Both the bullock-cart and the oxen-cart are represented in the art of the late third to early second millennium BC on a silver vase from the Louvre, the drawing on the vase depicting an A-frame chariot in a narrative frieze (Frankfort, 1992, 100). The remaining petroglyphes which depict the horse-drawn chariot cannot also be a surprise or a specific identifying feature of a much highlighted steppe community, since all the peoples, from Egypt and Anatolia to China, were using them during the second millennium BC (Frankfort, 1992, 100).The possibility of certain late Harappan communities replacing onager carts by horse carts brightens in view of the figurines of horse riders discovered from the Pirak valley of Baluchistan about the beginning of second millennium BC.

The Omnibus Ratha

The prevalence of spoked-wheel carts in the Harappan context, early or mature, seems to be a good basis of correlation between the literary and archaeological records of north-western South

Asia during the third millennium BC. In the *Ṛgveda*, the term *ratha* appears more than 650 times in the sense of a cart or carriage and, according to the needs of the people, the cart could be made for transporting goods, commuting or fighting battles. Further, *ratha* was a generic term for all types of carriages ranging from bullock-carts to horse-carts and donkey-carts. In one instance, a woman fighter Mudgalāni is seen driving a bullock-cart (10.102.2; 10.102.6) to fight enemies, the cart being repeatedly described as *ratha* (10.102.1-2; 10.102.11). In another instance, soldiers defeated in a war are seen hastening back to the safety of their home in a cart which too is called a *ratha* and driven by a pair of bullocks. Apart from bullocks, donkeys too were used for drawing carts, for example in the case of the Aśvins. In several other instances, carts described as *ratha* were used to transport goods from one place to another. Clearly, any attempt to suggest that the term *ratha* always meant a light war-chariot would be misplaced.

Coming to the different parts of the carriage, attention is at once focused on the description of the wheel fitted with spokes. In several passages, the spokes of a wheel are compared to the Maruts suggesting that spokes were of equal size just as Maruts were all equals (5.58.5; 8.20.14). The comparison with Maruts may also be a basis to speculate on the number of spokes fitted to a wheel. The Maruts are invariably represented by multiples of seven, such as seven, twenty-one, forty-nine, etc. Probably the prime number seven would do well to represent the number of spokes fitted to the wheel. The spokes appear to have been fixed between the nave and the rim by means of tight grooving, the terms for rim and nave being *nemi* and *nābhi* respectively. The bards frequently used the simile 'as the rim of the wheel holds the spokes' (*arān nemi na*, 1.32.15; 1.141.9) or 'as the spokes of the wheel are surrounded by the rim (*iva nemi arān*; 5.13.6). The grooving or fixing of the spokes into the rim and the nave is fairly well stressed by a passage which states that Indra bound all the Asuras together just as the spokes of the wheel are grooved into the rim and nave (*khe arān iva tānu sam it khedayā akhidat* 8.77.3). The terms *khe, khedayā* and *akhidata* are all derived from *kha*, which means a cavity, hollow, the whole of nave of a wheel through which the axis runs. The grooving or fixing of the spokes into the nave is also emphasized as in 10.78.4, which states that the spokes of the chariot wheel are bound to the nave or hub of the wheel (*ye sthūṇām ara na sanābhaya* 10.78.4).

Further information on the different parts of a carriage is furnished by two important passages of the third *maṇḍala*, which refer to the homeward journey of the Bharatas after they were defeated in the ten kings' battle (3.53.17; 3.53.19). The deity of these passages is described as Rathāngāni, meaning the parts of a carriage, although the cart in question is a bullock-cart driven by a pair of oxen. This is evident from the prayer, 'Let the bullocks be steady (*gāvau sthirau bhavatām*)'. Prayers are also made for the safety of different parts of the carriage till the Bharatas reach their home. Two types of wood appear to have been used in the making a cart. The *catechu* wood, which has a very hard texture, was meant for making the sitting area of the cart (*khadirasya sāraṁ*), whereas the *sisame* wood was used to make the axle. The expression *spandane śinśapāyām ojaḥ dhehi,* meaning 'put firmness into the axle made from *śinśapā* wood' (*dal bergia sisu*) is significant. The term *akṣa* meaning an axle also figures in these passages (3.53.17). The sitting area used to have a pulpit (*garta*) and the person seated in the pulpit was described as *gurlasadam*. As for the fore part of the carriage, two parallel poles were used in the case of a horse-cart and a single pole in the case of a bullock-cart. In either case, the pole or poles, *īṣā*, were fixed to a *yoke, yugam*. The different parts of a carriage appear to have been fixed by a kind of latch-pin (*pātalya*, 3.53.17) commonly used by most carpenters. In case a canopied cart was required, four additional shafts could be fixed at the four corners of the sitting area to hold a canopy made from leather or similar lighter material.

Language, Archaeology and Social Context

Reconstructing social contexts from language is a familiar method in historical linguistics. But when such attempts are made in relation to pre-historic societies, like Indo-Aryan and Dravidian, one would expect a certain amount of synchronism between the language and its speakers. While the Indo-Aryan of pre-history survives in a time-frozen liturgical text, the Dravidian of pre-history has to be reconstructed only through the back projection of modern Dravidian, the southern or the northern variety. Even a time-frozen text like the *Ṛgveda* may not always reflect the structural or lexical features of the dialect as spoken 4000 years ago, owing to a large number of recensions and redactions appearing in different regions and at different times. Similarly, the presumption that modern Dravidian is capable of representing diverse social contexts in prehistoric times in different regions and at different times is a little too unrealistic, linguistically as well as historically.

As for the social context, it can vary within a vast linguistic community inhabiting a large area as according diverse habitat conditions. Variations can also take place through contact with other languages or as a result of migration to new areas. The suggestion that the earliest Dravidian dialect represented a herding society, that the next stage of the dialect represented an agricultural society and that the final stage of the dialect represented an urban or state society (Southworth, 1995, 268) is based on a classification of existing Dravidian vocabularies. But it is difficult to say whether this classification can replicate historical stages more than 4000 years ago. In the Harappan archaeological context, herding societies preceded, coexisted with and even succeeded sedentary peasant societies and urban communities. In other words, social contexts not merely precede or succeed one another but also coexist and overlap, ruling out a simplistic linear equation of language and social context.

Curiously, Southworth's reconstruction also shows up with occasional lexical mix-ups. His suggestion that the name Maharashtra is the Sanskritized form of Marahaṭṭa or Maraghaṭṭa and that the latter contains the Dravidian suffix *haṭṭa* meaning hamlet or village (a Kannada form of *paṭṭi*) may or may not be correct but the entry number for *haṭṭa* in the *Dravidian Etymological Dictionary* (Burrow and Emeneau, 1960) is 3199 and not 3868. More intriguing is the observation attributed to Burrow (Southworth, 1995, 268, fn –13), who is said to note the existence of a word for horse, Tamil *ivuli* and Brahui (h) *uli* (*DED* 500), and which therefore must have existed in the earliest Dravidian language. However, *DED* 500 does not have any term for horse. Instead it has *utakku* in Tamil meaning 'to be fitted to the string of the bow', *utakku* in Malyalam meaning catch, latching, notch, obstruction. There is no trace of either *ivuḷi* or *(h)uḷḷi* in any of the supplementary vocabularies of Dravidian dialects furnished at the end of the dictionary. The terms *ivuḷi* in Tamil meaning onion, garlic (*DED* 605) and *uḷḷi* in Kannada meaning 'in this intermediate place, here' (*DED* 475) also do not help.

Ritual Drink and the Fire Cult

Attempts to identify the cultural remains of the Indo-Aryans, in particular archaeological assemblages sometimes overlook the plurality of ethnocultural formations underlying the Indo-Aryan society. The relatives of this ethno-cultural family shared many common elements but differed in many others in points of both time and space. The great diversity of archaeological cultures in any of the proposed Indo-Aryan homelands, whether south-central Asia, north-eastern Iran or north-western South Asia will bear this out in ample measure. The use of literary data also needs to be contextualized in time and space rather than treated as a loose baggage of information irrelevant to space or time. Expressions like 'Vedic literature' and 'Vedic funerary texts' are good examples of this approach.

The supposed correspondence between the association of the ritual drink and fire cult with west Iranian Grey ware burial site of Merlik in Māzandarān and similar practices in an unspecified Vedic funerary texts (Negahban, 1964; Kurochkin, 1990, 1994; Parpola, 1995, 359) calls for a more careful sifting of literary data than is evident. The *Ṛgveda*, which is the earliest document of the Indo-Aryan people and which provides details of diverse types of funerary practices has no signs of association of the ritual drink or fire altar with the burials. The divergent funerary practices, which include full burials, full cremations, post-cremation burials, post-exposure burials and disposal through exposure already emphasize the existence of several ethno-cultural categories within the Vedic society. Bronze Age archaeological sites in north-western South Asia, the home of the *Ṛgveda* hymns probably during the late third and early second millennium BC also bear a striking correspondence to funerary data detailed in the text. The funerary association of a model cart (*śakaṭa*), mortar (*ulūkhala*) and pestle (*muṣala*) in the Marlic tombs is said to be in striking agreement with the Vedic funerary text (Parpola, 1995, 359). Though the text is not named, Parpola invokes the authority of Caland who observes that these objects were to be placed at the legs of a deceased Indo-Aryan man who had established sacred fires (Caland, 1896). The funerary hymns of the *Ṛgveda* do not, however, mention any such practice.

The Fire Cult and Warriors

Similarly, Mandelshtam's observation (Mandelshtam, 1968), approvingly but incompletely cited by Parpola (Parpola, 1995, 359) compares square-shaped ritual fireplaces in men's graves and circular fire-places in women's graves found at Bishkent with the Āhavanīya and Gārhapatya fires respectively has no basis in the *Ṛgveda*. The term *āhavanīya* is unknown to the text and the term *gārhapatya* occurs several times in the sense of household management and only twice in the sense of a domestic fire. The practice may relate to a later stage of history, later-Vedic or post-Vedic by which time the funerary behaviour had changed radically under the influence of new peoples and new conditions of life.

Peacock in the Bronze Age Archaeological Context

Compared to these far-fetched analogies between widely separated textual and archaeological contexts, attention may be drawn to the representation of the peacock, a characteristic Indian word in the archaeological record of South Asia, Iran and Mesopotamia. Brentjes (Brentjes, 1981) furnishes important archaeological evidence and shows with cogent arguments that Indo-Aryans were in India much before the second half of the third millennium BC and that they moved to Iran and Iraq from India and influenced the people there culturally. He draws attention to the peacock element that occurs in Mitannian culture and art in various forms (to be eventually inherited by the Iranians), a motif which could well have come from India, the habitat of the peacock. The first clear pictures showing peacocks in religious contexts in Mesopotamia are the Nuzi cylinder seals of Mitannian times. There are two types of peacocks, the griffin with a peacock head and the peacock dancer, masked and standing beside the holy tree of life.

The veneration of the peacock could not have been brought by the Mitannians from Central Asia or south-eastern Europe; they must have taken it from the East, as the peacock is a native bird of India and peacock dancers are still to be seen all over India (Misra, 1992, 11). Peacocks are well represented in the Sindhi Harappan painted pottery style (Possehl, 1999, 220). There is also a little terracotta figurine from Harappa which may be a peacock in full plumage display (Vats, 1940, plate LXXVIII, No.14). Peafowl bones may be present at Rojdi (Stack-Kane 1989, 183). Since the bird is not given to long flights or migration by air, it could reach distant foreign lands only through the network of trade relations like it did in mesopotamia during the reign of surgon of Akkad (2334-2279 BC) when the import of live objects from Meluha or the Indus valley included peacocks besides black partridges, monkeys, a cat and a red dog (Kenoyer 1998, 98). In historical times, the bird was exported far and wide probably because of its exhibit and ritualistic value, reaching Rome by the beginning of the Christian era.

Chapter 4

The Environmental Crisis

The decay of civilization on the Indo-Iranian sub-continent during the Middle Bronze Age needs to be examined in the context of the geo-climatic devastations that took place throughout the civilized space, particularly the Northern Equatorial Desert Belt, which spread from Egypt in the north-east of Africa to the Thar desert in north-western South Asia. This region, which fell victim to the late Holocene geo-climatic disasters, cradled three of the world's greatest Bronze Age civilizations, viz. the Egyptian, the Mesopotamian, and the Harappan. The disappearance of Harappan civilization, which formed an integral part of an interactive world system based on a networking of trade and urban places, also needs some explanation in terms of the relative bench strength of different civilizations and the cumulative effect of diverse types of calamities visiting the area.

A recent interdisciplinary approach to the third millennium BC civilization collapse deserves mention here (Peiser, 1997).

> "During the last two decades, researchers have found evidence for abrupt climate change and civilization collapse as well as sudden sea level changes, catastrophic inundations, widespread seismic activity and abrupt changes in glacial features at around 2200±200 BC. Climatological proxy data together with sudden changes in lacustrine, fluvial and aeolian deposits are clearly detectable at the Atlantic-subboreal boundary in the archaeological, geological and dendro-chronological records from around the world".

The region-wise break up of affected sites include 260 in Greece, 350 in Anotolia, 200 in the levant, 30 in Mesopotamia,

> 230 in the Indian subcontinnent, 20 in China, 50 in Persia/ Afghanistan and 70 in Iberia. Although it is argued that the globally detected evidence for sudden downturns at the Atlantic subboreal boundary is chronologically interconnected, the main problem in correlating this vast amount of data chronologically is the application of incoherent and imprecise dating methods in different areas of geological and climatological research.

Except for the omission of the Nile valley civilization and a marked preference for catastrophic meteoric strikes as the chief agent of destruction, Peiser's investigations seem to throw much valuable light on the global destabilization of Early Bronze Age civilizations about the beginning of the Middle Bronze Age. Here, we may refer to certain independent studies on the same subject by way of corroboration.

Egypt

A reconstruction of Holocene climatic shifts in Egypt relates to Dakhleh Oasis in South Central Egypt, which provided twenty samples of ostrich egg-shells and hearth charcoal (Brooks, 1989, 139). These samples were associated, some firmly and some loosely with Basinal Lacustrine playa and sand sheet sediments responding to early pluvial Holocene. The gradual replacement of the early pluvial Holocene (8000 BC–4000 BC) by the Hyper Arid Late Holocene (4000 BC–present day) was complete in this area by 2700 BC. This date coincides with the Early Dynastic phase of the Egyptian Old Kingdom (2980 BC–2675 BC), which witnessed the decline of Southern dynasties and the ultimate unification of the Southern and Northern parts under Menes. A major segment of the lower or North Egypt comprised the Nile delta, which forms part of the Mediterranean eco system. The Mediterranean climate was much more hospitable during the late Holocene period than the North Equatorial Desert Belt.

It may not be without good reason therefore that throughout the Old Kingdom, the centre of politico-ecclesiastical authority always remained confined to the cities in the Egyptian delta, Memphis, Thinis or Heliopolis. A favourable hydrological regime in the Egyptian delta is also evident from the fact that in pre-historic times, probably up to the Early Dynastic period, the Nile emptied itself into the sea through seven different channels. The absence of any reference to the existence of and artificial channel between the Mediterranean Sea and the Gulf of Suez may suggest a natural waterway between the Mediterranean Sea and the Gulf of Suez. As things worsened during the mid-third millennium BC, efforts were made by the rulers of Twelfth Dynasty to link the Gulf of Suez with Mediterranean Sea via the Nile by digging a Canal. Another example of this type comes from the Suez inscription of Darius-I, suggesting that desert advances in this area were as unrelenting during the Achaemenian times as in the mid-third millennium BC and that strong administrative efforts were needed to create and maintain a continuous water link between the Mediterranean Sea and the Gulf of Suez.

The Egyptian Middle Kingdom appears to have witnessed considerable hydrological deficit to judge from a consistent policy of water management initiated by the rulers of the twelfth Dynasty. The most important of these developments was the construction of masonry retention walls measuring about 2,700 miles in length and equipped with sluices all around the Fayyum Basin. The total area of land reclaimed for agriculture with the help of Fayyum reservoir is said to be 27,000 square miles. Since the Fayyum was to receive additional water at the time of high flood, action was initiated to predetermine the annual runoff somewhere at the First Cataract, where the Nile emerged from its mountainous barriers for a smooth run upto the sea. The markings on the stone, which constituted a sort of Nilometer, can be observed even today.

North Carmel Coast of Israel

Compared to hyper-arid conditions in Egypt or abrupt changes in monsoon behaviour in Mesopotamia, geo-climatic disorders along the eastern coast of the Mediterranean appeared in the form of persistent marine transgressions which destroyed a large number of Neolithic and Bronze Age settlements in this area. A good study of the North Carmel coast of Israel between Haifa and Atlit shows that a series of submerged archaeological sites found on the continental shelf between Haifa and Atlit indicate a continuous marine transgression between 8000 and 1500 BP (Galili *et al*, 1988, 36). The sites are embedded in the upper part of a marshy clay that fills the trough between the coastal aeolianite (Kurkar) ridge and a ridge now submerged some 1000 to 1500 m to the west. The submerged prehistoric sites belong to two main chronological units: prepottery Neolithic Age (8000 yr BP) and late Neolithic Age (ca. 6500 yr BP). These were found at the depths of 12 to 8 m and 5 to 0 m, respectively. Bronze Age and Byzantine anchors were found at depths of 5 to 3 m and 4 to 1.8 m respectively. As the archaeological materials are firmly dated, these can help to reconstruct the rate of marine transgression from 8000 yr. BP to the present and the eastward movement of settlements through time as related to the transgression (Galili *et al*, 1988, 36). These archaeological events and the eastward movement of settlements may find correlation with the Biblical story of the great deluge and the escape of Abraham and his elk in the legendary Noah's Ark till the vessel found solid ground underneath on the top of Mount Ararat.

Mesopotamia

Things were not really different in neighbouring Mesopotamia. Scholars have shown that during the mid-third millennium BC, Sumeria was afflicted by severe drought, which substantially reduced the agricultural production and caused a thinning of population (Gills *et al*, 1993, 152). The resonance of advancing hyper-arid conditions during the mid-third millennium BC can be heard in the legend of Adoba the high priest in the temple of Ea in the city of Eridu. The submergence of the boat in which Adoba was fishing in the South Sea and the curse pronounced by Adoba against the south-eastern winds which caused the damage and the subsequent absence of rains in Southern Mesopotamia may appear significant here. This may also explain the shifting of political authority towards the northwest and the rise of Babylonia about 2000 BC. Comparing the two situations in Sumeria and Egypt, it would appear that the former gave way to an arid regime on its prowl whereas the latter rose to the occasion and made best out of a worsening situation.

Oman

Probably, the extent of pluvial regression in Sumeria and its adjoining area was much more intense and persistent in comparison to the Egyptian situation. The conditions operating in this area may perhaps be appreciated in the light of recent palaeo-climatic reconstruction of northern Oman based on carbonates from hyper-alkaline groundwaters (Clark *et al*, 1991, 320). The study shows that the area was characterized by playa lake formation and faunal remains typical of Savanna grassland during the late Pleistocene and Early Holocene pluvial regime (10,500 BC–4500 BC). From about the last quarter of the fifth millennium BC the late Holocene hyper-aridity began to cause widespread dessication. This hydrological calamity may have reached a high point in the region around Oman sometime about the second quarter of the third millennium BC. The hydrological crisis and the resulting agricultural decline faced by the Sumerians would thus appear to have been a related phenomenon in the whole area.

Iran and Afghanistan

The geo-climatic devastations, which struck the Early Bronze Age civilizations on a global scale and with terminal impact in the Greater Indus Valley could not have been any kinder to the settlements on the Irano-Afghan border lands. The proto-urban settlement of Shahr-i-Sokhta, which flourished between 3200 BC and 2400 BC registering a phenomenal growth of the urban area from a mere 17 ha in 3200 BC to 150 ha in 2400 BC (Tossi *et al*, 1992, 204), served as the nerve centre of proto-urban civilization in south-eastern Iran. Similarly, Mundigak together with Said Qala and Deh Morasi Ghundai, all lying within 60 km of the modern city of Kandahar, were the most important proto-urban settlements of southern Afghanistan during the third millennium BC. Mundigak, which together with Shahr-i-Sokhta is characterized as Helmand enclave, lies 55 km north-west of Kandahar city on the upper drainage of Kushk-i-Nakhod river, whereas Said Qala and Deh Morasi Ghundai lie near Kandahar in close proximity to the Argandab. The significance of Mundigak as the key player in the proto-urban civilization of Afghanistan can be gauged from the fact that the urban occupation at Mundigak expanded from a modest 6–8 ha to 55–60 ha during the early and mid-third millennium BC (Tossi *et al*, 1992, 204). However, after 2300 BC the same proto-urban settlements in eastern Iran, Afghanistan and South Central Asia entered a phase of rapid decline and were almost deserted by the end of the third millennium BC.

Differential Bench Strength

However, it is good to remember that although the Late Holocene hyper-aridity caused widespread desiccation throughout the North Equatorial Desert Belt, its impact on the civilizational process in the entire region was not uniform, either chronologically or spatially. In some regions, the desiccation began early while in others it took longer to reach a flash point. Human responses to a stressful environment were also differential. Perhaps things were not as bad on the western sector of civilization, which could withstand the onslaught of nature despite a sharp fall in agricultural production in Sumeria and a consequent thinning population in the area. Even the western sector, which could no longer draw upon the continental trade, became segmented into insular regions which lay dormant for a while and bounced back to intensify the politics of space as nature relented at a later date. In other areas, as in the Greater Indus Valley, the jerks must have been too severe and persistent to permit some breathing space for appropriate human responses to sustain the civilization. The several reconstructions of Mohenjodaro, which was repeatedly visited by natural calamity, may underline the ability of South Asians to contain the ravages of nature. But the cumulative effect of diverse types of environmental deterioration proved a little too much for the people of the area who could not sustain any longer the urban overarching of the Greater Indus Valley. Consequently, during the early second millennium BC (2000 BC–1800 BC), the urban archetype gave way to three regional culture formations, without any perceptible links among themselves.

The Harappan Experience

The growing amount of scientific data on geo-climatic shifts during the late Holocene would suffice to account for the decline of trade and urbanism on the Indo-Iranian subcontinent. The main contentions that try to explain the decline of Harappan civilization relate to tectonic activity, recurrent floods, shifts in river channels and a prolonged phase of hyper-aridity causing widespread desiccation, low precipitation, reduced runoff in the rivers, and the falling lake levels.

Monsoon Behaviour

"Studies on the variability of the South West monsoon for the last 19,000 years before present by using marine sediment records reveal that the South West (SW) monsoon started its intensification from 12,000 years BP, after a weak phase during the last glacial period" (Naidu, 1998, 69). Within the Holocene, greater values of upwelling indices have been noted between 10,000 and 6000 years BP, reflecting a strong SW monsoon during this period. The values of upwelling indices decrease abruptly at 5000 years BP, indicating the beginning of a weakening phase of the SW monsoon. The lowest upwelling indices in the Holocene occur between 3500 and 1200 years BP, suggesting that upwelling and the SW monsoon intensity decreased considerably during this period. Other evidences such as water levels in Ethiopian lakes (Gillespie *et al*, 1983), palaeo hydrological data from Western Tibet (Gasse and Van campo, 1994), benthic foraminifera records from eastern Arabian Sea, pollen records from Northwest India and $\partial 18^{C}$ values of peat deposits also suggest a weaker SW monsoon during this time. A similar pattern of dry conditions during the late Holocene is also reported from Africa and the regions around the Caribbean (Naidu, 1998, 72).

Independent evidence such as pollen studies from the eastern Arabian Sea (Caratini *et al*, 1994) and down core variations of calcium carbonate in the western Arabian Sea and $\partial 13^{C}$ data from Tibetan lakes also document the arid climate during this time (Gasse and Van Campo, 1994). This observation is further corroborated by an abrupt change in solar radiation, precipitation, temperature and south-easterly winds at about 3500 years BP in the Arabian Sea (Zahn, 1994). The declining strength of SW monsoon since 3500 years BP can therefore be interpreted as a result of the onset of arid climate throughout the tropics in general and the Asian tropics in particular." (Naidu, 1998, 72)

Recurrent Floods

Since Mohenjodaro lies close to the sea on the lower Indus Valley and shows evidence of several successive devastations, attention may first concentrate on heavy runoff in the Indus river and recurrent inundations. This is quite likely in view of recent reconstruction of Holocene precipitation on the basis of Lacustrine pollen. It has been argued that although the summer precipitation during the greater part of third millennium BC was double the present level, it was much lower than what preceded during the previous millennium. In other words, summer precipitation was fairly substantial till the last quarter of the third millennium BC. The overall precipitation during the period would, however, appear to be very impressive if we consider that winter precipitation in the area about the same time was at the maximum (Bryson et al., 1981, 144). No wonder the lower reaches of the valley were subjected to recurrent inundation and repeated destruction of the city of Mohenjodaro.

Tectonic Lift

Although floods may have played their role in undermining this southern centre of Harappan civilization, there are specialists for whom tectonic activity played a much greater role in destroying the civilization. The idea of tectonic lift was first suggested by German hydrologist Raikes (Raikes, 1964, 1979), whose findings were enthusiastically endorsed by the American archaeologist Dales (Dales, 1966). The tectonic lift affected the Indus delta by blocking the passage of the river and in turn forcing the river to deposit its water in the shape of a vast lake inundating large areas on either side of the river.

The tectonic lift may have been a reality but it does not explain the five successive devastations of Mohenjodaro and as many reconstructions of the city. For this, there would have to be as many tectonic lifts as the reconstruction of the city.

Wind-Blown Silt

Lambrick (Lambrick, 1967, 182; Possehl, 1967), who needed to contain both the theories of recurrent floods as well as dam impounding, suggests that the Indus suffered a great depletion of water on account of a channel diversion thirty miles upstream the city. The reduced drainage in the river may have affected the immediate agricultural environment thereby weakening the economic foundations in the area. However, Lambrick's suggestion that the city fell victim to wind-blown silt and sand in five successive phases seems a little flawed. If the city was running short of water because of a channel diversion upstream, what sustained its five successive reconstructions?

The controversial opinions of different specialists appear to leave non-specialists in dire straits. The time is not yet ripe and it may never be prudent to posit absolutist views on the decline of an ancient civilization, which conceals as much as it reveals. Perhaps each of the contentions has its own intrinsic merit and all need to be collated with one another towards a fuller understanding of the decline of the Harappan civilization.

Tectonic Lift and Marine Regression

As for the tectonic lift, its effects were much more disastrous and widespread than the mere creation of artificial inundation lakes near the city of Mohenjodaro. The more important of these consequences were the lifting of lake bottoms and coastlines, marine regression and the shifting of river courses. The entire area of Makran coast and the Sind littoral converges on the meeting point of three tectonic plates, the Arabian Plate, the Eurasian Plate and the Indo-Australian Plate. Roughly, the area of tectonic confluence covers 100 sq kms on the Makran coast, some 350 kms west of Karachi. This area, together with its outlying neighbourhood, is identified as a region prone to shallow earthquakes and for that reason can badly affect settlements along the Makran and Sind littoral as well as inland. No wonder, tectonic disturbances sometime during the late third millennium BC raised the coastal elevation with resultant marine regression. The location of Shehwan, an Indus port of the third millennium BC thirty miles inland from the modern port of Karachi, is mute witness to the calamity. Sutkagendor, the Western-most port city of the Harappans during the third millennium BC was much more vulnerable to tectonic activity since it lies very close to the meeting point of the three tectonic plates mentioned above. This ancient site now lies nearly 50 kms inland from the modern port of Gavdar on the Makran coast, slightly transgressing offshore.

The shallow earthquake region also covered the south-eastern part of Iran, particularly the area where Helmand river disappears into a vast intermittent lake. Tectonic disturbances like the one discussed above may have elevated the lake bottoms slightly, draining out its earlier volume of water, which could not any longer be compensated under the conditions of advancing aridity. One may feel tempted here to draw attention to a mythical story in the *Avesta* (Zamyâd Yast), which refers to a Turanian detractor of the Aryans named Frangrasyan who, in a bid to capture or destroy the splendour of the Aryans, thrice dived into the Vouro Kasha Sea or Helmand Sea. Every time, the water of the sea spilled over in the shape of a bay, frustrating the Turanian's attempt to capture the splendour of the Aryans. Probably the Helmand delta experienced three tectonic disturbances in quick succession some time during the Middle Bronze Age.

Geo-climatic deterioration also seems to have overtaken the Rann of Kutch and Dholavira, the most important resource centre in the area. Dholavira, which is recognized as one of the five major Indus cities, owed its predominance to the control of shipping activities and coordination of resource distributions between the coastal area and major Indus cities in the North and the East. The Rann of Kutch, which is a vast swampy tract today may have come into existence under the impact of tectonic lift and consequent marine regression sometime during the fourth-third millennium BC. Excavations at Dholavira suggest four major tectonic episodes, the last one happening during the fifth stage of occupation after which the city was deserted for a long time before its reoccupation during the sixth stage, which is extremely inferior in terms of habitational goods and planning, and has no comparison with the past grandeur of the city (Bisht, 1989). The tectonic movement may have affected the rivers, which brought fresh water into the Kutch region. As siltation increased, the discharge of fresh water diminished and the region slowly developed into a vast marshy tract with consequent marine regression. The whole process may have taken several centuries to give the Rann its present look. As the sea receded, a reorganization of the shipping routes further southeast on the Gujarat coast became imperative.

Late Holocene Hyper-Aridity

Although late Holocene hyper-aridity was already on the prowl, the third millennium began on an optimistic note to judge from high precipitation and heavy runoff in the rivers. The summer precipitation is said to have been double the present time and the winter precipitation was at the maximum (Bryson *et al*, 1981, 144). Taken together, this would create a warm and humid environment, which today characterizes the north-eastern part of the subcontinent. The figures of the tiger and rhinoceros on the seals and sealings of the Greater Indus Valley bear testimony to such a favourable climatic regime. Since both the tiger and rhinoceros were wild animals, their presence is hard to encounter in the available archaeological record. However, things began to change from the last quarter of the third millennium BC, by which time summer precipitation in the area may have reached its present status and left its indelible impression on vast stretches of desert.

An Extreme Cold-Dry Phase

There are indications that the late Holocene hyper-arid episode reached a critical point with the onset of Ice Age like conditions around 2200 BC. The event is said to have been triggered by a long period of solar inactivity, when the sun's magnetic field touched its mounder minimum, reducing solar radiation by a big margin. Reduction in solar radiation meant that the rays of sun were far less luminous and far less warm than before. Such a development may have simulated Arctic conditions and affected large parts of Asia.

It has been suggested that in the North Atlantic region and perhaps globally, there was a warm cold cycle with a periodicity of around 1500 years, starting about the beginning of the Holocene Age. Evidence from North Atlantic deep-sea cores reveals that abrupt shifts punctuated what is conventionally thought to have been a relatively stable Holocene climate. During each of these episodes, cool, ice-bearing waters from north of Iceland were advancing as far south as the latitude of Britain. At about the same time, the atmospheric circulation above Greenland changed abruptly. Pacing of the Holocene events and of abrupt climate shifts during the last glaciation are statistically the same. Together, they make up a series of climate shifts with a cyclicity close to 1470 ± 500 years (Bond *et al*, 1997; Crucifix, 1999). These brief cold–dry episodes are said to have affected climates across North Africa, Southern Asia, Europe, the Americas and Antarctica (Stager and Mayewski, 1997). The idea of 1500 years cyclicity of little Ice Age during the Holocene is also suggested by studies of ice-rafted debris in Northern Atlantic sediments (Broecker, 2000). Some of the computed dates are 9400 Y.A.= 7400 BC, 8100 Y.A.= 6100 BC, 5900 Y.A.= 3900 BC, 4200 Y.A. = 2200 BC.

As the desiccation began to cast its lengthening shadow on the whole area, large parts of Western Rajasthan and Gujarat became inhospitable deserts. The process seems to have reached its climax by 2000 BC, which coincides with the disruption of urbanism and trifurcation of the civilization into three regional cultures. Many of the freshwater lakes, which were the creation of heavy rainfall regime of late Pleistocene and early Holocene epochs registered a sharp decline in the water level and many were already turning saline. According to one study, the desiccation began, (or rather intensified) around 2250 BC and reached a flash point in 1500 BC (Swain *et al*, 1981, 5). The Rajasthan deserts were already in the process of formation by 2000 BC. Lake Sambhar had become saline by this date while

Lake Lukransar registered a drop of 250 mm in its water table. After about 1500 BC, the Lukransar profile indicated a desiccated lakebed with no pollen preservation (Swain *et al*, 1981, 5).

Widespread desiccation seems to have caused acute water scarcity in certain areas bordering the desert. The ancient city of Dholavira has brought to light an organized system relating to the harvesting of rainwater to be used during the lean season for domestic as well as agricultural purposes. This is well suggested by cisterns and reservoirs within the walled settlement and an additional reservoir outside the city (Kenoyer, 1998, 53). Within the city walls the reservoirs measured 17 hectares, which works out to 36 per cent of the inhabited area. This system of water management, which is not found anywhere else in the Greater Indus Valley, certainly points to an acute crisis of freshwater in the area, a definite marker of advancing arid conditions.

Shifting River Courses

The rivers, which were seriously disturbed by the tectonic movement, included the Indus, the Sarasvatī, the Sutlej and the Yamuna. Perhaps the best example of hydrographic change and its impact on settlement history during the third millennium BC is provided by the Hakra-Ghaggar river, which has frequently been identified with the Ṛgvedic Sarasvatī (Misra, 1994, 518). Non-perennial, only a short distance from the Shivalik hills, the dry course of Hakra-Ghaggar in Bikaner and Bahawalpur is two miles wide for a stretch of hundred miles and at places the width extends to nearly four miles (Spate and Learmouth, 1967, 536). Latest archaeological work in the Cholistan desert shows that between Rahim Yar Khan on the west and Yazman in the east, as many as 174 mature Harappan settlements were situated along the river. The existence of a perennial river, which flowed through Bikaner and Bahawalpur and then towards the Rann of Kutch with the eastern Nara in Sind probably being its continuation, was first suggested in 1893 (Oldham, 1893). But, latest studies have established the erratic behaviour of the river right from the beginning of the fourth millennium BC (Mughal, 1992, 191). Situated as it was in a flat plain, the river, despite a mighty perennial flow fell easy prey to diversions caused by either head-ward erosion by feeder channels or tectonic activity of a very small scale. The two mighty snow-fed rivers which once formed part of the Hakra-Ghaggar system turned away from the parent river, Yamuna joining the Ganges system and Sutlej developing its own network up to the sea. The event seems to have taken place between 1900 BC and 1700 BC followed by a series of devastations which threw the existing production organization out of gear. Studies based on aerial photographs and Landsat imageries clearly reveal the westward shifting of the Ghaggar river course (Ghosh *et al*, 1979 and Yashpal *et al*, 1984). Ghosh has noted the existence of four wide paleochannels located some 16, 30, 45 and 100 kms north of Jaisalmer (Ghosh *et al*, 1979). In fact, Ghaggar river continued to function as late as 3000 years ago in the extreme northern part of the desert (Misra, 1989, 3).

The emerging paleo-climatic picture would thus suggest that Harappan and other contemporary groups were operating not in an era of climatic opportunity but in one of increasing climatic stress which affected food-producing strategies (Shaffer and Lichtenstein, 1989).

Differential Ecozones: The Central Indo-Gangetic Plain

Interestingly, what was happening in the Greater Indus Valley did not happen in the immediate eastern neighbourhood of the region. This may be attributed to a differential eco-system such as we have on the western and eastern sides of the Aravali range. The region east of Aravali was warm and humid about the time the Greater Indus Valley was experiencing hyper-aridity and perhaps also increasing cold. The lakes on the western side of Aravali suffered regression and salinity while the one on the eastern side of Aravali continued in good shape.

A recent study of clay minerals and fluvial pedo-genesis of samples in the Central Indo-Gangetic Plains, North Central India between the Ramganga and Rapti rivers (Srivastava *et al*, 1998, 230) shows an interesting contrast of palaeo-climate in this region. The results of the study, though a little incomplete, show that between 8000 BC and 4500 BC the region experienced an arid climate, just about the time when the large parts of north western South Asia, Iran and Central Asia were experiencing an intensive pluvial phase characterized by playa lake formation and Savanna grasslands. No specification is put forward for the period 4500 BC–1800 BC. But the period from 1800 BC onwards is recognized as the period of a warm and humid climate. If this can be taken as the indication of warm and humid climates towards the east and south-east of the Greater Indus Valley, this may provide some convincing explanation of the movement of late Harappan people (2000 BC onwards) towards the east and south-east. But this is a different story and may call for greater investigation of population shifts, directional preferences, artefactual mutations, ecological adaptations and differential lifestyle surfacing during the early second millennium BC.

Epidemics and Pathogenic Disorders

The Harappan urbanization has frequently been viewed from the artefactual and architectural angles, and stratified accordingly, though unsatisfactorily, into Pre-Harappan, Early Harappan, Mature Harappan and Late Harappan phases of the civilization. But, the origin, maturity and decay of an urban phenomenon also need to be considered from the environmental and human resources angle.

The role of natural calamities in the decay of Harappan urban centres has been discussed by different specialists over the last five decades, as outlined above. As the problem continues to be investigated from different angles, literature on the subject keeps growing. But, the mental and physical ability of a people, who negotiated these calamities, is also worth focusing. If the people were constrained by hereditary disorders, the ability to withstand these calamities would already be much reduced. This is more so when such disorders affected the people who figured somewhere in the power structure. Perhaps one such disorder was widespread porosity of bones caused by hereditary Thalassemia and Sickle Anaemia. Both these conditions relating to inheriting abnormal haemoglobin are said to have been present in the Harappan population (Kennedy, 1984, 430). The two diseases resulted from hereditary nutritional disorders in which the metabolism is unable to pump adequate levels of iron into the blood even though the intake of iron is quite sufficient. According to one estimate, nearly twenty-five per cent of skeletons reported from different burial sites of the Harappan culture and belonging to both sexes and all age groups ranging from 12 to 40 are found to have suffered from chronic, hereditary, anaemia (Kennedy, 1984, 430). The fact that these skeletons from Harappa and Mohenjodaro belong to different periods of the Indus civilization would suffice to underline the presence of a pathogenic hereditary disorder, which, in times of a civilizational crisis, would have an insurmountable compounding effect.

The other killer agent was the Anopheles mosquito, which would have a field day in the insanitary conditions afflicting Harappan cities during the decaying stages of the civilization. It is understood that the Anopheles mosquito is the host of the Plasmodium parasite, and that this carrier achieves highest fertility rates in undrained regions, as in areas with stagnant ponds or abandoned irrigation channels. The unquestionable deterioration of civic standards in the later phases of Mohenjodaro and the intermittent recurrence of abnormal and devastating floods which Wheeler (Wheeler, 1968) laments, would provide the social setting for virulent and endemic malaria. Although it might be a careless overstatement to speculate that malaria or any other pathogenic condition was a cause of the Harappan decline, the toll of such stresses on a society are felt nevertheless in the demographic shifts, in the number of men employable as labourers or capable of bearing arms at any given time in defence of the state (Kennedy, 1984, 430).

Though, the skeletal remains from different Harappan sites provide good evidence of widespread pathogenic disorders within the Harappan population, these do not automatically suggest that the entire Harappan population was afflicted by a traumatized state of mind. For, the skeletons, which invariably come from burial sites and belong to certain members of the power elite, need not represent the large masses of people. Also, since trauma is always the consequence of an unexpected deadly calamity afflicting a large population, one must look for more potential factors than hereditary diseases of a terminal nature in a limited number of families. The families afflicted by these disorders would have been fairly well aware of the fact that death would be premature for certain relatives thereby ruling out the possibility of any trauma-like situation. Moreover, in the archaeological sense, the signs of trauma can be read either in the shape of inscribed record or the products of art featuring the afflicted human face, neither of which is forthcoming from Harappan context.

As shown above, the Harappan archaeological record preserves in good measure catastrophic events striking various settlements separately or simultaneously. Some of these calamities have been studied in respect of single settlements like the recurrent floods of Mohenjodaro, earthquake at Kalibangan and Dholavira, siltation and marine regression in the Rann of Kutch and epidemics or starvation deaths at Harappa. Besides, the civil war, of which some evidence is encountered at Mohenjodaro, may have been much more widespread and covered other important urban settlements in the Greater Indus Valley. Persistent desiccation and desertification, both of which are fairly well documented, the former in the shape of regressive precipitation and increasing siltation and the latter in the form of Thar desert, may have been other potential factors of civilization collapse in this area.

Chapter 5

The Decaying Settlements

Myth and History

The determination of the relative age of 10,000 plus compositions in the *Ṛgveda* cannot perhaps ignore the large number of myths appearing in the text. This is an area of Ṛgvedic history, which calls for much greater attention in terms of demystification of these passages and their correspondence with historical developments in nature and society. Myths are said to be true inside and false outside. In other words, a myth is a reality which a particular people experience at a particular point of their history. For other peoples far removed in space and time, the reality would surely appear like a figment of imagination. Take the example of the *Vendîdâd*, which refers to creation of sixteen excellent settlements by Ahura Mazda and the destruction of these settlements by Angra Mainyu. The two categories of information which surface in two consecutive chapters seem to focus on two different stazes of habitat history on the Indo-Iranian subcontinent, possibly during the Bronze Age. If one can set aside existing ideas and preconceived notions and take care of myths appearing in the *Ṛgveda* and the *Avesta*, an upper limit of Ṛgvedic chronology and also perhaps of the Avestan tradition may not be too difficult to ascertain.

Nature Myths in the *Ṛgveda*

Myths in the *Ṛgveda* can be classified under two major heads—encounter myths and nature myths. Frequently, the two types get mixed up, creating further confusion for the investigator. For instance, the term Vṛtra appears in both encounter myths and nature myths. But a careful reader will notice that encounter myths relating to Vṛtra are fewer in number and refer to the suppression of rival chiefs inhabiting walled resource centres, the walls around the settlements representing a circle or semicircle (*vṛtta*). Vṛtra-related nature myths also turn out to be encounter myths inasmuch as the term Vṛtra in all these examples represents hydraulic constructions for the purpose of controlled drainage which deprived distant peasant localities of much-needed drainage facility. These hydraulic constructions represented the Gabarband type of barrages erected by the Harappan state throughout the Greater Indus Valley during the Bronze Age. In Baluchistan, the dams were made of stone and, accordingly, were much too difficult to dislodge. Occasionally, Vṛtra also signified clouds blocking rains. Hydraulic myths relating to Ahi are not very different from the Vṛtra related myths highlighting low precipitation and insufficient drainage. Two other characters projected in these myths are Vala and Śuṣṇa. Vala, in addition to symbolizing various natural detractions, characterized paucity of rainfall and river water. Vala also represented a mountain-demon, who held back valuable resources and accordingly, had to be ripped open by fire spark (*arken agnim)* and digging a tunnel (*parvaṇ*) for reaching out to the hidden wealth, probably in the shape of valuable ores and precious stones. The other character who surfaces as the demon of drought is Śuṣṇa. From √śuṣ meaning to soak out, Śuṣṇa would be a symbol of desiccation and a creator of arid regions. This demon of drought occasionally figures in association with Kuyava or the demon of bad harvests. Elsewhere, śuṣṇa represents a desert chief with a mobile entourage and portable homes preventing access to meagre water resources in the deserts (Nandi, 2001).

We may now take a good look at the quantitative value of hydrological myths in the text. The term Vṛtra alone appears in 196 passages. Add to this, another 185 compounds of the term. The term Ahi makes more than a hundred appearances in the text whereas the terms Vala and Śuṣṇa appear in 25 and 40 passages respectively. There are several passages in which Vṛtra appears with Ahi or Vala. Notwithstanding this overlap, the references to the demons of drought account for nearly five per cent of the 10,000 odd invocations recorded in the text. One needs to spare a thought as to why the earliest Vedic speakers were so obsessed with the fear of drought. Possibly, the focus is on an aggravating hydrological crisis, which the bardic composers would be only too justified to blame on the rapine of a drought demon.

Hydrological Regression East of the Indus

Probably, these passages underlined a perceptible deterioration of habitat conditions, which seriously undermined the whole range of human activities in the civilized world during the Middle Bronze Age. We have argued that a persistent period of aridity, which began around the beginning of the third millennium BC, reached a highpoint by the end of the millennium. An extreme cold-dry phase towards the end of the third millennium BC meant lower rates of snowmelt and lesser drainage of water in the rivers. Part of the blame must also be taken by tectonic activity, which disturbed the river flows, reduced the runoff to the sea and increased the amount of silt in the deltaic regions. Tectonic lift may also have caused regression of the sea, which was then more than two feet higher than at present near the Rann of Kutch. A similar plight may also have overtaken the people along the Sind littoral and the Makran coast, where the seaports today lie quite a distance inland, 30 kilometres at Sehwan and 50 kms at Sutkagendor.

The Iriṇa or the Rann of Kutch

It may be useful here to examine the correspondence of textual and geo-morphological data relating to the great marshy plain, which goes by the name of Rann of Kutch. The term Rann is a modern Indic form of Iriṇa, which occurs several times in the *Ṛgveda*. Going by the meaning of the term Irina in early Indian literature, three stages in the geo-morphology of the region can be underlined during the second and first millennium BC. In the *Ṛgveda*, the earliest portions of which may synchronize with the beginnings of the Middle Bronze Age in north-western South Asia, the term Iriṇa occurs in the sense of a water course or rivulet, suggesting perhaps the shrinkage and fragmentation of the large rivers draining through the area into the Arabian Sea. Two of the seven stanzas, which mention the term Iriṇa may appear particularly significant in this context. In one of these (1.186.9), Maruts or the rain bearing gods are implored to fill all the dried up channels with water *viśvam iriṇam pruṣāyantaḥ*. The term *pruṣāyantaḥ* (from *pruḥ*, meaning 'to sprinkle, shower, wet, moisten') shows that many of the rivulets (*viśvam iriṇam*) were past drying up under the heat of hyper-arid conditions. Evidently, such shallow watercourses became unfit for human use and were left to be taken care of by the animals. This is the precise import of the other stanza (8.4.3) in which a thirsty deer is stated to be descending into the rivulet which has been discarded (*apākṛtam*) by human beings (*yathā gauraḥ tṛṣyan apākṛtam iriṇam ava eti*). By the time of the *Atharva Veda,* most of these rivulets may have become hollow, dried-up channels justifying their description as hollow, excavated ground in the text. Still later, in the *Manusmṛti* and the *Mahābhārta,* the term means a desert, an inhospitable region, a bare plain, barren soil, salt soil. The marshy plain was already underway about the beginning of the third millennium BC, if we go by the evidence of Dholavira excavations which brought to light marshy encrustations at the subsoil level during the earliest phase of Dholavira settlement.

Parisāraka and the Sarasvatī

The rivers, which were seriously disturbed by the tectonic movement and or advancing aridity included the Indus, the Sarasvatī, the Sutlej and the Yamuna. Perhaps the best example of hydrographic change and its impact on settlement history during the third millennium BC is provided by the Hakra-Ghaggar river, which has frequently been identified with the Ṛgvedic Sarasvatī. The first blow to this mighty perennial channel came around 2400 BC and the next about 2100 BC (Mughal, 1992). The hydrological regression continued on its prowl till the end of the Middle Bronze Age when two of its powerful snow-fed channels, the Sutlej and the Yamuna changed their course, the Sutlej joining the Indus system on the west and Yamuna turning to the Ganga system on the east.

The event is said to have taken place during the period 1900 BC–1700 BC. Although the river continued over ground till 1000 BC, it frequently changed its course, judging from the existence of several palaeo channels of the river north of Jaisalmer. After this time the river became underground and non perennial.

Some of these happenings could not go altogether unnoticed in the literary record of the area. In the *Ṛgveda*, the river is always described as a mighty perennial channel with a large volume of water and strong velocity running all the way from the mountains to the sea. In these compositions, there is no idea of any hydrological disorder suffered by the river except one stanza (6.61.14) which refers to devastating floods driving people away from settlements on either bank. Since people living on the banks of the large perennial rivers are always familiar with the annual inundations, this passage seems to underline an extraordinary situation in the behaviour of the river. In the absence of two mighty feeder channels, siltation of the river belt may have increased and, situated as it was in a level plain, the river could easily cause frequent inundations over a large settled area.

The *Aitareya Brāhmaṇa*, the earliest of *Brāhmaṇa* texts and probably coterminous with a major part of the *Ṛgveda* hymns dealing with fire rituals and Soma oblations has much more valuable information on the hydrological behaviour of the river. The passage which draws attention to annual recharge failure of the river Sarasvatī (Keith 1920/1998, 148) relates to contesting groups of priests over the right to offer Soma oblations to gods and inhabit the area known as Parisāraka. Derived from the term Parisar, which means 'to go round and round', 'circumambulate', 'wander about', Parisāraka seems to be an apt description of the region around the Sarasvatī, 'the dear home of the gods' and the pure Brāhmaṇas'. This may be a good indication of the fact that by the time of the *Aitareya Brāhmaṇa*, the river could no longer complete its journey up to the sea. The reference to the 'welling out' of river water on the chanting of prayers is also a priestly way of stating that for most part of the year, the river remained underground and that water could be obtained only by digging small ponds in the river bed. Also interesting is the fact that prayers to the rain-god Parjanya were necessary to bring water to the river, a suggestion that about this time the river depended on rain water rather than snow-melt.

Hydrography and Settlements West of the Indus

The geo-climatic devastation which affected Punjab, Sind and Rajasthan on the eastern side of the Indus could not have been any kinder to the settlements on the western side. The three prominent river systems noticed in the *Vendîdâd* (Chapter 1), as part of sixteen excellent creations of Ahura Mazda lay, as now, on the Indo-Iranian borderlands. These are Haitumant, Haraiti and Haroiva. Haitumant is represented by modern Helmand, which, after originating in the northern mountains travels nearly 1,450 kms before disappearing into desert swamps in south-eastern Iran. The proto-urban settlement of Shahr-i-Sokhta, which flourished between 3200 BC and 2400 BC registering a phenomenal growth of the urban area from a mere 17 ha in 3200 BC to 150 ha in 2400 BC (Tossi *et al*, 1992, 204), served as the nerve centre of proto-urban civilization in south-eastern Iran.

Haraiti, the Arachosia of Greeks and Argandab of today, also originated in the central mountains and makes a detour of Mundigak before joining the Helmand. Mundigak together with Said Qala and Deh Morasi Ghundai, all lying within 60 km of the modern city of Kandahar were the most important proto-urban settlements of southern Afghanistan during the third millennium BC. Mundigak, which together with Shahr-i-Sokhta is characterized as Helmand enclave, lies 55 kms north-west of Kandahar city on the upper drainage of Kushk-i-Nakhod river, whereas Said Qala and Deh Morasi Ghundai lie near Kandahar in close proximity to the Argandab. The significance of Mundigak as the key player in the proto-urban civilization of Afghanistan can be seen from the fact that the urban occupation at Mundigak expanded from a modest 6-8 ha to 55-60 ha during the early and mid-third millennium BC (Tossi *et al*, 1992, 204).

As for the Haroiva, it is identified with the Sarayu of the *Ṛgveda*, Aria of Greeks and Harirud of the present time. Like the other two rivers, the Harirud also originates in the central mountains, travelling nearly 600 kms due west before turning north to travel another 400 kms as the boundary between Iran and Afghanistan and finally disappearing into desert swamps. Along this longish route, several settlements must have flourished during the Chalcolithic and Early Bronze Ages, but the one that is well documented in the archaeological record lay in the ancient delta of the river and is represented by the Chalcolithic and Early Bronze Age settlement of Geoksur in the oasis of the same name.

All these settlements flourished till 2300 BC and may, accordingly, justify their description in *Vendîdâd* Chapter 1 as excellent regions. On the contrary, after 2300 BC, the same proto-urban settlements in eastern Iran, Afghanistan and South Central Asia entered a phase of rapid decline and were almost deserted by the end of the third millennium BC. This may be a poetic representation of the destruction of sixteen excellent creations of Ahura Mazda by Angra Mainyu, also described in the same *Vendîdâd*, Chapter 1. Perhaps the sixteen excellent creations of Ahura Mazda, all of which lay between eastern Iran and eastern Rajasthan coincide with the closing decades of urban growth about 2300 BC, whereas the subsequent destruction of these settlements by Angra Mainyu may represent the widespread decay and desertion which engulfed the whole area by the close of the millennium.

Habitat Myths in the *Avesta*

The Helmand today disappears into vast swamps, but during the early Holocene pluvial phase, it constituted a mighty river and its delta a vast pool of water resembling a sea. The river and its delta continued in this shape till widespread dessication struck it towards the beginning of the third millennium BC. In the vast adjoining desert and semi-desert tracts of Iran and Afghanistan, the Helmand thus constituted as at present the sap of life for the people living along its banks and the deltaic region. The river has a special quality insofar as it is relatively salt-free, unlike most other land-locked rivers of Afghanistan. This may have added to its sanctification by the concerned people and subsequent elevation to the position of a river goddess in the Old *Avesta*.

In the *Avesta*, there is frequent reference to the sea Vouru Kasha and the mighty river called Ardvisura Anahita. The river Ardvisura, which took its rise from Mount Hara and reached out to sea Vouru Kasa, seems to represent Haitumant of *Vendîdâd* Chapter 1 or the Helmand. In the Old *Avesta*, there is no reference to Haitumant although a full *Yasna* is devoted to the praise of river Ardvisura joining the sea Vouru Kasha. In the Zamyâd Yast (Yt-XIX), however, Haitumant is connected with the sea Kasao or Vouru Kasha. The identification of Vouru Kasha with Hammun-i-Hilmund (Gnoli, 1989, 58) would thus appear to be justified. The name Haitumant (Vedic Setumant), meaning 'abounding in bunds' may have been a later coinage following hydrological regression throughout the third millennium BC. The reduced runoff caused increasing silt formations, which slowly stabilized as small patches of hard land obstructing the flow of water in the delta. Although the number of bunds increased with the passage of time, these were not entirely unknown, when the earliest Avestn poets were singing their praise of the river. In *Yasna-LXV*, the poet states that all the gulfs in the sea Vouru Kasha were stirred up when the mighty Ardvisura downed its water into the sea. The existence of gulfs in a deltaic sea would be possible only when the underwater surface is undulated, rising above the water level at many points.

Apart from hydrological regression, some amount of tectonic lift may also have disturbed the earlier morphology of Hammun-i-Hilmund. The geological event appears to be graphically described in the Zamyâd Yast (Yt.19.), which refers to Turanian Frangrasyan, who was out to capture or destroy 'the glory of Aryan peoples'. For this purpose, he thrice downed himself into the sea Vouru Kasha, but each time 'the glory spilled over in the shape of a bay'. Subsequent to the over-flooding of the sea Vouru Kasha or Hammun-i-Hilmund, vast areas in the neighbourhood were destroyed beyond habitation. The people who inhabited these areas and thrived on the basis of agricultural activity and trade were economically unsettled and forced to migrate to new areas and restart pastoral and agricultural activity. This is also well described in *Vendîdâd II,* in which Ahura Mazda entrusted to Yima the task of creating new settlements and re-establishing peoples in them. The over-flooding of Vouru Kasha or Hammun-i-Hilmund recorded in the Zamyâd Yast is also corroborated by Seistanic legends relating to Jamshid or Afrasiab (Gnoli, 1989, 58). The event must have taken place during the late third millennium BC to judge from the fact that Shahr-i-Shokta, a flourishing urban centre of the Helmand delta, which expanded from a mere 17 ha in 3200 BC to 150 ha in 2400 BC (Tossi *et al,* 1992, 204) became completely deserted after 2300 BC. A similar plight also befell other smaller settlements in the area.

The natural phenomenon which led to the reduction of Hammun-i-Hilmund into a swampy tract also affected yet another of Ahura Mazda's sixteen creations. The *Vendîdâd-1* refers to the settlements along the river Haroiva (Ṛgvedic Sarayu), which is the Avestan name of the modern river Harirud. As already stated, the Harirud, after descending from the mountains runs westwards for a distance of 600 km within Afghan territory before turning north to form the border between Afghanistan and Iran. The river finally disappears into desert swamps. Like the Hammun-i-Hilmund, this swampy tract was also a vast lake at least till the end of the third millennium BC and this is the lake, which is mentioned in association with Haroiva in *Vendîdâd* Chapter 1.

If it was desiccation of lakes and rivers which affected settlements in some areas, it was the severity of winter which devastated life in other areas, particularly in the high mountainous regions. This is what the *Vendîdâd* Chapter 1 seeks to convey when it refers to Airyena Baijaha, the first of Ahura Mazda's sixteen creations. According to Chapter 1 of the *Vendîdâd,* Angra Mainyu, the arch enemy of Ahura Mazda whittled down a deadly winter demon to this region afflicting its inhabitants with debilitating cold. There were ten winter months and only two summer months in this region. Even during these two summer months, the earth was cold, the water was cold and the trees were cold, providing little respite from the deadly winter.

Perhaps it is passages like these, which enthused certain Western scholars to argue that the ancestors of the Avestan Iranians and the Vedic Indians had lived side-by-side with Finno-Ugric populations in the Arctic Circle before migrating to the areas, which they occupy today. With such ideas as the starting point of investigation, it may not be too difficult to associate the Avestan Iranians and the Vedic Indians with Nordic ocean and the polar lands (Bongard-Levin, 1981, 112). This appears to be the result of some mix-up between geo-climatic conditions prevailing in the great mountain ranges running from the Hindu Kush to the Pamir and the Himalayas with their Arctic temperatures on the one hand and the Nordic, Polar elements in the Arctic Circle on the other (Gnoli, 1989, 17). This could be the explanation of the story of the severe climate of Airyena Baijaha rather than that deriving from theories about Nordic origins and reminiscences favoured by Bongard-Levin and Grantovskij (Gnoli, 1989A, 44).

However, the identification of Airyena Baijaha with a major part of Hindu-Kush-Pamir-Himalays would be clear from a good look at the temperature chart round the year at Kabul.

	Max. (°C)	Min. (°C)
Jan.	2.2	– 7
April	18.8	6.1
July	17.7	16.1
Oct.	22.7	5.5

By this token, the two-month summer mentioned in the *Vendîdâd* Chapter 1 would be as cool as the early winter in India and Pakistan during the second half of December. This is only natural since the Kabul valley is situated at a height of nearly 6000 ft. and surrounded on all sides by high mountain ranges.

The Possibility of a Mini Ice Age

However, Arctic condition does not simply mean Arctic temperature. It also means a six-monthly night and a murky six-monthly day. Neither is normally possible in any part of the Indo-Iranian subcontinent, described in the *Avesta* and the *Ṛgveda*. Probably, the killer winter whittled by Angra mainyu relates to a Mini Ice Age like condition in a major part of this whole area some time during the Middle Bronze Age. Such a possibility also seems to be suggested by certain Ṛgvedic passages, which register the laments of bards over a truant sun (8.89.7; 1.51.4). Expressions like 'where has the sun disappeared', 'where have its rays vanished', 'who knows' are interesting inasmuch as these may signify a long murky day as one in the Arctic. There are also passages stating that after destroying the demons, which caused such disaster, Indra once again restored the sun in the firmament. This may signify the end of a brief spell of Ice Age like conditions, probably caused by solar inactivity, when the sun's magnetic field touched its maunder minimum, reducing solar radiation by a big margin.

Reduction in solar radiation meant that the rays of sun were far less luminous and far less warm than before. Such a development may have simulated Arctic conditions, which badly affected visibility, at least in the northern fringes of mountainous South Asia. Misty winter days in vast tracts of north-western South Asia reducing visibility to almost nil are a characteristic feature of high winter months. On such occasions, the sun does not come out even once during the whole day. In certain bad years, there may be several such successive days. With the sun's magnetic field at the maunder minimum, conditions much worse than these may have prevailed for months together, making the winter look like unending and deadly. The reconstructions suggested here on the basis of coincidence between Avestan and Ṛgvedic passages and a correlation of such information with relevant data on geo-climatic depredations during the early second millennium BC may or may not be conclusive. But, it certainly underlines the relevance of such an exercise in an uncertain domain of history.

It has been suggested that in the North Atlantic region and perhaps globally, there was a warm-cold cycle with a periodicity of around 1500 years starting around the beginning of the Holocene Age. Evidence from North Atlantic deep-sea cores reveals that abrupt shifts punctuated what is conventionally thought to have been a relatively stable Holocene climate. During each of these episodes, cool, ice-bearing waters from north of Iceland were advancing as far south as the latitude of Britain. At about the same time, the atmospheric circulation above Greenland changed abruptly. Pacing of the Holocene events and of abrupt climate shifts during the last glaciation are statistically the same. Together, they make up a series of climate shifts with a cyclicity close to 1470 $\pm$ 500 years (Bond *et al*, 1997; Crucifix, 1999). Accordingly, the Holocene optimum (7000–3000 BC) may have been punctuated by a severe cold and dry phase that affected climates across North Africa, Southern Asia, Europe, the Americas and Antarctica about 8,200 years ago, perhaps lasting for a century or two before a return to warmer and wetter conditions (Stager and Mayewski, 1997). One of these episodes is assigned to 2200 BC, when the urban and proto-urban civilizations in North-western South Asia, Iran and South Central Asia were coming to an end. The idea of a 1500-year cyclicity of little Ice Age during the Holocene Age is also suggested by studies of ice-rafted debris in Northern Atlantic sediments (Broecker, 2000). After about 5,000 years ago (3000 BC), there was a further cooling and drying in many areas (again, often sudden and stepwise), and conditions became more similar to the present day. This may have reached a high point during the first quarter of the second millennium BC.

Prolonged winter months, combined with reduced solar activity could also affect the immune system in human beings and animals besides upsetting faunal and floral balance in the concerned areas. Probably, the *Vendîdâd* chapter I drops a hint to this affect, which needs to be further investigated on the basis of scientific studies in palaeo-botany and palaeo-zoology, particularly, during the late third and early second millennium BC. In the *Vendîdâd* list, there are two regions which fell victim to the side effects of drastic environmental changes. The first of these two areas are Gava or Sugda, which is identifed with Sogdiana, north of Bactria across the Oxus river. The other settlement was Haroiva or the Harirud valley in western and northern Afghanistan. Gava or Sogdiana is said to have been afflicted by a poisonous fly called Skaitya, which caused a cattle epidemic and devastated the settlement. In the Haroiva or

Harirud valley, it was a scented mosquito, which caused an epidemic among the people in this area. In either case, osteological studies conducted on the remains of animals and human bones from these areas can alone prove or disprove the veracity of observations made in *Vendîdâd* Chapter I. In any case, the investigations will have to be qualitative rather than quantitative, in view of the limited nature of archaeological recovery and still more limited chances of surviving specimens.

As for the remaining settlements in the *Vendîdâd*, Hapta Hindu is the only one which was affected by a stressful environment, excessive summer in this case. Although the Punjab and Sind lie south and south-east of the Indo-Iranian borderland, where winter would be less severe than in the northern and north-western regions of this area, a detailed examination of climatic conditions may alone provide reasonable date for such a calamity, if at all. Another settlement on the South Asian side of the Indo-Iranian subcontinent was Varena, which has been identified by Gnoli with Buner in the Swat territory (Levi, 1915; Henning, 1947; Gnoli, 1989). The region was afflicted by the snake Azi Dāhak and even subjected to foreign rule. The Gāndhāra country with Swat valley as its nucleus is said to have been inhabited by a Dāsa people, who worshipped the snake and spoke a local dialect, probably an early form of Northwestern Prakrit or the Gāndhāra Prakrit (Dani, 1986) during the third millennium BC and afterwards. As for the foreign occupation of the Swat valley, the story seems well documented in the fourth *maṇḍala* of the *Ṛgveda*, which Witzel assigns to the earliest phase of Ṛgvedic compositions (Witzel, 1999). These passages have to be read in association with a hymn of the eighth *maṇḍala* to produce a meaningful historical episode (Nandi, 1993).

Chapter 6

The Urban Fiasco

The Breakdown

The Harappan urbanization, which was the culmination of a long process relating to integration of resource zones and communities, has consistently been viewed as a harmonious development overlooking the reactions and responses of communities thus exploited. The symbiotic relationship based on the interdependence of assets and interests left several latent interstitches in the same area in the form of ambitious individuals and groups preying on the resources and their control. The construction of walled enclosures made of mud bricks or stones around every resource centre, which emphasized the need for protecting the resources and their owners against competing individuals and groups, may have symbolized the organization of accumulation and contradictions inherent in such organization. That such conflicts caused occasional ripples in an otherwise smooth relationship of cooperation seems borne out by the possible evidence of arson and the consequent reduction of the settlements at several places. Two of such settlements, which may have witnessed violent destruction within the pre-urban phase are Nausharo, which lies six miles from Mehargarh and Kot Diji, which lies opposite Mohenjodaro across the river Indus. Ash layers at the site of Kot Diji may represent the intentional destruction of the site followed by a rebuilding. A similar pattern of burning and rebuilding has been documented at the site of Nausharo (Kenoyer, 1998, 42). Signs of fire, accidental or intentional have also been reported from Bronze Age sites of Hathala and Gumla near Rehman Deri.

Attempts to explain the signs of violence at whatever places they occur as accidental and to attribute the rebuilding of the resource centres to their original inhabitants may not be well reasoned. The argument advanced for wishing away the intentional destruction of resource centres by competing individuals or groups is that there is no evidence of large-scale killing of inhabitants at either of the sites (Kenoyer, 1998,42). Large-scale killing of the inhabitants of the resource centres would be relative to the nature of resistance put up by the latter. If the killing or capture of the station chief and a few of his diehard supporters could clinch the issue in favour of the attackers, there would be no point in undertaking unnecessary killing of people, who alone could facilitate rebuilding activities at the site. In case no rebuilding was necessary, the original inhabitants would still be quite helpful in perpetuating the control of the resource centre by the intruders. That resistance against the attackers was negligible can be assumed from the fact that, unlike their Mesopotamian and Egyptian counterparts, the Harappan political authority did not care much for raising and maintaining large armies, manufacturing heavy battle weapons and a state of military preparedness. The continuity of ceramic assemblage at the concerned sites (Kenoyer, 1998, 42) also does not mean much, since the fights were in the nature of neighbourhood conflicts involving the same or different groups of people belonging to a common cultural matrix. Differences of dialect, physical features like skin colour and marginal rituals without any structural involvement would also remain beyond archaeological determination.

Such conflicts, if at all, would be few and far between during the mature phase of Harappan urbanization in which the rival groups could gain more by co-operation than by conflict. But, after the decay of towns began towards the end of the third millennium BC, individuals and groups aspiring for a greater share of resources appear to have had a field day. There may have been communities, in particular resource zones no longer willing to co-operate with the distant ruling elite and trying to shape their own destinies under stressful conditions of life. Latest archaeological research shows that agricultural communities existed side by side with resource zones like shell workers of the coastal area and mining communities in the highlands. However, archaeological evidence may not be as specific as to suggest how different communities in disparate resource zones were reacting to the new situation. One can only speculate that an urban phenomenon, which was no longer in a position to deliver the goods created niches of social protest which soon took the form of a widespread political conflagration in which every community, deprived or entitled, was led by a political authority trying to capture as much resources as it could lay its hands on in the immediate neighbourhood.

With the breakdown of a relationship based on interdependence of assets and interests, the resource centres in different regions became isolated and impoverished, further intensifying conflicts for the resources. With deteriorating civic conditions, encroachment on streets, squatter colonies and marginal structures, these centres no longer looked like a town, even in the physical sense of the term. At the most, these places looked like ramshackle bastions of some sort of authority, when compared to the countryside homes of the less affluent people. These could, however, function well as the centres of local chiefdoms.

In the countryside, much more important than competition for the control of resource centres between powerful families was the scramble for bare subsistence among the masses. The people, who were forced out of their homes and hearths in the wake of severe economic regression were either crowding the dwindling urban places or taking to migration in search of food and shelter. The more enterprising families moved on to far-away places in search of a more hospitable habitation. The desperate ones, who were unwilling to take so much trouble, thronged the decaying urban places and carved out a subsistence by snatching it from others. The meek and the feeble, who could not muster so much strength, preferred to subsist by begging. As overcrowding increased in towns, it paralyzed whatever little civic administration was trying to take care of the citizens. Increasing insanitation may have caused epidemics, which claimed a heavy toll of life.

The urban freebooters were already making life and properties insecure for the residents. The several huddled groups of skeletons discovered at Mohenjodaro may have been the result of these encounters between competing chiefs or the doings of organized groups of wandering marauders. As epidemic and insecurity continued, tens of hundreds of people may have perished throughout the region. With no one around to offer even a collective funeral to the dead, the corpses lay bare scattered in the open for beasts and vultures to take care of them, like at Mohenjodaro.

Political Unrest

The post-urban scenario outlined here is beyond archaeological reconstruction but is well suggested by textual evidence which seems to synchronize quite reasonably with the turn of events during the Middle and Late Bronze Ages. It is not for nothing that the text provides so much space to encounters relating to the possession of walled resource centres, hydraulic constructions like dams and barrages, and fertile agricultural land. The walled Harappan structures, which lay on the trade routes and were surrounded by rich agricultural land and a river flowing nearby with or without hydraulic constructions for water management would be natural targets in terms of neighbourhood political conflicts. Every group, Vedic or non-Vedic, knew that control of the fortified settlement would also give control over revenue from trade, the produce of vast agricultural lands in the surrounding countryside and hydraulic works, already in place and functional. The bracketing of a water management system and fertile agricultural land with the acquisition of fortified settlements may not therefore be without a contextual significance. In a low intensity conflict, the countryside, adjoining hydraulic works and the unguarded caravan halts outside the city gates would be soft targets for raiders. When such conflict became persistent and widespread, it snapped the lifeline of the city and undermined the very existence of urban places. In case the cities were the targets, this could be achieved during the day when the city gates would be wide open and everybody would be on some job or the other and vulnerable to a sudden rush of armed men resorting to wanton killing or capture of the people both inside and outside the fortified area, large-scale arson and vandalism, all of which would suffice to bring the administration to its knees. In any case, battle-related damages to city walls would be uncalled for.

The term *pur*, which occurs more than 80 times in the *Ṛgveda*, has invariably been understood as 'citadel' or 'stronghold'. Consider where else the Vedic communities would come across walled settlements made of mud, mud brick or stone, except in the Greater Indus Valley during the Bronze Age. As for the 'destruction' of citadels, this is easier said than done and can never be the intent of a people who viewed the walled settlements as the source of wealth, power and security and fervently aspired to possess these through capture or construction. Encounters for possession of walled resource centres would be all the more relevant about the close of the third millennium BC when the decline of cities and civic life in the Harappan mainland of Sind, Punjab, Rajasthan and Haryana had reached a flashpoint. Judging by the names of rivers, these are the regions which figure prominently in the descriptions of Vedic poets. The conflicts relating to the capture and occupation of fortified resource centres would perfectly fit a situation in which availability of resources became scarce, triggering conditions of small scale but widespread political disturbances and social unrest.

Fortified Settlements: Pur, Vṛtra, Vṛjana and Durga

In the Harappan context, the town is almost invariably represented by a fortified area, whether it is a citadel, middle-town, downtown or religious complex. Jostling crowds in busy marketplaces, networks of roads and drains and constructional features of different types of buildings, all would be shut out inside the fortification. It would be naive to suppose that marauding chiefs and their troops were unfamiliar with these features of fortified urban life. Occasionally, the interior of these walled settlements, with the built-up area criss-crossed by some sort of passages or pathways, was compared to similar crisscross sections in a spider's net (*aurṇa vābha*, 2.11.18). This is fairly well suggested by the Harappan archaeological record from the early urban phase. Perhaps even these features of urban life would not any longer be as prominently visible during the decaying stages of an urban system. For succeeding generations of the late urban phase, the only prominent thing on view would be the fortification, some ruined and completely deserted and some others still in tact with a thinning population.

The *pur* represented a settlement, which was invariably enclosed by a wall made from stone, mud-brick or mud, all of which have been encountered in the Harappan excavations. The two other terms *durga* and *vṛjana* also represent fortified settlements, the likes of which would be too many during the late third millennium BC. The term *durga* means 'difficult to access'. In one case, it appears as an adjective of the term *pur*, suggesting thereby a 'settlement difficult to access' (1.41.3). In another case, the term appears in association with a word for house, both in the locative case, *duroṇe durge* meaning a 'house or settlement difficult to access' and refers to Indra's destroying thousands of enemies hidden inside these strongholds (4.28.3). As for the term *vṛjana*, (from vṛ, to cover + *jana*, people), it too means enclosed habitation, probably a prosperous village community protected by mud walls on all sides resembling German 'Mark'. After the complete disappearce of urban places sometime after 1500 BC, it was these walled semi-urban or rural settlements which served as the seat of political authority. The siege of forts mentioned in certain later Vedic texts like The *Taittirīya Samhitā*, The *Aitareya Brāhmaṇa*, The *Śatapatha Brāhmaṇa*, The *Gopatha Brāhmaṇa*, etc. may relate to these walled centre shop of political power. In traditional India, villages used to be walled settlements of some sort till as late as the early British times, the purpose of such walling being to prevent brigands and wild predators in the surrounding jungles from barging in. The other term *vṛtra* (from *vṛ*, 'to cover', 'to enclose'), also signified a walled settlement, but the plural *vṛtrāni* refer to the inhabitants of such settlements. The stories relating to destruction of *vṛtra* fall into two categories. In most instances, Vṛtra represents a demon who obstructed the passage of rivers and withheld the clouds from releasing the rains. But, in several other instances, the episodes relate to actual fights for the capture of walled settlements and irrigation dams.

Perhaps the Vedic-speaking community was just one of several ethno-linguistic communities which inhabited north-western South Asia during the Bronze Age. Like other peoples in the area, the Vedic speakers also prospered and suffered with the turn of events in the Greater Indus Valley. Each of these communities reacted to the turbulent events in its own way. Those who possessed literary skills created small and big oral texts, recording the events and the destruction which followed these. These oral texts could be Vedic as well as non-Vedic. Non-Vedic texts, if at all created, could not evidently survive in the absence of a oral mechanism of preservation and transmission. This is where the Vedic poets seem to have scored considerably over all others and made good use of their literary skills to dish out information on diverse types of calamity in nature and society, the *pur* encounters being just one of them.

In the snatching of resources, there were no good guys or bad guys, notwithstanding claims by one section of people who described themselves as 'noble' (Ārya) and denigrated all others as enemies (Dasyu). There are compositions relating to conflicts between one Ārya chief and another, between one Ārya chief and one Dāsa chief, besides fights like the ten kings' battle in which one Ārya chief was combating a coalition of Dāsa, Vṛtra and Ārya chiefs. Pejoratives used by the composers in relation to non-Vedic people always relate to a conflict situation and the poets overdoing to please their patrons. When these groups came together for a common political purpose, abuses disappeared into thin air. As for the walled settlements, these belonged as much to the Ārya as to the Dāsa or the Vṛtra. Bardic compositions frequently refer to Vedic-speaking communities inhabiting the strongholds together with their priests, armed companions, subjects and herds of cattle. Clearly, the walled settlements were needed as much by the Dāsa or Vṛtra as by the Ārya and fights undertaken to this effect. Remember Sudāsa, an Ārya chief belonging to the Tṛtsu segment of Bharata lineage ruling on the banks of Paruṣṇi (Ravi) and capturing the strongly built fortifications (*dṛmhitāni puraḥ*, 7.18.13) belonging to Aṇu and Puru, who too where Ārya chiefs ruling on the banks of Yamuna. The omnibus Indra, who seems to have been a warrior par excellence of Vedic antiquity, was later raised to the position of a divinity supposed to ensure success in battles and, accordingly, registered his shadowy presence in every encounter, including those relating to the capture of walled settlements. No wonder, he was as much a breaker of fortified settlements (*purandara*) as the lord of such settlements (*puḥ pati*, 1.183.10).

Going by the semantics, there are chiefs with non-Vedic sounding names, like Pipru and Dhuni, just as there are chiefs with Vedic-sounding names, like Karañja and Praṇaya, both categories of chiefs possessing several fortified settlements. Pipru is called a Dāsa (8.32.2) and an Asura (10.138.3) having a black brood (1.101.1) and allied with dark-skinned people (4.16.13). No such pejorative is used either for Karañj or Pranaya (1.53.8). As for the dark skin colour, it cut across Vedic and non-Vedic speakers. Trasadasyu, an Ārya chief of the Swat valley, is called a dark-skinned leader (8.19.37). Divodāsa and Sudāsa, who were Dāsa converts to the Ārya faith, may also have been dark-skinned chiefs. Similarly, Kaṇva, the chief poet of the eighth book, is described as black (10.31.11).

The descriptions of walled settlements appearing in the *Ṛgveda* bear characteristic similarity to walled habitations and citadels found throughout the Greater Indus Valley and belonging to different stages of Harappan urbanization. There were mud-brick ramparts, like at Amri, where the wall was made of sun-dried bricks (Kenyor, 1998, 44) and stone-built citadels, like at Kot Diji. Many of these settlements, particularly the mega cities, ranged between 100 and 250 hectares which matches fairly well with bardic description of forts as broad and large. The mud or mud-brick rampart is simulated in the expression *āmāṣu pūrṣu* (2.35.6), meaning 'raw' or 'unbaked structures', while the stone rampart is characterized as *aśmamayī* (4.30.20; 2.35.6) or 'built of stone'. In certain areas, the bards may have come across structures in which limestone was the principal construction material or structures with a thick shining coat of lime on the outer walls to motivate the simile 'forts like crystal' or 'crystalline forts' (*puraḥ na śubhrā* 5.41.12). Despite the usual mix-up with unrelated water myths, this part of the stanza surely relates to fortified settlements at certain sites like Dholavira, Rojdi and Surkotda, where limestone was liberally used as a construction material. Depending on availability, limestone was also used at other sites, liberally or sparingly. The excavator of Dholavira informs that during the earliest three stages, limestone was used on a large scale with certain prominent parts of structures getting a lustrous polish (R.S. Bisht, personal communication). At its prime, the whole structure surely gave the appearance of a huge white mansion. The understanding of commentators and translators that the term *śubhrāḥ* in this passage means 'crystal' also needs clarification. Crystals do not make houses, but limestones do and polished limestone resembles marble (also limestone) more closely than crystal. So far as pillared citadels are concerned, Marshall's (Marshall, 1931) excavation at Mohenjodaro has brought to light many such buildings, particularly one in the area L, which shows a large building with 20 masonry pillars arranged in five rows with four pillars in each row. Even otherwise, pillars would be an integral feature of massive masonry structures, like forts.

The bardic descriptions relating to walled settlements fall into four categories. The first relates to the stanzas which highlight the elaborate nature of enclosed settlements and the second underlines prayers for possessing similar settlements, either by way of capture or construction. The third type of invocations refers to Vedic-speaking communities actually inhabiting such walled settlements and worshipping their gods inside these structures. A fourth group of hymns highlights that despite several successful accounts of *pur* encounters, the Vedic community was actually living under a constant fear of death and destruction caused by other competing chiefs, like they themselves caused to other inhabitants of walled settlements. This is reflected in the compositions which fervently appeal to various gods for the protection of strongholds inhabited by Vedic speakers.

As for the structural dimension of walled habitations, a

passage of the first book implores the fire god to provide spacious and manifold castles (1.189.2, *naḥpṛthvī ca pūḥbahulā ūrvī bhava*). In another passage, Maruts are urged to protect the Vedic-speaking people with pillared strongholds (1.166.8 *śatabhujibhiḥ purvhiḥ rakṣata*). A poet of the tenth book prays to the gods to make the forts invincible, as strong as metal and provide these with many arms or pillars (10.101.8 *adhṛṣṭāḥ āyasīḥ puraḥ kṛṇudhvam*). The prayer is a characteristic of a people already inhabiting fortified settlements which were frequently targeted by neighbouring chiefs and peoples. In yet another example, Indra is described as the lord of the fortified settlement (1.173.10 *pūḥpatim yajñaiḥ upaśikṣanti*). A similar expression is found in another passage of the first book, which states 'in this fortified place may be dwell with our brave sons under your protection' (1.51.15 *asmin vṛjane sarvavīrāḥ asmat sūribhiḥ tava śarman syāma*). A Vedic community in possession of fortified settlements again surfaces in a passage of the first book, which implores the Maruts to preserve 'our fame and also our strongholds' (1.139.8 *dyumnāni mā jāriṣuḥ uta asmat purā jāriṣuḥ*). Even where the Vedic communities severely damaged the fortified settlements, they were careful enough to preserve one of these for their own habitation (4.26.3, etc.).

Strongholds and citadels were herding places for cattle (8.6.23) and also a safe habitat of the community itself. Strongholds built or captured by the Vedic speakers were broad and wide (*pṛthvī/ūrvī*, 1.189.2), many pillared (*śatabhuji*, 1.166.8; 7.15.14), made of stone (*aśmamayī*, 4.30.20; 2.35.6), made of mud or mud-brick (*āmāṣu pūrṣu*). Raiding of strongholds was also intended to dislodge the station chief and capture all his cultivable land and drainage facilities (*tvam ayajñyum martyam śāsaḥ mahīm pṛthvīm imāḥ apan amuṣṇāḥ*, 1.131.4). There are prayers for many-pillared strongholds (1.166.8), built or captured for plenty of fertile land and spacious citadels (1.189.2). Gods are frequently described as protectors of walled habitations (*vṛjanasaya gopā*, 1.91.21).

Ruined Settlements

As for the ruined settlements, littered with burials, there is a single expression (*armake vailasthāne*, 1.133.3), which occurs twice in the same passage of the first book. In both these instances, the words are used in the locative case with the first part serving as the adjective. Taken together, the expression means 'in the ugly or awesome place of the dead'. However, the term *armaka* does not have a satisfactory derivation in the Vedic dialect. Probably, it was the Vedic synonym of a Dravidian vocable *ara-mana* or *armana* meaning 'house of the king' or 'palace', used here in a derogatory sense. In the Harappan context, many of the decaying settlements were erstwhile centres of political power and could accordingly be described as 'palaces'. But, the fortifications which enclosed these 'palaces', also contained several sprawling graveyards as at Harappa. These burial grounds appear to be well represented by the term *vailasthāna* or *mahāvailasthāna*. From *vila* or *bila*, which is a regular term for a pit or hole, *vailasthāna* would mean 'an extensive burial ground'. From Tamil *vil*, meaning 'crack, split, to be separated from', *vailasthāna* may also mean the place where the dead are finally separated from their relatives, a burial ground. This is precisely what the city of Harappa may have looked like within fifty or hundred years of its desertion. Interestingly, the term *vailasthāna* anticipates the much later place-name Mohenjodaro or 'the mound of the dead', given to it by brick robbers, who encountered massive graveyards and numerous unburied skeletons at the site. The terms *armaka* and *vailasthāna* appear to justify a situation such as this. Even the passage in which these two expressions occur refers to large scale killing of the inhabitants of these places by armed groups of attackers. The clusters of unburied skeletons, which fired the imagination of certain archaeologists, who thought of a massacre taking place at Mohenjodaro (Wheeler, 1947, 55) may have been the people dying in large numbers from natural calamities punctuated by civil war like conditions.

Antique Homes

Consider how the walled settlements might have looked another couple of centuries later. As many of these places were completely deserted, the structures became worn out and dilapidated, justifying the bardic expression 'dwellings of ancient times' (*pratnasya okasaḥ*) and 'in the dwellings of ancient times' (*pratneṣu dhāmasu*). Some of the ancient Harappan settlements may still have been partly habitable, which encouraged some of the Vedic speaking communities to settle at these places. The term 'ancient settlements' may relate to the compositions of bards, who witnessed for successive generations the progressive decay and desertion of Harappan settlements. In one case, it is stated that god Rudra showed up at all those ancient settlements (*pratneṣu dhāmasu*, 8.13.20), where the bards prayed in his honour. Another passage of the eighth *maṇḍala* refers to the Priyamedha section of the Angirā family as lodging themselves in settlements belonging to antiquity (8.69.18). Priyamedhas, who is enumerated after Dadhīci and Angirā, and before Kaṇva, Atri and Manu (1.139.9), seems to match fairly well with the antiquity of the deserted Harappan settlements in Sind, Punjab, and Rajasthan. That the Priyamedhas belong to this area can be inferred from their reference to the land of seven rivers, which flowed into the sea (*saptasind havaḥ kākudam anukṣaranti*, 8.69.12), a phenomenon, which may synchronize with the time when apart from the Indus, other rivers, particularly the Sarasvati, modern Hakara-Ghaghar reached out to the Arabian Sea. This would be sometime around the close of the third millennium BC. Such descriptions may have continued until the deserted Harappan structures slowly developed into large mounds. Such mound formation may have taken a couple of centuries from the time when depopulation of Harappan centres started. After the mound-formation was complete in most of the major Harappan settlements, the Vedic communities, already a residual existence in the area would not have much occasion either to occupy these settlements or narrate such events.

A Regressive Economy

Although the urban networking had disappeared and the interactive regions disintegrated by the close of the third millennium BC, small-scale production and distribution of prestige goods continued even after the decay of urban centres.

These prestige goods came from marine shell-workers along the coastline, miners, metal workers and gem designers in the highlands, while subsistence goods came from agricultural and pastoral sectors in the fertile plains. Overland exchanges of goods dropped to a minimum and took the character of transit trade, involving small groups of entrepreneurs. Enterprising people were still going out to the high seas for the disbursal of prestige items, like *lapis lazuli* among distant customers. Sometimes, there were shipwrecks, resulting in loss of life and property, as in the case of the chiefs Tugra and Bhujyu. As for the caravans, the main components comprised camels, mules, bullocks and horses, depending on the nature of tracts negotiated. Prayers for the safety of journeys to distant lands and back home are frequently mentioned. All these activities were organized more on a private basis by groups of individuals, with or without marginal support from chiefs along the way.

The incidence of metallic money was limited, the bulk of trade being carried on through barter. Terms for sale, purchase and lease were known just as terms for customs duty. Loans were taken and repaid along with interest, but failure to repay led to the enslavement of the debtor by the creditor. The exchanges took place through pedlars moving either in singles or groups. Frequently, the bardic composers themselves acted as the medium of commodity exchange between far-off places. On other occasions, they were part of long-distance caravans. The term *vaṇik*, which means 'trader', occurs twice in the *Ṛgveda*, once referring to a bardic caravaneer and once to a crafty trader. Some idea of the commodities exchanged is also provided by the goods collected by Ṛgvedic bards from their patrons. These included horses, camels, donkeys, cattle, goats and sheep, chariots, objects of gold and brass as well as solid blocks of these metals, textiles of different type, precious gems, metallic money, slaves, brides with glittering jewellery and items of food. A part of this was consumed by the recipients, but the rest was disposed of through barter or money transactions, besides presentation to prospective chiefs and queens. All this would give some idea of how things were shaping upon the commercial front during the dying stages of the Harappan civilization. The exchange of goods, howsoever marginal, would surely bring the producers and manufacturers of these goods into sharp focus. As such, a quick look at the information relating to craftsmen and craft-working in the text would be quite in order. The information, which surfaces from every portion of the text, includes all the major categories like metal-working, wood-working, leather-working, pot-making and weaving. All this knowledge would be commonplace in north-western South Asia during the late third and early second millennium BC. Judging by the content and context of the textual evidence, it would be unrealistic to wish away synchronism with the Harappan cultural milieu.

Deflated Urban Classes

Crestfallen from a hyperactive urban networking of market economy, different professional groups were trying to find as flattering a space as they could manage in the decaying urban milieu. The most important of these professional groups was evidently the religious elite, who headed a new belief system, mastered a liturgical dialect for its propagation and projected and exclusive social identity for all who fell in line. The followers of the new system came from all sections of the society—political patrons, merchants of trade, physicians, craftsmen, navigators, peasants, the miracle man–and all others who enjoyed varying degrees of importance in a fast–decaying society. Through their literary creations the poets and seers raised each one of their benefactors to the position of a demi-god. But all others who did not subscribe to the new religious system were denounced as enemies and abused in every possible manner. Chiefs who could win battles and offer lavish gifts to the priests were the most important characters of the literary creations, followed by merchants, craftsmen and peasants.

The importance of physicians and miracle healers in a society constantly threatened by death and disease needs no over-emphasis. The physician was also in great demand in the political and military circles following recurrent wars and wanton destruction of life and property. The importance attached to Bhiṣak Athrvan and Dadhīci, who belonged to the Athravan family and whose special relationship with Aśvins, the physicians par excellence enraged Indra and the conflict between Indra and Aśvins over the possession of a secret therapeutic knowledge would suffice to highlight the role of professional medical practitioners in the early Vedic society and may correspond to conditions prevailing in the decadent Harappan society.

The other competing groups were bankers, barterers and the craft workers. Although the urban system was fast disappearing, the importance of prestige goods for the marginal political, religious and commercial elites continued. Necessarily, the production and distribution of these commodities involved the participation of various categories of craft workers, who produced these goods and pedlars and hawkers, who marketed them. These necessities would naturally bring the workman closure to the court, the latter rewarding the former for their consummate skills. The bardic composers also needed a part of these prestige goods and necessities of day to day life and, accordingly, praised the craftsmen and even raised some of them to the position of divine artificers. At the same time, they did not take too kindly to the munificent benefaction justifiably showered by the court on these workers. This may have led to the castigation of craftsmen and stories, real or fabricated, relating to their humiliation, as in the case of Tvaṣṭā and Viśvarūpa.

Chapter 7

The Chants of Disaster

The hymns of the *Ṛgveda,* which were composed in the same region as the Greater Indus Valley, probably during the decaying stages of Harappan civilization, seem to provide *in situ* description of persistent catastrophic events in nature and society. The times were stressful and the instincts of self-preservation reigned supreme. The values and emotions of family relationship were falling apart with the relatively well-to-do preserving food stocks at the expense of friends and relatives, who were driven out of the household (10.117). Families which were wiped out in the wake of natural disasters and civil war (7.58.1), however, escaped such depravity. Some of the people forsaken by their families eked out a bare subsistence by performing odd jobs while others joined the ranks of bandits and beggars. The brigands, who were particularly active in the forest, overpowered passers by and looted all their belongings (10.4.6).

Disaster Terminology in the *Ṛgveda*

The stanzas in which calamity related words make their appearance emphasize that misfortune is the result of man's irreligious conduct. These also underline a deep distrust of all human efforts to overcome the calamity and an abiding faith in the forces of nature for deliverance. One of the terms, which occurs throughout the text and makes as many as 26 appearances is *nirṛti,* meaning 'the lady of death'. It also means dissolution, destruction, calamity, evil, and adversity. Literally, the term means 'devoid of *ṛta* or right conduct', suggesting that abhorrence of righteous behaviour invites destruction. The term *amati,* which represents want or scarcity, literally means negation of mati or devotion, prayer, worship, hymn. Once again it is bad conduct which invites abject poverty. A third vocable is *anira* or *anirā,* meaning destitute of vigour. Derived from *ir,* meaning 'to go', masculine *anira* or feminine *anira* would literally mean inability to move, signifying lack or want of vigour. Combined as it is with another term *anāhutim,* non-praying, it may mean that it is the negation of worship through prayers, which causes poverty and which in turn leaves people languishing for want of vigour. The term *asunītī,* which is understood as a personification of death or simply a demon representing death, derives from *nītī,* meaning 'right conduct' or moral behaviour; *asunītī* therefore means abhorrence of right conduct or moral behaviour. It would follow from this that death overpowers those who neglect righteous behaviour. The term *ducchunā,* which appears in over a dozen passages belonging to different portions of the work, is understood as misfortune, calamity, harm, mischief. The term *amīvā* also occurs in about 30 passages belonging to different portions of the work. Depending on the context, it means distress, terror, fright or tormenting spirit, demon or affliction, disease. Other words denoting calamity or misfortune are *viṣūcī* and *upadru.* The term *viṣūcī* (6.74.2) means 'destruction, falling asunder and the term *upadru* means to oppress, attack'.

Disaster Events in the *Ṛgveda*

Apart from these, there are separate words and contexts signifying disaster of different types, flood, famine, earthquake, epidemic and probably meteoric strike. Two such potential words are *dhvasmā* and *dhvasir,* both derived from √*dhvas,* meaning polluting, darkening, destroying. Going by the contexts, both the terms mean earthquake, deluge, and desiccation. One of the passages mentions a terrible instance of the subsidence of earth (7.83.3). The expressions *bhūmyāḥ antāḥ dhvasirāḥ sam adṛkṣata* and *divi ghoṣaḥ ārūhat* in this passage are quite significant. The first expression means 'all the lands have subsided' and the next expression means 'the tremendous roar is rising from earth to the sky'. Although, this passage occurs in relation to the battle of ten kings, it does not indicate any organic connection with the event. Moreover, battles fought with the help of foot soldiers, chariots and horses can hardly cause any subsidence of earth worth a mention. The stanza, surely an earlier composition describing a major episode of earthquake, is used here with characteristic bardic desire for projecting the intensity of the battle and the destruction which followed it.

Widespread subsidence of earth can be the result of a terrible earthquake, meteoric strikes and devastating floods, a huge roar invariably accompanying all three episodes. In a passage of the eighth book (8.66.15), we hear of a bard assuring his people not to panic since the dreaded calamity is now gradually receding (*dhvasmā apa it ayati eṣaḥ svayam apa ayati*). In Griffith's translation, *dhvasmā apa it ayati* is understood as 'darkening sorrow going away'. The term *dhvasmā* may suggest widespread earthquakes or floods, either of which can shake the ground, bringing down structures and uprooting settlements. In the Harappan context, Mohenjodaro experienced repeated floods while Kalibangan was destabilized by earthquake sometime between 2450 BC and 2300 BC (Ghosh, 1989, 78). The city of Dholavira in Rann of Kutch also experienced several earthquakes, the last one being instrumental in the desertion of the city. The family of the bard Kali may have been one of the numerous bardic communities which experienced different calamities in different regions during the dying moments of the Harappan civilization.

Although no attempt has so far been made to assess the importance of meteoric strikes in the destruction of the Harappan civilization, recent scientific investigations underline the role of such episodes in the destruction of Early Bronze Age civilizations (Peiser, 1997). Recent studies by Indian geologists reported in *Current Science* suggest the possibility of the destruction of the Harappan civilization in Kutch and Rajasthan in the wake of meteoric strikes. A circular crater measuring 1.2 kms east-west and 1.2 kms north-south, is suspected by scientists to be formed by the impact of an extra-terrestrial object, near Luna village in the north-western Banni plains of the Great Rann of Kutch. The site, the third in the country after Lonar in Maharashtra and Ramgarh in Rajasthan, is located about a kilometre away from a human settlement belonging to the Harappan period and may have found reference in ancient Sanskrit texts, which mention the impact of a burning extra-terrestrial object in western India some 4000-5000 years ago (Times, 2006). Certain portions of the *Ṛgveda* mention the episode of falling meteors resulting in the subsidence of land (10.68.4—*arkaḥ bṛhaspati dyauḥ ulkām iva bhūmyāḥ tvacam udnāiva vi vibheda*). The passage has two parts joined by a simile. First, it refers to the falling of a meteor (*ulkā*) from the sky. Second, it refers to the subsidence of earth caused by heavy rains, which is compared to the subsidence caused by a large herd of cattle. Subsidence of earth is caused by meteors in the form of craters. Marginal subsidence of land is also caused by continuous and heavy downpour, but the hoofs of the cattle, howsoever large the herd may be, do not cause any subsidence of the earth. As such, this can be dismissed as a figment of bardic imagination. Probably, the bard was more concerned with the activities of his herd and used the memory of a meteoric episode to highlight it by way of poetic hyperbole.

Listening to bardic cries against calamity and prayers for its prevention may be instructive, if contextualized. Some of the clinching passages come from the sixth and the seventh book, which are said to form part of the family portions of the text and supposedly representing an early phase of the Ṛgvedic society. One of these passages refers to families wiped out by calamities (7.58.1—*uta avamśāt nirṛte kṣodanti*). In another passage (6.74.2), the poet implores Soma and Rudra to save him and his kinsmen from falling asunder or from destruction (*viṣūcīm vivṛhatam*), to drive away the distress that has entered the houses (*amīvā yā naḥ gayam ā viveśa*) and to caste away the calamity (*nirṛtim parācaiḥ āre bādhetām*). Similar sentiments are echoed in respect of Varuṇa, who is implored to purge the calamity (1.24.9—*nirṛtim parācaiḥ dūre bādhesva).* Likewise, a composer of the Tenth Book (10.59.4) prays to Soma for deliverance from death and destruction. At another place (2.32.2), Indra is prayed to for protection against calamity (*naḥ ābhyaḥ ducchunābhyaḥ mā rīraghaḥ).* The consistency with which the expression *nirṛtim prācaiḥ,* meaning 'remove the destruction' occurs throughout the text points to a longish period of disaster afflicting different Ṛgvedic communities.

Drought and Scarcity

Though the disaster came in many forms, one that is fairly well recorded in archaeology and literature relates to a persistent hydrological crisis represented by low precipitation and drought, which caused repeated crop failures and created conditions of widespread scarcity. Archaeologically, it is already well known that the Greater Indus Valley was passing through a difficult period of mid Holocene hyper-arid conditions, particularly during the Middle and Late Bronze Ages. Difficulties were further compounded by the disappearance of south-west monsoon from the area and tectonic lifts bringing about changes in the course of rivers. In the bardic parlance, the focus is on myths relating to Ahi, Śuṣṇa, and Vṛtra. Ahi, who held back the clouds from raining was the demon of low precipitation, Śuṣṇa who caused reduction in groundwater was the demon of aridity. The Śuṣṇa story or its fragments surface in forty different passages of the text, in three of which Śuṣṇa is brackted with Kuyava. If Śuṣṇa was the demon of drought, Kuyava was the demon of bad harvest, suggesting that famines in the Greater Indus Valley would be a matter of asking during the Middle and Late Bronze Ages. Vṛtra, also a demon of hydrological crisis, represented dams and barrages blocking the smooth flow of rivers and preventing distant peasant communities from using the water of the river.

Match this information with frequent prayers for rains and plentiful crops. Almost every important divinity, Indra, Agni, Soma, Varuṇa and Puṣan is prayed to usher in rains and drench the cornfields. Prayers to Puṣan, the god of nutrition are particularly significant. The Maruts, who appear as monsoon winds in certain portions of the text, like the fifth book, not only drive the clouds to their destination but also create the clouds by lifting and condensing water vapours from the sea. Besides, there are complete hymns addressed to Parjanya, the rain god who not only irrigates the fields during the winter and summer monsoons, helps raise plentiful harvest, but also drenches the deserts and make them negotiable for the travellers. This is besides the famous Frog Hymn of the sixth book, which has all the characteristics of frog behaviour during the monsoon.

The misery brought about by long spells of drought and subsequent famines appears to have haunted the earliest Vedic speakers of South Asia on a recurrent basis. To tide over the crisis, special sacrifices were held to please the gods in the heaven and bring the downpour to the scorched earth below. The famous drought hymn (10.98.1-12) of the tenth book captures the experiences of people afflicted by frequent drought and crop failures. The sacrifice being performed by priest Devāpi on behalf of King Śāntanu was to continue so long as angry gods holding back the rains did not respond to the prayers of the priest.

Famine and Starvation

An inevitable consequence of recurrent droughts and crop failures would be to create famine-like conditions, giving rise to widespread scarcity of foodstuff and deaths from starvation. The relationship between hunger and want is repeatedly stressed by the bracketing of the terms *āmati* and *kṣudh*, the former meaning 'want' or 'indigence' and the latter denoting hunger. In several instances, the gods are implored by the bardic composers to spare them and their kinsmen the misfortune of poverty and hunger, the indignity of wearing tottered clothes and provide safeguards against demons in the dwellings and in the forest (10.43.3; 7.1.19; 8.66.14). At other places, gods are implored by bards not to place them and their kinsmen into houses stricken by poverty and hunger (1.104.7—*naḥ akṛte yonau mā kṣudhyatabhyaḥ vayaḥ āsutim daḥ).* The widespread nature of starvation can be seen from the helplessness of people who project hunger and poverty as the curses of divinities. Hunger created by gods is truly mortifying as is observed by one of the composers (10.117.1—*devāḥ kṣudham na daduḥ Vadham* it. The killer hunger is once again mentioned in a passage of the eighth book (8.60.20—*anirām kṣudham rakṣasvinaḥ/parogavyuti apa sedha).*

Brigands and beggars constitute an important marker of every decadent society, like the one in north-western South Asia during the late third and early second millennium BC. Both are destitutes devoid of any secure means of livelihood. But, the former are strong enough to snatch their requirements from the hapless survivors in decaying settlements. The latter, who are weak, can only resort to begging their morsel of food from the same hapless survivors. But, many may not oblige as indeed one can see from a poignant hymn of the tenth book (10.117). Interestingly, the theme of this composition is the seeking of subsistence from those who have it and the composer is described as Bhikṣurāngirasa or a beggar of the Angira family. The very first stanza (10.117.1) refers to killer hunger ordained by the gods ostensibly as punishment for the deviant actions of the people. It then praises the virtues of the gifts of food and curses the miserly non-givers. Continuing the curse further, the bard states that a man, who is possessed of grain stores, but without a kind heart does not care for the tottering beggars and guests in front of himself and helps him happily with morsels of food. Such a person has no happiness in life (10.117.2). Many of the beggars who frequented the decaying settlements were rickety and weak on account of continuous starvation (10.117.3). The subsistence crisis even compelled the householder to deprive friends and dependants of their share with a view to preserving foodgrains for worse days ahead. The deprived friends and dependants left the householder for good and set out on an uncertain journey thereby further swelling the ranks of alms seekers (10.117.4). He who offers neither to the gods nor to the friends or guests and feeds only himself is said to be a sinner sure to die uncared for (10.117.6). Making a poignant reference to highly unequal resources of different families (10.117.8), the poet goes on to add that a liberal person, who gathers his wealth from agriculture and spares part of it for the needy is far better than the knowledgeable seer, who does not do anything to either enrich himself or provide succour to the destitute (10.117.7).

The description of the pangs of poverty and hunger are interspersed throughout the text, but these need not synchronize with the portions in which they are found in the present redaction. Instead, all these compositions together with those reflecting on various types of natural disasters as a whole should relate to a specific period of time, a longish one in the history of Ṛgvedic communities.

Death and Disease

Chronic malnutrition caused by widespread poverty and hunger would be only a short distance from death and disease. While a large number of people may have died just because of persistent low intake of calorie following widespread famines and scarcity, malnutrition of a chronic type could have given rise to metabolical disorders of a serious nature, like atrophy or hypertrophy. Rickety people, obviously victims of malnutrition, are mentioned to be moving from door to door in search of a morsel of food (10.117.3). Premature death could result as much from starvation of this type as from pathogenic disorders caused by malnutrition. The fear of premature death casts its shadow on many of the compositions, like the few from the eighth book. In one case (8.67.5), the poet implores the collective gods Ādityas to arrive for rescue before people are overcome by death. In another instance (8.67.20), the poet is more specific when he implores the gods to spare people from falling to death before attaining old age. Some archaeological evidence of premature death caused by chronic malnutrition of a hereditary nature has been noticed at Harappan sites in Punjab and Sind (Kennedy, 1984). That the affliction was of a deadly nature can be inferred from the fact that it covered as much as 25 per cent of the population in the age group of 12 to 40 years.

Chronic hereditary anaemia, which affected 25 per cent of the population in the Indus Valley may have triggered chronic infertility, of which there is some indication in the bardic account. There are several passages dilating on diseases of uro-genitals, particularly sperm and ovum-related disorders resulting in chronic infertility. There is a clear reference to sperm-related disorder in which the sperm is unable to reach the target. This is figuratively described as an evil spirit licking away the sperm and preventing it from fertilizing the ovum (10.162.4; 10.162.3). Chronic anaemia or other uro-genital disorders could also induce miscarriages and even lead to still births (10.162.3). Both possibilities are mentioned in a passage of the tenth book, which refers to the miscarriage of foetus and still-born child (10.162.3). The importance attached to mental disorders and trauma in certain bardic compositions, particularly those bracketed with the onslaught of calamity, may not therefore be out of context. In one instance (10.164.1), the deity of calamity is implored not to torment the mind which is already afflicted by frightening thoughts. The nightmares which tear apart the mind day in and day out, the phobia which keeps men awake at night may be dispelled by the fire god (10.164.3). In the bardic context, the term *duḥsvapnaḥ* or 'bad dreams' will translate fairly well for neurosis of a chronic type. In pregnant women such deadly fright of a raging calamity might well have induced miscarriages and stillborn births (10.162.6).

The lengthening shadow of death and disease within a shattered community can also be measured by the repeated mention of the term *yakṣmā* in different portions of the work. *yakṣmā* meant 'disease', *rāja yakṣmā,* 'an incurable disease', and *ajñāta yakṣmā* 'a disease defying diagnosis. When diseases failed to respond to medicines, the only alternative would be a divine remedy, *haviṣ* or oblation, which was supposed to placate angry gods and win their blessings as curatives. Although, diseases are a normal feature of human existence, some of the earliest Ṛgvedic communities appear to have been much more vulnerable to such contingencies. A longish catalogue of various types of ailment listed in a portion of the tenth book reveals the bardic awareness of human anatomy and physiology. There are diseases of the eye, ear, nose, throat, diseases of glands and motor nerves, cardiac ailments, diseases of bone joints, diseases of lungs, liver and kidney, disorders of gastroenteritis, uro-genital disorders, dermatological diseases and, of course, mental disorders. The portion of the text in which these disorders are listed project some evil spirits as the cause of these ailments and appeals for divine remedy through prayers and oblations, giving the impression that communities had reached a terminal stage when medicines or medicine men would not be around or effective.

Elsewhere in the text, the contingent nature of diseases in the life of bardic communities is underlined by the importance attached to medicines and medicine men. Consider the importance of the Aśvin twins, who, on account of excellent medical expertise, were raised to the position of divinities. In the tenth book, there is a complete hymn consisting of twenty-three invocations, all addressed to Oṣadhi or herbals and composed by a physician called Bhiṣag Atharvan. The deity of herbal plants is called a mother, Ambā, who resides in hundreds of places and takes thousands of forms (10.97.2). Herbs, which are collected from far and near (10.97.21) and brought to the house of the physician (10.97.6) drive away ailments from every part of the body, limb by limb, joint by joint (10.97.12). Herbs are urged to work in harmony to give the best of results in the treatment of a patient (10.97.14). There are herbs, which bear flowers and fruits, but there are others, which do not (10.97.15). Probably, the latter refers to roots, which had to be dug out from the earth. Safety is prayed for persons digging out herbal roots from the ground in unknown areas and freedom from diseases for bipeds and quadrupeds (10.97.20). The fee of the physician was computed in terms of horses, cattle and garments (10.97.4).

In a warm, humid and densely forested country like India there would be no dearth of poisonous snakes and insects. A medical system here would be always incomplete in the absence of information relating to poisonous creatures and anti-venom applications to guard against them. A full text of the first book on toxicology (1.191) underlines the familiarity of Ṛgvedic medicines with different types of poisoning and their respective remedies. Different types of snakes residing in different types of grasses are mentioned, though neither the snakes nor the shrubs are named (1.191.3). Many of the toxic substances appear to have been neutralized through exposure to sunlight

(1.191.10). A small bird called Śakuntikā (francoline partridge) was capable of removing toxicity from an afflicted person without itself getting harmed (1.191.11). Further, twenty-one types of bird, not named are said to perform a similar function (1.191.12). The ninety-nine unnamed herbal plants are said to be effective in the treatment of poisoning (1.191.13). She-peacock or Mayūrī is also said to be capable of removing poison (1.191.14). Small poisonous insects like Kuśumbhaka are mentioned as the agents of poisoning (1.191.15) and, finally a poison doctor coming from the mountains is said to hold the secret for scorpion bites (1.191.16).

The Ominous and the Auspicious

The fear of death, particularly pre-mature death, and the desire to prevent such incidents gave rise to certain beliefs associated with particular birds and beasts. The mention of the Śakunta bird to which nearly six invocations are addressed in the second book shows that certain birds and animals, depending on their behaviour, real or attributed, were gradually being associated with the well-being or otherwise of humans in life and after life. Staying as it does on the southern part of the house (2.42.3 *gṛhāṇām dakṣiṇata ava kranda*), the Śakunta makes auspicious sounds as the boatman brings the boat safely to the shore (2.42.1), suggesting thereby that the bird is capable of assuring a safe passage in life to the inmates of the house. It is urged to ensure good fortune (2.42.1—*sumangalaśca bhavāsi*) to all members of the house. The auspicious sounds made by this bird are compared to the singing of Sāmam melodies by Udgātā priest and the invocations chanted by the Brahma priest at the sacrifice (2.43.2). Like the singer of Sāmam, Śakunta is said to be proficient in both Gāyatrī and Triṣṭubh meters (2.43.1—*gāyatram traiṣṭubham ubhe vācau*) and protection is prayed for it against the attacks of prey birds like śyena and Suparṇa as well as armed intruders (2.42.2).

Just as Śakunta was the bird of good fortune, Kapota (pigeon) and Ulūka (owl) were considered to be the harbingers of misfortune. Prayers were chanted to drive away the pigeon, the messenger of the lady of death (Nirṛti) trying to enter the house (10.165.1-2). Prayers were also chanted to prevent the pigeon as well as owl causing harm to bipeds and quadrupeds of the house (10.165.3-5).

Turning to the Harappan funerary record, one can notice a good deal of importance attached to certain birds and beasts, whose bones were interned with or without the dead man's bones or ashes. The funerary paintings encountered at Cemetery-H also underline the association of birds and animals with the after life journey of a dead person. In certain depictions, birds in flight are seen carrying the soul men within their bellies. The birds may be identified as peacocks or pigeons.

Chapter 8

The Beginning of an Ideology

Ideology and Social Disorder

A major premise of the present work underlines the fact that geo-climatic depredations and consequent social upheavals exercised profound influence on the historical processes throughout civilized space in ancient times. It is another matter that such linkages are not well reflected in the available sources. Yet, considering the fragmentary nature of historical sources and their interpretations, too much importance need not be attached to absence of evidence, which at any rate is no evidence of absence. Sources of the ancient civilizations are not always exclusive to the remains of the monuments, artefactual goods and inscriptions, damaged or well preserved. The historians and archaeologists dealing with past situations also need to reckon with the myths and legends encapsulating social processes as in the case of text-based Biblical archaeology. In the following passages we will see that the myths and legends are characteristic reflexes of the popular mind fields and tend to camouflage a historical reality experienced by a particular people at a particular point of time. A careful investigator of these materials would notice that in all ancient civilizations, catastrophic events in nature and society gave rise to new ideologies and thought processes frequently reflected in art and literature. In the present context, the focus is on north-western South Asia during the Middle Bronze Age, which was a global disaster time.

Witness the didactic literature of the Middle Kingdom of Egypt, which emphasized accountability of political, administrative and religious leaders to the people and how attempts were made at all these levels to remove different forms of injustice and inequality. The accountability of the rulers for their actions and policies is also well reflected in the artistic creations of the middle kingdom particularly the statues of kings with grim and thoughtful expressions quite unlike those of the Old Kingdom. Such concerns are uncharacteristic of an ancient state in which the kings were thought to be the representatives of god and therefore not accountable to anybody for their actions. Such a change of mind therefore came about under very compelling conditions following centuries of anarchy compounded by natural depredations in the form of hyper-arid conditions and the diminishing returns from fields and workshops. In lower Mesopotamia, the disaster came in the form of the absence of monsoon winds and the accompanying rainfall, which caused a sharp decrease in agricultural production and depopulation of the region, finally resulting in the end of the Sumerian civilization at the close of the third millennium BC. This event finds its mythical resonance in the famous legend of Adoba which relates to the capsizing of high priest Adoba's vessel by the winds in the southern sea and the angered priest's banishing the monsoon winds from the southern sea altogether. Similarly, the northern Carmel coast of Israel from Atlit to Haifa was the victim of marine transgression from the Neolithic to the Byzantine period resulting in the submergence of historical settlements in this area and the foundation of new ones further east. This may relate to the Biblical story of the making of Noah's Ark and accommodating in it all the species of life in anticipation of the great deluge and the final escape of Abraham in this vessel to a safer high ground, also in the east. On the eastern fringe of the Middle East, the destabilization of proto-urban civilization in Iran, Afghanistan and adjoining south Central Asia and the civil disorders which followed it are fairly well documented in the *Avesta*, which encapsulates mythical stories relating to creation and subsequent destruction of civilized space in this region by Ahura Mazda and Angīra Mainyu respectively. The *Vendîdâd* story of Ahura Mazda advising Yima, the founder of civilization to preserve the seeds of all the species of life in a *varah* so that civilization could be recreated after it was destroyed by a killer winter at the end of a long year of twelve millennia. In north-western South Asia the geo-climatic disorders and the subsequent disintegration of the Harappan civilization gave rise to a new religious ideology which blamed these disturbances on the sinful acts of human beings but at the same time assured the afflicted people of divine deliverance by means of a prayer liturgy in honour of the forces of nature.

In the context of north-western South Asia, the political ideology of the third millennium BC addressed itself to the functional aspect of political cooperation between unrelated peoples and territories, and adequately supported by a continental networking of trade and urban places. Compared to this, a religious ideology may have been the work of a small but dominant religious elite, much delimited spatially but trying to integrate as many divergent peoples as it could. As such, the term 'Harappan' or 'Indus Valley People' does not have any ethnic significance, just as the term 'Ārya' does not signify any ethnic exclusiveness. If Harappan urbanization brought divergent peoples together for mutual material gains, the ideology of the Ārya tried to bring together divergent peoples by means of certain rituals representing a cult or form of worship, which provided emotional support to the afflicted communities and promised deliverance from distress, natural or manmade. Since ideologies do not originate in a social vacuum, one must look for overbearing reasons, which triggered a system of nature worship and an abiding faith in the norms of good behaviours.

The natural calamities, which struck the Early Bronze Age civilizations on a global level, may have been a little too deadly for the people of the eastern fringe, forcing them into a state of utter helplessness. The calamity record, which dominates different portions of the *Ṛgveda*, appears to be *in situ* observations of these catastrophic events or the haunted memories of these episodes. In either case the bardic composers who refer to these events could not have been too far removed from the time of this disaster. From this angle, the crisis would appear to have been a powerful motivation towards the development of a system of nature worship in north-western South Asia during the decaying stages of the Harappan civilization.

How do people cope with a personal (or natural) calamities like flood, earthquake and famine, all of which are signs of human powerlessness and the final inability to govern the circumstances of their life? Such flashpoints in the life of an individual or community are characterized as breaking points (O'Dea, 1969, 5). Contingency, powerlessness and scarcity are said to be the three realities of human experience during these breaking points. In these terms, religion is the most basic mechanism of adjustment to these delimiting elements.

In times of crisis, religion also provides a transcendental relationship through cult, worship and ritual, which act as emotional grounds to give man a new security and firmer identity amidst the flux and change of history. Religion also helps humans cope with their deviance and lapse from social norms, which are rampant and widespread during a crisis. It also offers ways to expiate guilt resulting from such deviant action and to reintegrate with the social group.

In the face of uncertainty, men need emotional support and consolation when confronted with disappointment and reconciliation with society when alienated from its goals and norms (O'Dea, 1969, 7). Breaking beyond ordinary or normal experience they raise questions, which (supposedly) can only be answered by spiritually evolved people who intercede between ordinary mortals and the Beyond.

Since the Beyond does not communicate with the common man, the latter would turn repeatedly to spiritually evolved people for an interjection. Some of the ethnic communities on the Indo-Iranian subcontinent appear to have done just this. The composers of the Hymns of the *Ṛgveda* and the *Gāthās* of the *Avesta* may have been highly evolved spiritual leaders capable of psychic healing and motivating afflicted minds to reintegrate and surge forward in diverse regions. The sayings and sermons of these preachers frequently interspersed by mundane materials by way of illustration slowly develop into religious texts of great significance, long circulating in the form of lyrics and songs and finally compiled and codified for exclusive religious purposes. As fellow sufferers in a calamity, the reactions and responses were much the same until dissidence forced the parting of the ways.

The two basic ideas of the original Indo-Iranian religion emphasized that there is a law in nature, which makes everything fall in place eternally and universally, and that this was the doing of an all-powerful and omniscient supreme divinity. This divinity was the god Varuṇa of the *Ṛgveda* and Ahura Mazda of the *Avesta*. The other basic principle originally underlying the Indo-Iranian religion was that there was a continuous struggle going on in nature between the good and the bad, the former identified as a divinity and the latter denounced as a demon. In the *Avesta,* the struggle involves Ahura Mazda, the god of high intellect, and Angra Mainyu, who was all death and disaster. In the *Ṛgveda,* the struggle involves Indra, the chief of the storm gods who is armed with lightning and thunder and the demons Ahi and Vala, who represented low precipitation, Śuṣṇa, the demon of desiccation and Vṛtra, the demon of river blockades or dams. Ahi is a serpent demon who has carried off the Dawn and the rivers, the former personified as a goddess and the latter as milch cows and who keeps them captive in the folds of the cloud. In the *Avesta,* the same myth appears in a simpler form and involves Atar (fire) and Azi, the serpent demon. These myths underline a long-drawn hydrological crisis which gets much more emphasized in the *Ṛgveda* than in the *Avesta* and appears to corroborate archaeological data, particularly from north-western South Asia during the Middle and Late Bronze Ages.

Divine Law (Ṛta) and Right Conduct (Vrata, Supatha)

Considerations of moral behaviour and ethical values, which are sidelined in normal times, tend to dominate collective thinking of a people in times of widespread decay and destruction. Great emphasis is put on the pursuit of right conduct and abhorrence of all types of misdeed, for it is the latter which invites divine wrath in the form of natural calamities. These misdeeds, which were a violation of the divine ordinance (*ṛta)* angered the gods, hence the destruction.

Surrender to the will of the gods, obedience to the laws of nature, and prayers for benevolence underlined the surest route to deliverance from sufferings. Since the episodic disasters were caused by the forces of nature, these became spontaneous objects of awe and reverence, leading to the divinization of each of these elements and a system of nature worship. Many of the elements may already have been sanctified in different ethnic circles in some form or other.

Nature worship is not named anywhere in the text but the elements are detailed everywhere, particularly the significance attached to *ṛta* or cosmic ordinance and the large number of hymns relating to various aspects of nature like heaven and earth, storm and rain, rivers and the sea, fire and water, sun and moon, night and dawn, besides trees, mountains, forests. The followers of the new religion were distinguished as noble people, Ārya. The method of worship was prayer, which consisted of rhythmic, soulful chants sung in honour of the gods. The mode of propagation was to undertake wandering missions and target influential people in the region to convert them to the new faith. For the faithful, the practice of the faith consisted of a firm belief in divine truth or cosmic ordinance, *ṛta* and the observance of a code of right conduct, *vrata*, the two concepts being causally related. For, in the absence of abiding faith in the divine truth, the observance of right conduct was infructuous. Though not recurrent, the linkage is fairly well underlined by the expression that pursuit of divine truth is known as the observance of right conduct (*te ṛtam anu vratam iti āhuḥ*, 3.4.7; 3.7.8) and that the followers of right conduct enlighten themselves by uttering the right prayers (3.4.7; 3.7.8).

The importance attached to these concepts is evident from their repeated appearance in different portions of the text. For instance, the term *ṛta* appears 578 times, including a very large number of compounds. The term *vrata* also appears nearly 150 times and the term *supatha*, which is not really different from *vrata*, appears 13 times. The term *sumati*, meaning 'good thoughts' or 'right-mindedness' surfaces in over 100 passages. Besides, there is a large number of vocables, like *amhas, enas, agas, agha, duritā paripā, pāpa*—all of which signify some kind of blemish or deviant action on the part of repentant mortals praying for divine forgiveness. These terms draw a clear distinction between good deeds and bad deeds, the former bringing good fortune and divine bliss, the latter causing persistent misfortune and divine wrath. The frequency with which these terms occur in every portion of the text is significant. Of these, *agas* makes nineteen appearances, *enas* makes thirty-one appearances and *anṛta* makes twenty-five appearances. Similarly, the term *duritā* appears in nearly sixty passages and *agha* in nearly ninety stanzas. The number of stanzas which mention these terms and other vocables denoting some kind of deviant action and their deadly influences account for nearly 10 per cent of 10,000-odd stanzas in the text, a fact which needs reckoning in any historical reconstruction of the document.

Varuṇa—Lord of the Universe

Although every major god is associated with the maintenance of the divine law and the protection of righteous people, there is a clear dividing line between those who operated at the cosmic level, like Mitra and Varuṇa, and those who functioned at the terrestrial level, like Indra, Agni and Maruts. The prayers relating to Mitra and Varuṇa may be the earliest of the series and perhaps also the earliest of the Ṛgvedic compositions. Varuṇa always leads people along the right path (*supatha,* 1.25.12) and rules ordained by him are always obeyed by people (1.25.1). He is the upholder of right conduct (1.25.6) and never discards the upholders of right path (1.25.6—*na pra yucchataḥ*). He is all viewing, *viśvadarśatam* (1.25.18) and omniscient, *urūcakṣasam* (1.25.16). The faithful are in constant fear of the divine wrath caused by their sinful acts but are hopeful of removing these sins and escaping divine punishment through fervent prayers, oblations and salutations (*te helaḥ namobhiḥ ava imahe havirbhiḥ yajñebhiḥ,* 1.24.14). Those who serve Mitra and Varuṇa (*yaḥ janaḥ mitrāya varuṇāya avidhat,* 1.136.5) and follow their laws (*yaḥ enoḥ vratam;* 1.136.5) are always saved from sin.

Among a host of divinities, the pre-eminence of Varuṇa or Mitrāvaruṇa is unmistakeable, not by the number of invocations but by the qualities assigned to them. The qualities attributed to Varuṇa, Mitrāvaruṇa or occasionally Aryamā are seldom spoken of in relation to other gods, though the bards in their bid to enhance the prestige of other divinities, sometimes appropriate some of these qualities and functions, like a passage of the first book in which the divine ordainer is Indra, whose ordinance is followed by other gods, including Varuṇa (1.101.3). This may signify a later stage in the development of the ideology when Varuṇa was being gradually sidelined in favour of other gods, specially Indra. Together, Mitra and Varuṇa uphold and rule the earth and sky, together they guard the world, together they promote religious rites and together they avenge sinful acts. They are possessed of divine truth *ṛtāvānau* (1.151.4; 1.151.8), they are the upholders of right conduct (dhṛtavratāḥ) and they are the proclaimers of cosmic laws (1.25.6, 8). Varuṇa ensures the conformity with divine laws and destroys all types of falsehood (1.151.1).

The distress, which inevitably follows from the commission of sinful acts, can be overcome by avoiding such deeds and following a righteous conduct. The idea of righteousness simulated the laws of nature, which govern the universe and are unbreakable. The various forces of nature projected as divinities are also bound by such dispensation. The inviolable nature of the laws promulgated by the divine ordainer is repeatedly stressed by the fact that not even the gods are able to transgress these laws (*vām dhruvāṇi vratāni amṛtāḥ devāḥ na ā minanti*, 5.69.4). With gods following the right conduct (*devāḥ ṛtasya vratā anu guḥ*, 1.65.2), the earth became heavenly (*dyauḥ na bhūma*, 1.65.2) and quests began everywhere (*pariṣṭi bhuvat*, 1.65.2). The 'quests' may relate to search for promoters and followers of the new faith in and otherwise hostile surrounding given to non-conformist religious practices. The beginning of a new religious system appears to be suggested by a passage of the first book in which the bards implore Indra to patronize the newly formed liturgical knowledge (*asya navīyasaḥ vedhasah navīyasaḥ me manma ā śrudhi*, 1.131.6). The need for wooing Indra, the warrior par excellence is understandable because he is the one divinity who appears in numerous passages as the tormenter and destroyer of the non-believing enemies or Dasyus.

Ārya—The Righteous One

In the bardic circles, the term Ārya, which appears in nearly 37 passages signified respectable, noble, faithful, devoted or righteous. None of these meanings has any ethnic significance. If anything, the term meant a righteous person who strictly followed a religious ideology. Those who subscribed to the ideology of Daiva worship were recognized as Ārya or noble, and those who did not were denounced as Dasyu or enemy. This is the precise import of a passage (1.51.9) in which Indra is implored to recognize the Ārya, who are the followers of right conduct and the Dasyus or the enemies who are non-believers (*avratān*) or the followers of false doctrines (*apavratān*) and to destroy the latter for the sake of the former (*anuvratāya*). As such, a Dāsa, a Vṛtra, a Paṇi, a Paktha, a Bhalana, a Śiva or a Viṣāṇin, all of whom represented divergent ethnic groups—could become an Ārya, physical features and dialect being of little consequence in this ideological overarching. These peoples continued to speak their respective dialects and follow their life-styles and even retain their ethnic names after subscribing to the ideology of Daiva worship and patronizing a particular bardic family. The point can be illustrated by referring to a passage of the sixth book, which states that Dāsas were converted into Āryas (*yayā dāsāni Āryāṇi karaḥ*, 6.22.10). Sayana's explanation of *dāsāni* as *karmahīnāni* (devoid of righteous action) and of *āryāni* as *karmayuktāni* (endowed with righteous action) seems appropriate. This seems to have been the manner in which many friendly ethnic chiefs, like Sudāsa and Divodāsa, became followers of Ārya religious ideology. Several *dānastuti* passages in honour of a Paktha (Pakhtoon) chief appearing in the eighth book also fall in place. Compared to this, non-friendly hostile chiefs and peoples were either eliminated or captured and reduced to a lowly position. If neither could be achieved, they were simply denounced as irreligious or bad people and enemies of the first order. However, differentiation within the Ārya ranks may have surfaced as new peoples joined in and replenished the cult in their own way like in the case of all major religions of the world.

Although conflicts between the Ārya and their enemies centred round the politics of space and influence, the dividing line is always a religious one. This is evident from a large number of invectives used by bardic composers in relation to their non-believing opponents. To this category belong terms like *adeva* (without Gods, 5.61.6), *amanta* (mindless, 10.22.8), *arādhas* (uncharitable, 5.61.6), *atrātar* (not protecting, 5.61.6), *ayajñyān* (not sacrificing, 7.6.3), *aśraddhān* (disrespectful; 7.6.3), *amitrā* (unfriendly, 1.133.1), *anindra* (disrespectful of Indra, 1.133.1) and *akarmā* (non-sacrificing, 10.22.8). Other categories are also on view like *apavratān* (followers of false beliefs, 1.51.9), *anyavratān* (practising other rituals, 10.22.8) and *anṛtadeva* (worshippers of false gods, 7.104.14) and *śiśnadeva* (worshippers of the phallic god, 7.21.5; 10.99.3).

The Early Promoters

As the doctrine of divine prayers became widespread, every bardic community appears to have claimed its origin. In a passage of the third book, Viśvāmitra describes himself as first among the poets, who spoke the prayers of the gods (3.4.7; 3.7.8). Elsewhere, the Angirāses family claims the honour by stating that the best of the Angirāses was the first to say divine prayers (*tvam agre prathamaḥ angirastamaḥ kavi devānām vratam paribhūṣasi*, 1.31.2). At still another place, Trita, and epical Soma oblator assumes the guardianship of Deva worshippers inviting five leading priests (*pañca hotṛn cakriyā avase abhiṣṭaye na tritaḥ*, 2.34.14) to the cover of his protection and patronage and ensure the success of their spiritual missions. The *pañca hotṛn* may represent the spiritual heads of five different ethnic communities which are variously described as *pañca jana, pañca kṛṣti, pañca śreṇi, pañca carṣaṇi*, and *pañca kṣiti* in different portions of the text.

Subversion of Varuṇa's Authority: Schism and Split

With the passage of time, the original doctrine relating to divine laws and right conduct lost its importance and attempts were made to subvert the authority of Varuṇa or Mitrāvaruṇa. Bardic groups, who were more interested in material gains rather than the purification of the soul, showed special favours for Indra, who personified a hardened fighter and a mundane lifestyle. If Varuṇa belonged to the world of spirituality and transcendental experience, Indra belonged to a temporal world of hard reality. Varuṇa was supposed to punish sinful acts by triggering natural calamity and reward righteous action by ensuring happiness. He could not descend to the earth to save righteous people from the attacks of non-believing enemies. But, Indra, the warrior par excellence, was quite capable of such violent actions, probably the need of the hour. Accordingly, Indra was elevated to a position of divine ordainer and all other gods including Varuṇa and Sūrya were supposed to follow his command (1.101.3). Perhaps this marked a dividing line between the time of the first seers, who believed and practised the doctrine of righteousness and the time of later generations of poets which misused this doctrine for inciting local chiefs to perpetrate violence in order to gain material prosperity. Much later, the descendants of the earliest seers bounced back to pre-eminence and revived the supremacy of Varuṇa and established the Ahuric doctrine of subline monotheism in Eastern Iran.

The origins of the dissent, perhaps as old as the ideology itself, are manifest in the *Ṛgveda*. The devolution of the term Asura from divinity to demon appears to be diachronic and the latter meaning may have something to do with the development of a monotheistic Ahuric doctrine. 'In the *Ṛgveda*, the Asura of heaven was often invoked in company with Mitra, the god of the heavenly light, and he let him share with himself the universal sovereignty. But Ahura Mazda of the *Avesta* could not bear an equal, and accordingly Mitra became one of his creatures. His Indic name Varuṇa was lost in Iran and instead Varena remained only as the name of mythical heaven' (Darmesteter, 1887/1992). Both Varuṇa of the *Ṛgveda* and Ahura Mazda of the *Avesta* are endowed with heavenly wisdom or Medhas (Mazda). Both Varuṇa and Ahura Mazda are considered as the supreme gods of the cosmos and both are supposed to punish sinful acts. In the *Ṛgveda*, Varuṇa together with Mitra and Aryaman are described as Pracetasa meaning 'possessed of truth'. Ahura Mazda (Asura Medhas) of the Zoroastrian circle also means 'a divinity possessed of right wisdom'. Compared to this, most of the important gods of the Ṛgvedic pantheon including Indra, Sūrya, Nāsatya and Sarva are reduced to the position of demons. The term Deuu (Ṛgvedic Deva) in the *Avesta* also means a demon and is frequently associated with Angra Mainyu, who is all destruction.

'Indeed seldom has a man approached the truth so closely and then departed from it so widely' (Darmesteter, 1887/1992, 17). In terms of the frequency of invocations, Varuṇa of the *Ṛgveda* is way behind Indra or Agni. Perhaps this is suggestive of an originally almighty divinity (10.121; 10.125; 10.129; 10.190) slowly losing ground to secondary terrestrial and celestial divinities in the wake of polytheistic tendencies and increasing priestly indulgence in superstitious rituals for appropriating larger shares of social goods. This may have been just the point where a dividing line was drawn between superstitious faith and reasoned intellect, between polytheism and monotheism.

Perhaps the Ahuric doctrine symbolized just one of several dissident anti-Daiva groups motivated by pre-existent ethnic ideas in different regions. There were dissident groups among the Daiva worshippers themselves to judge from rivalry of Indra and Aśvins or the myths relating to conflicts between Indra and solar divinities like Uṣas. Although all the principal Ṛgvedic gods are invoked in different parts of the text, a careful examination of related geographical data would show that particular gods were region specific and accordingly more popular among the people of the concerned area. Such a scenario appears to have prevailed for many long centuries both before and after the rise of organized opposition against the system of Deva worship.

Devas and Deuus

The Ārya dissidents of Iran, who later became ardent followers of Zoroastrian reforms, condemned the Deva worshippers as bad people and even bracketed Mazainya Deuus and Varainya Deuus with the Turānian rapime. Interestingly, Zoroastrians retained the term Ārya in the sense of a noble person, but denounced the term deva (Avestan Deuu) as the symbol of heresy. As for Mazainya Deuus, they may relate to Deva worshippers in the vicinity of Mount Mujvant of the *Ṛgveda* (Avestan Muj) whereas Varainya Deuus seem to represent Deva worshippers of Varenu or Buner region in the North-West Frontier Province of Pakistan. This hatred of Deuu worshippers is also stressed by the fact that several counter creations of Ahreman, namely Varena (Buner), Hapta Hendu (Punjab) and Raṇha lay on the Indo-Pak borderland. Also important is the reference to a plague-like epidemic, which Angra Mainyu caused in these areas.

Such hatred notwithstanding, the Mazda worshippers always tried to enlist followers from among non-believers, just as the Deva worshippers of much earlier period were trying to incorporate diverse groups of people into a religious community, each member of which called himself Ārya. The *Farvardîn Yast* is explicit in this sense, since the text calls for the worship of the Fravashis of just men and women in the Airya, Tūirya, Sairma, Sāinu and Dāha lands and in all lands (*Yt*. 13. 143-144; Malandra, 1971, 218; Gnoli, 1989, 58). The mention of Ārya as the first in this list shows that the Ārya was considered in the Ahuric circles much superior to others like Tūirya, Sairma, Dāha, etc.

However, there was no immediate success for the followers of the Ahuric doctrine. This is well suggested by the laments of early Ahuric preachers, like Zarathustra, over the extreme unwillingness of people to accept Mazdian faith and the insignificant number of Mazdian followers. We may also recount here, lamenting Ahuric preachers asking Ahura Mazda about a region where the Mazdian faith will have greater success. These laments already appear in the Gāthic literature, suggesting thereby that the earliest followers of Ahura Mazda did not meet with any immediate success in the prevailing religious milieu dominated by Daiva worshippers on the Indo-Iranian subcontinent and that unsuccess trailed them to several places where peoples' response varied from naught to partial. Even among the Ahuric followers, there were dissident groups quarrelling among themselves, each one abusing the other as the followers of a false doctrine. We also hear Zarathustra calling out to dissident Ahura worshippers as well as Daiva worshippers to acknowledge the Ahuric faith being advocated by the preacher. The *Vendîdâd* Chapter 1, which refers to sixteen excellent regions created by Ahura Mazda and the devastation of these by Angra Mainyu, mentions that a few of these settlements like Nicaya were plagued by utter disbelief of people in the Ahuric faith.

Chapter 9

Priests and Patrons

The Milieu

Some signification of bardic enterprise in relation to shifts in continental economy and the consequent changes in the hegemonic situation may be pertinent here. The bardic composer, who moved from one place to another in the course of bardic enterprise, mobilizing patronage from new customers of Vedic ideology and collecting huge gifts of mobile assets, also freely participated in the exchange processes current at the time. In the initial stages, the distinction between the bard and barterer paled into insignificance. While many of the bards were good at trade, some of the traders were also not too unfamiliar with the bardic skills. Occasionally, the bard may have been a member of the caravan while at other times a caravaneer acted as a profound bard. Whether bard or trader, neither thought of a permanent residence for reasons of professional promotion. But, either was conscious of increasing accumulation of goods and their speedy disposal through barter or money transaction. The only difference between the two is that the former acted as a missionary of new ideology, which is also a selling point in the accumulation of wealth. Although the constant journey of bardic missionaries facilitated commodification of the gifts and their exchange with locals *en route* in return for other goods, the task of propagating Vedic ideology prevented the bard from moving out of the new destinations as quickly as the traders.

Considering the gripping influence which the priestly class has exercised on the South Asian mindset for millennia, even single families of priests or bards could be quite effective in motivating people towards the new ideology. In the old world conditions of cultural fluidity and frequent paradigm shifts, the bardic ideology, which involved invocations to different divinities and marginal fire rituals, and which promised enhancement of material goods and temporal power, may have found many enthusiastic takers among ethnic South Asians, most of whom were passing through a traumatic phase.

With its characteristic phonology, morphology and the manner of recitation, the Mantric lore was the guarded preserve of the priest's mental skill. All this was unintelligible and mystical to the locals and inspired a sense of awe and reverence towards the priest and his compositions. But the divinities who were expected to listen to these invocations and grant the wishes were all too familiar to the locals everywhere. Consider who were to be invoked—the earth, the sky, the rivers, the sun, the high seas, the medicine man, the dawn, the dusk, the rains, the storm, the successful leader and so on. And what was to be prayed for—wealth and fame, happiness and longevity, children and subjects, livestock and grains, protection from diseases, protection from predators and protection from calamities.

If bardic prayers could usher in all this, already a tall order, the local chieftain would only be too willing to offer to the priest subsistence, security and a place in the chief's entourage. If things went wrong, the blame could always be laid at the door of the chief, on shortcomings in arrangements and provisions or misdemeanour on the part of an unknown someone in the entourage. If things went right, it only fattened the priest and increased his authority. Occasional hiccups at some of these destinations were not unlikely. But the entrepreneurs of priestly craft were gifted enough to overcome such minor tiffs. Take the case of Taranta, a chief in the neighbourhood of Gomal Valley, who refused to entertain the visiting bard and was duly criticized by the latter as *adeva* (godless), *arādhas* (uncharitable or without wealth) and *atrātar* (not protecting). However, the bard had already influenced the spouse, Śaśīyasī who offered two red horses and other gifts to the priest and gave directions for the next destination.

Stratifying the Liturgy

At the earliest stage of bardic interaction with the uninitiated, the whole emphasis was on the spoken word, which was supposed to contain uncanny powers and could therefore force the divinity to grant wishes. These early prayers may have meant just a few words or even a few syllables and without metrical regulations to admit phonological variations. Even in the present text, one comes across several words with unaccented syllables. Gradually, as the prayer became a mechanism of control, more and more emphasis was put on metrical regulations. This falls in line with the fact that in the beginning, the chants contained only the Svarit accent and that the Yajurvedic priests, in a bid to prevent aberrant chants, added the Udātta and Anudātta accents to the *Ṛgveda* mantras. The warning that even the slightest mistake in the proper use of accent would produce just the opposite result further sanctified this.

The conviction that effective poetic compositions (*kavya*), which also served as the oblation (*havya*) sufficed to please the divinity making fire rituals and oblations redundant, appears to be the guiding principle of bardic exercises. From this angle, the present text of the *Ṛgveda* would appear to be a book of the prayer cult. It is not without some good reason that out of over ten thousand invocations recorded in the text, only a small number specify the objects of oblation to the fire. The importance of sacrificial fire considered to be the carrier of oblations to different gods increased, with a corresponding decline in the *kavya-havya* (prayer as the oblation) conviction among the bardic people and their customers.

The significance of prayer cult is as much evident from a large number of references to poetic composers in the *Avesta* and the *Ṛgveda,* as from the mention of common composers in either text. In the *Ṛgveda,* the number of named poets is more than 250 while terms like *kavi* (poet) and *kāvya* (poetic compositions) appear in 240 and 50 passages respectively. The Gāthic text was also the work of a large number of poets. To judge from the younger Avestan texts, which provide a list of twenty-seven *kauui* composers of the Gāthās. The list would have been much longer if a major part of the text had not been lost through careless transmission.

As for the common composers, Uśanā must have been among the earliest bards who received adoration even after the separation of the Avestan and Ṛgvedic dialects. The Kauui Uśanā of the *Avesta* is the same as Kavi Uśanā or more appropriately Kāvya Uśanā who figures in about score of passages in the *Ṛgveda*. Many of these compositions project Kāvya Uśanā as the model poet and his compositions as most distinguished poetry by succeeding generations of Ṛgvedic bards. The name Uśija, which figures in the *Avesta* as well as in the *Ṛgveda,* is also significant. In the Vedic dialect, the term is said to derive from *vas*, to control, regulate. The Avestan etymological derivation could not be too far from the Ṛgvedic connotation, in view of the fact that in both the bardic traditions, the poet was considered to be the mentor of both gods and people.

Although the earliest bardic prayers were without phonological regimentation and unaccompanied by any fire rituals, considerable concern for the freshness of new compositions is evident. Since the divinities were expected to enjoy the invocations, the repetition of the same material over and over again would be monotonous and therefore fruitless. At this early stage, the dominant idea was to use the power of prayer to good effect and to articulate a frozen literary style for this purpose. When these verses were chanted with articulate accent before a stranger, the latter was immediately attracted by the power of sonorous rills emanating from these chants, although he did not understand anything of the whole utterance. A new literary style does not also call for too many originators. Even single bards with gifted intellect, command over the spoken word and entrepreneurial abilities would do well for the beginnings of a new literary style and even its diffusion to new areas. From this angle, the role of itinerant bards interacting with local chiefs in different parts of the Indo-Iranian subcontinent would become significant.

The inflation of priestly functionaries has an interesting history in the text. The process was gradual rather than sudden and may have covered three distinct stages of development. The first stage was marked by bardic prayers unaccompanied by any fire rituals. The next stage marked the introduction of marginal fire rituals, which could be managed by single priests. This single ritualist was the Adhvaryu, who is regularly mentioned in different portions of the text, the references totalling more than seventy. The Adhvaryu (*adhvar*, sacrifice) had to measure the ground, prepare the sacrificial vessels, build the altar, fetch wood and water, light the fire, bring the animals for immolation. While engaging in these duties, he had to repeat the hymns. In the final stage, this bundle of priestly functions was parcelled out and earmarked for new priestly functionaries, like Hotā, Potā, Praśāstā, Neṣṭā, Udgātā and Agnidh.

The Hotā (the inviter) was the priest who called out to divinities to listen to the prayers being uttered for them and receive whatever oblations were being made. The Potā (the cleanser) was expected to purify different objects associated with the fire rituals. The Agnidh (the fireman) priest was the functionary who was entrusted with the responsibility of keeping the flames at a particular level throughout the duration of the sacrifice. The Udagātā (the singer) priest was required to set particular mantras to particular tunes and sing these according to the requirements of the rituals. The Praśāstā (the supervisor) was the functionary who supervised the whole affair from the beginning to the end and was expected to point out lapses on the part of any of the priestly functionaries. The Neṣṭā (the herald) was required to ceremonially bring forward the chief and/or the spouse into the sacrificial circle for the legitimation of his or her political authority.

Considering however, the wide gap in the number of references to Adhvaryu and those to the other functionaries, it is unlikely that the latter functioned on a large scale during the greater part of the Ṛgvedic age. For instance, Adhvaryu appears in over seventy passages of the text whereas other functionaries taken together do not account for even one-third of this number. More important, the Adhvaryu dominates every portion of the text whereas the other functionaries remain confined to particular books. Thus the seven references to Hotā, Praśāstā,

Potā, Neṣṭā, Agnidh, Brahmā and Udgātā are found in the second book, but occasional references to some of these priests are also not wanting elsewhere in the text. However, the ritualistic phase marked by Adhvaryu in the *Ṛgveda* witnessed development of a different kind. This relates to the introduction of the calendar man or the Ṛtvij. The unstated purpose behind the induction of this functionary, who appears in all the portions of the text except the fourth book for a total number of sixteen times, was to prescribe and multiply the days and durations of the sacrifice. Probably, this is how the number of priestly functions and related functionaries were inflated in the course of time. There are several passages referring to sacrifices continuing for full one year. The yearlong sacrifice (*samvatsara*), which is mentioned several times in the text, may have been the handiwork of this functionary.

The Politics of Prestation

The praise of gifts was not merely intended to sanctify the donor's political authority. It was also intended to publicize such authority in the court of another chief. This provoked the other chief to outmatch the gifts made by former donor. It also occasionally triggered hegemonic conflicts between two or more chiefs to fight out a legitimacy crisis. From this angle, a *dānastuti* passage is as much a praise of the donor as it is of the composer himself. The power of composition was thought to insure success in battles, good fortune, wealth and progeny, besides providing cure for incurable diseases. It could also bring rains to arid tracts and help river crossings on foot. It is not known whether the five modes of saying the prayers had already been articulated during the early stages of the prayer cult. But, considering that the power of the prayer mattered most under the given conditions, attempts to develop these methods of recitation may not have been unlikely. The more complex the method of chants, the greater was the efficacy of the utterance and the influence of the person concerned.

Bardic attempts to monopolize priestly authority at the political centres may have occasionally been influenced by ethnic considerations. This is logical as well since the bardic composers were drawn from different ethnic groups irrespective of physical features, dialect use and life-styles. As such there could be fair-skinned bards as well as dark-skinned poets. Kaṇvā, who is described as *kṛṣṇa* and *śyāva,* meaning 'dark-skinned' appears to have been a victim of ethnic discrimination. A passage of the tength book (10.31.11), states that no other divinity except the fire god Agni extended patronage to the priest (*atra asmi nakiḥ apipeta*) and that the fire god became radiant and caused the Udders or sources of wealth to overflow for *Kaṇva* (*kṛṣṇāya rūśat udhaḥ ṛtam apinvata*). The discrimination may also relate to an ethnic dialect spoken by Kaṇva poets and the influence of this dialect on their compositions in the Eighth Book in the form of declensional deviants.

Apart from ethnic considerations, professional jealousy and the desire to appropriate all the gifts and customers in a particular locality embittered social and political relations in the concerned area and even across the localities. The observations of the bards sound like dealers in a market place trying to attract the largest number of customers. This is the precise import of passages in which the poets implore the gods (or chiefs) to denounce priests at other sacrifices and come to the ones performed by themselves (8.33.14; 8.66.12; 2.18.3).

The introduction of Soma oblations appears to have further intensified the infighting. In many quarters, the Soma sacrifice was suppose to be more appealing to the gods and therefore more beneficial to the priests and their political patrons. Accordingly, a distinction was made between those who made Soma offerings and those who did not (4.25.6; 4.25.7; 5.34.5). Even those groups which were familiar with the Soma plant but did not make Soma offerings were sought to be sidelined (6.41.4). Damnation was also reserved for those sacrificers who were friendly to bad people, made a false display of their wealth and publicized vanity by decorating their bodies (5.34.3). Since Soma offerings would provide benefits to whoever priests made these oblations, the space for gift sharing narrowed down with diminishing returns to competing priests. A desire to edge out the rival priests from the Soma sector would be natural. An alibi was not far to seek. Soma juice prepared carelessly and or offered without proper chants would suffice to discredit and disentitle the concerned groups (6.41.4; 7.26.1).

Soma-related conflicts soon reached a crescendo, to judge by the accounts of Trita and Kavaṣa. Trita was an Apical Soma oblator of the Ṛgvedic and Avestan tradition who enjoyed considerable leverage on account of his newly developed expertise in the extraction and offering of Soma drink to different gods (2.34.14). But it was the same expertise and the attendant high position, which proved to be his undoing and eventual expulsion from the Indic homeland. The fact that in the Avestan tradition Trita ranks next only to Vivasvān (Avestan Vivangvān) would suffice to suggest that following his humiliation Trita escaped to Avestan circles in eastern Iran, which is also confirmed by his reference to Persians (*parśavaḥ*) tormenting him like co-wives (1.105.7). The mention of oppression caused by co-religionists (*stotāraḥ*) would also suffice to indicate that it was the rival priests in the Indic homeland who humiliated the poet and forced him to leave the country (1. 105.8). The lament over the loss of righteousness and the lack of Varuṇa's surveillance over good and bad people in the Indic homeland shows that the behaviour of Daiva worshippers on the Indo-Iranian subcontinent had reached a flashpoint and needed a strong reformist movement to neutralize it (1.105.6).

The reference to Persians in these compositions underlines the fact that the majority of Iranians during the early second millennium BC were followers of either Daiva priests (the 'Deuus' of *Avesta*) or followed some local religious beliefs. The laments of Trita expressed in these passages resemble the outcry of Zarathustra against competing groups of Daiva worshippers, who did not subscribe to the Ahuric doctrine of monotheism.

The Persian tormentors of Daiva worshippers surface once again in the compositions of Kavaṣa Ailūṣa, an important poet of the eighth and the tenth book. Like Trita, this composer also refers to the Persians tormenting him, like co-wives (10.33.2) and the mental agonies devouring him like the mice eating up tentacles (10.33.3). The passages may be an adoption of previous compositions or these may reflect the actual hostilities experienced by Kavaṣa Ailūṣa in Iran. But, unlike in the case of Trita, the humiliation of Kavaṣa Ailūṣa at the hands of fellow priests had a social angle as well. This is underlined in the *Aitareya Brāhmaṇa,* which belongs to the *Ṛgveda* and almost synchronized with the redaction time of the bardic text. In the Aponaptriya section of *Aitareya Brāhmaṇa* (Pañcikā – II, Adhyāya – III, Para – II.19; VIII.1; Keith, 1920/1998), the basis of this humiliation seems to be the low birth of Kavaṣa, who is denounced as the son of a slave woman, a cheat and a non-Brāhmaṇa. Considerable anguish and surprise are expressed at the presence of Kavaṣa in the midst of rightful sacrificers. The tormentors of Kavaṣa debarred him not only from offering Soma oblations but also from inhabiting the banks of Sarasvatī. Kavaṣa is driven to a desert tract where he may be afflicted by thirst and die ultimately. Although a large part of north-western South Asia had developed into a desert tract by 2000 BC, the mention of Persians by Kavaṣa himself and of desert ostracism in the *Aitareya Brāhmaṇa* can only assign the poet and his family to a contiguous region of Iran and Afghanistan.

The passage drops several interesting hints relating to the claims and counter claims of rival groups of priests. The consignment of Dāsa to a lowly position within the Ārya order is already noticeable in certain portions of the bardic text and it is likely that children born in Dāsa families were being increasingly discriminated and sidelined in every sphere of life.

Together with the considerations of high and low people, this passage of *Aitareya Brāhmaṇa* also emphasizes emerging ideas relating to pure and impure regions to be inhabited by the high-born and the low-born respectively. This may be an early indication of ethno-genetic formations based on purity of life and habitat, which is so characteristic of later Brāhmaṇical ideas.

The descendants of Kavaṣa are, however, treated differently in the *Kauṣītakī Brāhmaṇa,* which too belonged to *Ṛgveda,* but postdated the *Aitareya Brāhmaṇa* by a couple of centuries, coinciding perhaps with *Upaniṣads* and *Śatpatha Brāhmaṇa.* True to the spirit of the time, the *Kauṣītakī Brāhmaṇa* acknowledges Kavaṣa as a rightful priest and does not use any invectives for him. Clearly, the Kāvaṣeya or the descendants of the Kavaṣa family had come a long way from the days of their humiliation and set themselves firmly on the path of a protest movement. These sentiments are very well reflected in the *Āraṇyakas* and the *Upaniṣads*. In the *Aitareya Āraṇyaka* (3.2.6; Sarup, 1920-27), Kāvaṣeyas are seen straightaway denouncing the study of the *Vedas* and performance of sacrifices as useless actions. In the *Maitrāyaṇī* and *Kauṣītakī Upaniṣads,* the condemnation is more severe as the study of the *Vedas* is called *avidyā* or false knowledge.

Conflict over Therapeutic Knowledge

As in the case of Soma-related conflicts, the familiarity of certain priests with therapeutic knowledge and the prestige it brought to them was the cause of great concern for those priests who did not possess the knowledge. It is clear enough that neither the Bhiṣag Atharvan, the promoters of knowledge relating to health and healing nor Ghora Āngirasa, the advocates of magic and miracle, were conceded the same prestige as was enjoyed by the Udgātā priests, the Adhvaryu fire ritualists and the Soma oblators and, accordingly, the oral literature developed by these two streams of knowledge was not given the status of revealed knowledge. Thus it may have become imperative for both Bhiṣag Atharvan and Ghora Āngirasa to organize into a sect and fight for a rightful place in the Vedic circle.

The programmes and ideologies of these people are fairly well reflected in Atharvan Āngirasa, the name by which the *Atharva Veda* was originally known. The expression Atharvan Angirasa combined two parallel but mutually complementary programmes, one, health and healing (Bhiṣag Atharvan) and the other, magic and miracle (Ghora Āngirasa). Taken together, the two programmes exercised considerable influence on the minds of the masses, which is why perhaps the two programmes or rather their promoters came in for so severe a denunciation. In many portions of the *Ṛgveda* itself, one can notice hostility of this nature, like in the conflict of Indra and Aśvins relating to a secret healing knowledge and decapitation of Dadhīci, a descendant of Atharvan in this connection. From the materialistic position of healers and magicians in the Atharvan Āngirasa, it was not much difficult for the promoters of these programmes to launch a tirade against the authority of *Vedas* as revealed knowledge and mobilize intellectual opinion in favour of anti-Vedic thoughts and movement.

This is brought into fuller relief by the later Vedic texts, the *Brāhmaṇa*, the *Āraṇyaka* and the *Upaniṣad*. The *Gopatha Brāhmaṇa*, which belongs to the *Atharva Veda*, relates stories to establish the superiority of the *Atharva Veda* over *Ṛk*, *Sāma* and *Yajus Samhitās*. In the first story, Vāk or the speech divinity asks all the four *Vedas* one by one to try their ability in taming a wayward mare. The three *Vedas*, *Ṛk*, *Sāma* and *Yajus* found that the mare, instead of being tamed filled each of them with terror and turned east, west and north respectively at the approach of *Ṛgveda*, *Yajurveda* (*Vājasaneyī Samhitā*) and *Sāma Veda*. Finally, all the three *Vedas* sought the help of Atharvan, who, in his turn, sprinkled the water of tranquility on the animal, which then calmed down and stood in salutation before the Atharvan. In the other story, the gods asked Indra to protect the sacrifice and find a shelter for the gods. Indra took the form of *Ṛk*, *Yajus* and *Sāma* one by one and stood before the gods in the east, west and north respectively to achieve the task. But each time the gods were dissatisfied. Finally, Indra took the form of *Atharva Veda* and the gods conceded that now Indra could provide the greatest protection to gods as well as sacrifices (*Gopatha Brāhmaṇa*, 1.2.19; Sarup, 1920-27/1984).

Persian Chiefs and Priests

In the present text of the *Ṛgveda*, there is ample evidence of close cooperation between Irano-Afghan and South Asian followers of the Deva ideology. The evidence surfaces in the form of Iranian ethno-geographical terms like Persia and Parthia, typical Avestan proper names like Vadhṛyāśva, Śyāvāśva and Iṣṭāśva, and the names of several important rivers of Afghanistan and Baluchistan, besides words like Karkandhu, which signified a particular type of Iranian wells fitted with wheel. The mention of desert tracts, camels and camel-carts in these contexts, also points to a vast geographical area dominated by deserts and semi-deserts as in Iran and Afghanistan. The text also refers to Persian chiefs like Cāyamāna Abhyāvartī, and Tirindir.

In the absence of any dependable studies relating to the historical geography of Iran during the pre-Christian era, it is difficult to ascertain what names were used at which periods to denote a country or a part of it. The name Iran, which today refers to a vast country resulted from a rediscovery of the Iranian pride in the Aryan descent. Compared to this, the Ṛgvedic term *parśu,* (the Avestan *pareśu,* the Assyrian *parsua,* the Old Persian Fars and Greek Persia) has a much longer history dating back to the late third and early second millennium BC, when the earliest hymns of the *Ṛgveda* were being composed. The Ṛgvedic term *parśu* appears as a locative singular *parśau* (8.6.46) in relation to a chief of Persian origin and the nominative plural *parśava* (1.105.7; 10.33.2) in the sense of the Persian people. The other term *pārthava,* which figures in a *dānastuti* passage relating to a Persian chief named Cāyamāna (6.27.8), is an adjectival form of *parthava* derived from the nominative singular *'parthu'*. Depending on the phonological behaviour of different groups of ancient Iranians, the dental S could become sibilant Ś of the palatal class and *vice versa.*

According to one study, the name parthia (a Greek form of the Old Persian parthava and the Ṛgvedic Parśava) refers to the ancient land corresponding roughly to the modern regions of Khurasan in Iran (*Encyclopaedia Britannica,* 2001). The first certain occurrence of the name Pārthava is in the Bisutun inscription (c. 520 BC) of the Achaemenian king Darius I. Pārthava may be only a dialectal variation of the name Parśava (Persian). The name Khurasan, literally the 'land of the sun', represents a vast territory now lying in north-eastern Iran, southern Turkmenistan and northern Afghanistan. According to Arab geographers, its boundaries extended as far east as India (*Encyclopaedia Britannica,* 2001). It may have been so even much earlier since Afghanistan was sometimes part of Persia as during the Achaemenian period and sometimes part of India as during the reign of Aśoka.

It is also not necessary to judge facts of historical geography on the basis of current geographical demarcations. For instance, the term *fars*, which derives from Ṛgvedic *parśu*, Avestan *pareśu* and Assyrian *parśua*, today denotes a small western province of Iran contiguous to Iraq. Similarly, the name Elam today refers to another western province of Iran contiguous to Iraq. But, during the third millennium BC, the cultural and political influence of both Fars and Elam extended as far east as the frontiers of Afghanistan and Baluchistan. This is testified as much by the presence of proto-Elamite seals in the eastern parts of Iran from the beginning of the third millennium BC as from the mention of *parśu* and *parśava* (1.105.7; 10.33.2) in the *Ṛgveda*, the earliest compositions of which may date back to the late third millennium BC. As time passed, ethnic Iranians represented by the Elamites and Persians lost ground and made way for other ethnic peoples.

In this background, some understanding of the episodes relating to the prestation activities of Indo-Afgan and Iranian bards and their patrons may be in order here. The episodes relating to the bards Śyāvāśva, Vadhṛyaśva, and Kakṣivān and the chiefs Tirindir, Caidya Kaśu, Cāyamanā Pārthava, Yadu, Turvaś and Citraratha provide valuable information in this connection. The episodes relating to flight of Yadu, Turvaś and Kakṣivān from an unnamed homeland underline the growing intensity of the politics of space and influence in the concerned region. The acrimonius relationship between Iṣṭāśva, who may have been the same as Vistapes, the patron of Avestan doctrines and the poet Kakṣivān may provide some insight into these conflicts. Śyāvāśva, on the other hand, appears to have been an Avestan poet on an enduring gift collection mission in Afghanistan, Baluchistan, the Indus Valley, Punjab and Northern Rajasthan. As for the chiefs, Tirindir was a Persian ruler, Cāyamanā, a Parthian ruler and Citraratha an 'Afghan' ruler while Caidya Kaśu appears to have been a Kassite ruler.

Turning to the evidence of personal names, one would notice that names ending with *uṣṭra* and *aśva* are very frequent in the *Avesta*, the most important examples being Zarathustra and Vistaspa, the founder and political patron respectively of the Mazdian faith. But, such personal names are almost unknown to the *Ṛgveda*, notwithstanding a large number of common bardic names in the two texts. The three examples of names ending with *aśva* suffix, which surface in the *Ṛgveda,* are Vadhṣyāśva, Śyāvāśva and Iṣṭāśva. Vadhṣyāśva, who appears to have been the principal chaplain of Divodāsa, formerly an Afghan chief who is mentioned just once in the sixth book (6.61.1) authored by the poets of Bhāradvāja family. According to one study (Hillebrandt, 1891, 343), Divodāsa, who figures in association with the priest Vadhṛyāśva and the river Sarasvatī (Avestan Haraiti, Modern Argandab) may have fled his Afghan homeland under the heat of hegemonic conflicts and established a new chiefdom on the banks of Paruṣṇi, modern Rāvi in the Punjab. In the Vedic mainland, the priest of Iranian descent lost his importance and the priesthood of the family was taken over by the native Bhāradvājas.

As for Śyāvāśva, it is in connection with the itinerary of this poet that we come across references to almost all the major rivers of Afghanistan. The two rivers, which do not figure in this account, are the Sarayu (Modern Harirud) and the Sarasvatī (Modern Argandab). However, both these rivers appear in close proximity to one another, as today, in a portion of the eighth book. The mention of the Argandab and the Harirud, both of which originate in the northern Afghan mountains but travel very different courses, the former disappearing in the desert swamps of Seistan and the latter vanishing in the sandy marshes of south Central Asia brings the eastern part of Iran closer to the area, which gave rise to the ideology of Daiva worship, sometime during the Middle Bronze Age.

A close look at geographical information surfacing in different parts of the text shows that the present territory of Afghanistan was a focal area of bardic gift collection missions and of hegemonic conflicts involving Āryas and Dāsas. Two contexts, one in the fourth *maṇḍala* (4.30.18) and the other in the eighth *maṇḍala* (8.21.17-18) deserve attention here. The first of the two contexts relates to a fight between two groups of Āryas on the banks of Sarayū resulting in the elimination of Arṇa and Citra. The river Sarayū of this passage appears to represent Avestan Haryu, Old Persian Haroiva and Modern Harirudh. King Citra of this passage may be the same as

Citraratha who figures in two *dānastuti* stanzas of the eighth *maṇḍala* (8.21.17-18), which eulogize the king as greatest among the chiefs ruling on the banks of Sarasvatī. The river Sarsavatī of this passage appears to represent Avestan Haraiti, Old Persian Haraiti and Modern Argandab. The eulogistic reference to King Citra of the Sarasvatī valley and the slighting of other chiefs is underlined by the use of the term Rājā (king) for Citraratha and Rājakā (diminutive king) for other chiefs. This seems to be a bardic ploy to both publicize and legitimize the authority of the donor chiefs and belittle the non-patronizing ones. Such publicity, which passed from mouth to mouth, had the effect of encouraging political rivalry among those who were not praised or legitimized in this manner and inducing them to emulate the chiefs patronizing Vedic poets. It also had the effect of weaning away other potential composers from their erstwhile patrons to a more superior benefactor, further intensifying the political animus.

The bardic description of Indo-Iranian chiefs and poets provide occasional hints which may or may not suffice to reconstruct certain political and religious events about the beginning of the second millennium BC in north-eastern Iran. An interesting episode of the first book refers to two chiefs, one of whom Iṣṭāśva has a distinct Avestan name and may represent king Vistaspa of the Gāthic tradition. The account (1.122.13-15) surfaces in connection with the acrimonious reference to this king by Kakṣivān, an important composer of the first book who may have originally belonged to the court of the Iranian king but later picked up a quarrel as the king began to show disrespect to Daiva gods like Mitravaruṇa (1.122.6, 9, 15). In the Gāthic portions of the *Avesta*, Vistaspa appears as a chief, who is constantly haunted by fear of agitations and suppression of his authority. This may point towards political instability in north-eastern Iran, following hegemonic conflicts among local chiefs. Since the poets or priests had to take sides, they could fall victim to oppression by the rival contenders. Some such kind of development may have forced the Kakṣivān family to leave the country and look for patrons in neighbouring South Asia (cf.1.122 and 1.126). It is also likely that some of the hegemonic conflicts focused on the widening gap between the Daiva worshippers and the followers of Ahura Mazda, both of whom might have been turning their backs on one another on a permanent basis.

From the available information, we come across three important persons named Vistaspa. The first in this list was Vistaspa, the father of Darius-I, who belonged to the sixth-fifth (522-486 BC) century BC and, for that reason, is out of reckoning in the Ṛgvedic context. There are no indications either that Zarathustra was a contemporary of this Achemenian chief. According to one estimate, which is based on the absence of any reference in the *Avesta* to Western Iran, Media or Medes, Zarathustra belonged to early eleventh century BC, 1080 BC to be precise (Humbach *et al*, 1991; Skjaervo, 1995). This would refer Kakṣivān to the late twelfth century or early eleventh century BC. A third possibility relates to the Zoroastrian tradition, according to which Zarothustra is said to have been born on 26th March 1767 and visited the court of Visṭaspā in Seistan at the age of forty. This would suggest that the movement of Zarathustra, which was just one of several anti-Deuu sects took off about the middle of the eighteenth century BC. This may coincide with the acrimonious relationship between Vistaspa and Kakṣivān, the latter leaving the court along with his merchant father for a new destination in South Asia.

The importance of Iranian patrons in the dissemination of Daiva ideology seems well suggested by three *danastuti* passages (8.6.46-48) composed in honour of the Persian chief, Tirindir. These Pragātha one-liners were composed by a branch of the Kaṇva family, which is named Vatsa Kāṇva (8.6.46-48). A much clearer allusion to a Persian chief is recorded in a *danstuti* composition of a Bhāradvāja poet in the sixth *maṇḍala* (6.27). The chief was Cāyamāna Abhyavartih or Abhyavartī, the son of Cāyamāna who has the rare distinction of being described as Maghvā (very affluent 6.27.8), a characterization normally reserved for Indra. The same passage also describes Abhyāvartī as Samrāt (emperor) and a Parthava (parthian or persian). The chief figures in relation to a fight involving two detractors, who were decimated at Hariyūppiyā and, as usual, the act is ascribed to Indra (6.27.5). The charities (*dakṣiṇā*) of this chief are eulogized in the same concluding passage of the hymn (6.27.8).

A word needs to be said about the Kassites, the eastern branch of which may have lived in north-eastern Iran contiguous to the Indo-Pak borderland, the home of the *Ṛgveda* poetry and the ideology of nature worship. In three passages of the text (8.5.37-39), we come across Caidya Kasu, a generous chief who patronized bards from neighbouring South Asia. The Kassites are first mentioned in the Elamite inscriptions of late third millennium BC. Besides the Elamite inscriptions, Kassites are mentioned in the Old Iranian language (Avestan) as 'kāsva'. The Akkadian form of Kassites is 'kassu', which is almost identical with the Ṛgvedic 'Kaśu'. The Old Śakas pronounced the term as 'kāssa' whereas the Middle Iranian, Median and Old Bactrian form of the term is 'Kāsp', which became 'Kaspioi' in the Greek accounts. According to Herodotus, one group of Kaspioi lived in the neighbourhood of the Caspian Sea and another lived in north-eastern Iran (Harmatta, 1992, 370). It is the north-eastern branch of the Kassites, which was first exposed to the Daiva ideology of the Indo-Iranian subcontinent during the late third millennium BC and moved away from this area towards the west in the wake of widespread geo-climatic devastations about the same time or a little later. Two important Vedic deities, Surias and Maruttas, appear as the names of Kassite gods in an Elamite inscription of eighteenth century BC.

Chapter 10

Ideology and Ethnicity

The study of ethnic formations in pre-history generally depends on a classification of diverse archaeological cultures occasionally supported by textual information. The great diversity of cultural assemblages exposed by archaeological excavations in north-western South Asia during the early and Middle Bronze Ages may suggest the existence of several ethnic and subethnic boundaries in the area. The archaeological record provides a good view of habitat conditions and the corresponding lifestyles and technologies, but ethnonymic identities are out of the reckoning. Probably the makers of these cultures were the ancestors of the same people who are known from the historical records of a later period.

For a literary corroboration of ethno-cultural locations in north-western South Asia, one may turn to the present text of the *Ṛgveda*, which is a religious document of the Middle Bronze Age and mentions a large number of ethnic groups by their names and traits. The tracts occupied by many of these are identifiable and may relate to one or the other cultural assemblage in the concerned area, like the Bolanese people of the Bolan valley, the Śivas or Śibis to the east of the Bolan valley, the Pakthas of eastern Afghanistan, the Gāndhārīs of the Swat valley, and so forth. In cases where the ethnonyms do not help, the correlation becomes all the more tentative. Conscious of these limitations in the correlation of archaeological and literary materials, the present section concentrates on a classification of ethnic communities and their love–hate relationship with and ideologically overarching, supralocal, and trans-ethnic religious community, which describes itself as Ārya. The Ārya of the *Ṛgveda,* who inhabited north-western South Asia, spoke a common dialect, shared common religious beliefs and practices and distinguished themselves from all others who did not share these features would thus appear to qualify as a homogeneous ethnic community. However, a closer examination of textual information underlines certain gaps in this homogeneity. In the first place, the system of religious beliefs outlined in the *Ṛgveda* was inclusive rather than exclusive. Any group which subscribed to the system could be designated as Ārya but in terms of language, lifestyle and physical features they maintained their own separate identities. From this angle, the ethnic identity of Ārya would be as strong or weak as that of the members of any of the major religions of the world today. Some understanding of these fineries of articulation in their historical context and of the relationship between the Ārya and other ethnic communities as perceived by the bardic composers themselves seems imperative here.

Geo-diversity and Ethnic Plurality

Ethnic groups or 'Ethnos (in, the narrow sense of the term) are said to be an aggregate of people, historically established on a given territory, possessing in common relatively stable particularities of language and culture, and also recognizing their unity and difference from other similar formations (self-awareness) and expressing this in a self-appointed name (ethnonym)' (Bromley, 1975, 11). These particularities are a product of divergent habitat conditions and the available material equipment and the ability of the concerned people to make the best out of the given opportunities. According to another opinion, 'ethnic groups are categories of ascription and identification by the actors themselves, and thus have the characteristic of organizing interaction between people' (Barth, 1969, 10). Barth may be right in insisting that it is the traits themselves which in the end allow the ethnic distinctions to be made, but a study of their emergence, however important, may not be within the domain of ethno-genesis.

The views of Bromley and Barth are, however, mutually complementary rather than contradictory or incongruous.

Traits are the markers of ethnic identity (Bromley) and the evaluation of these traits is the result of interaction of one group with its neighbour (Barth). Both are equally significant. In fact, identity itself is the result of a long process of complex inter-community interaction.

Some awareness of geo-diversity in north-western South Asia and its neighbourhood lends well to divergent forms of life in this area. During the Early and Middle Bronze Ages, there were peoples at different levels of material culture in the hills, the plains, the forests, the deserts and the coastline. As for the divergence in physical biology, the whole area was already being inhabited from as early as the mid-fifth millennium BC by four of the five major physical types, the proto-Austroloids, the Mongoloids, the Mediterraneans and the Alpines. The proto-Austroloids appear to have constituted the bulk of population. An examination of the skeletal data from Harappa and elsewhere also indicates the relative strength of these physical types within the Harappan population. However, these physical types were neither homogeneous nor exclusive, each group being differentiated on the basis of habitat and culture. This would suffice to anticipate an ethnic mozaic developing in the area through interactions and differentiation in terms of physical features, lifestyles, dialect use and mindsets. The concentration of these groups may have varied according to the subregions and their proximity to non-South Asian neighbourhoods.

The bardic information recorded in the *Ṛgveda* appears to underline some degree of correspondence with such pluralism notwithstanding the quagmire of bardic similes and metaphors. However, before using the text for any determination of ethnic types and their mutual relations, it is necessary to remember that it includes the compositions of Vedic-speaking Āryas, Vedic-speaking non-Āryas, and bards of Iranian origin. Some of the composers were surely interactive but others were quite distant from one another in both time and space.

The Primary Category

The ethnic or sub-ethnic groups, which occupied the centre-stage in the *Ṛgveda* can be classified into two broad religious categories, one which believed in the ideology of Daiva worship and the other which did not. The believers described themselves as Ārya and decried the non-believers as Dasyu. The term Dasyu does not have any ethnic significance as believed by certain scholars (Erdosy, 1989, 37). It merely distinguished the believers in Ārya ideology from the non-believers.

A careful reader of the text may notice that apart from the Ārya, the two other broad categories, which occupied the ethnic canvas, were the Dāsa and the Vṛtra. There are many passages, which refer to friendly relations between the Ārya on the one hand, and the Vṛtra and the Dāsa on the other, friendship or hostility being determined by hegemonic conflicts in the politics of space. When the Dāsa or the Vṛtra were not on friendly terms with a particular Ārya segment, the poets would repeatedly denounce the former by whatever terms of abuse came their way. It is on such occasions that the skin colour, nasal index and dialect use came into prominence. A friendly Dāsa or Vṛtra would not be denounced in this manner even though they did not conform to the Ārya ideology, but simply lent military or political support to their Ārya friends.

Friendly ties such as this may occasionally have induced a Dāsa or Vṛtra to embrace the Ārya religion and thereby establish his claim to the Ārya status like in the case of Paktha in the eighth book and Śibi Auśīnara in the tenth book. In the first instance, a Kāṇva priest praises the charities of the Paktha ruler and in the other example, Śibi Auśīnara is the name of the priest, who composed a full *dānastuti* hymn. Although, however, a non-Ārya could convert to the Ārya status, the reverse could not happen under any circumstances. At least the text does not provide any instance in which an Ārya was relegated to the position of a Dāsa or Vṛtra.

The understanding of ethnic boundaries and interaction in the *Ṛgveda* can be instructive if viewed in the light of information furnished in the Dāśarājñaḥ hymn or hymns related to the battle of ten kings. The expression *dāsa ca vṛtra hatam āryāṇi ca*, which occurs in a passage of the seventh book (7.83.1) and elsewhere, is of considerable significance. The expression is used by a poet priest of Sudāsa to describe the enemies of his patron. Clearly, the Dāsas, the Vṛtras and the Āryas had joined hands to humiliate another Ārya chief Sudāsa. Although there is no indication that the Vṛtras and Dāsas in this particular example followed the religious practices of the Ārya, the coming together of three different peoples could not have taken place without a strong common interest and the continuous process of bilingualism, which enabled them to communicate with one another.

However, a distinction between the Ārya on one hand and the Dāsa and the Vṛtra on the other could not be lost sight of, at least so long as the two latter groups did not fall in line with the practice of Ārya religiosity. This is very well brought out in a passage of the sixth book (6.33.3), which uses the expression *tvam tān ubhayān amitrān vadhiḥ dāsā vṛtrāṇi āryā ca* to state that Indra eliminated Dāsas, Vṛtras and Āryas for the benefit of another Ārya chief. The expression *ubhyān amitrān*, which means both types of enemies clearly classifies the three peoples into two groups, first Ārya and second Dāsas and Vṛtras. However, the scope of selective strikes featuring only non-Āryas was increasingly being reduced with the gradual expansion of Ārya ideology engulfing many resourceful Dāsas and Vṛtras within the Ārya fold.

The Secondary Category

However, the study of ethnicity in the *Ṛgveda* neither begins nor ends with Dāsa-Ārya dichotomy based on religious distinctions, as supposed by Erdosy (Erdosy 1989, 37). Ārya was a broad religious category, but within it there were subdivisions characterized by physical features, lifestyles and dialect use. Somewere dusky (*kṛṣṇa*), somewere dark-brown (*śyāva*) and some others were light-skinned (*śvitna, śvityañca*). The legitimation of divergent modes of the disposal of the dead like burial, cremation, post-cremation burial, post-exposer burial and exposure in the funerary portion of the text (10.14.16; 10.18) also underlines divergent life-styles followed by diverse groups of Vedic speakers in disparate regions. Similarly, the vedic dialect was common to all Vedic speaking communities, but the dialect varied from chaste to pervert depending on the association of particular groups of vedic speakers with the speakers of region specific non-vedic ethnic dialects. Likewise, the Dāsa and the Vṛtra also appear to have comprised several sub ethnic groups, some of whom are camouflaged by ethnonyms, of which a large number is mention in the text. Besides there were professional groups, like the Paṇis who represented banking entrepreneurs of the late third and early second millennium BC.

Vṛtras—People of Enclosed Settlements

As for the term Vṛtra (*vṛtta*, circle), it seems to identify certain groups of people, who lived in enclosed settlements. Enclosures could be made from mud, mud-brick or stones, all these examples being available within the Harappan context. The bardic comparison of such settlements with spider's net (*aurṇavābham* 2.11.18) is quite interesting. The spider's net is a circular structure enclosing several chambers. This very well simulates many walled Harappan settlements of the Bronze Age on the Indo-Iranian subcontinent during the late third and early second millennium BC. The destruction of these enclosures, which prevented access to the goods inside is a recurrent theme of Indra's encounter with Vedic as well as non-Vedic speaking peoples. However, the term 'destruction' is not appropriate in all of these contexts since the purpose of attack was to clear these strongholds of the enemies and occupy them. Vṛtra also represented chiefs guarding hydraulic constructions for control drainage. Elimination of these chiefs and the diversion of dammed water towards fields not getting share of the river water also figure prominently.

Paṇis

Compared to the Dāsa and the Vṛtra, Paṇis appear to have been a professional group comprising bankers and barterers, who may have belonged to one or more of the several ethnic communities in north-western South Asia. As is characteristic of moneylenders and marginal barterers, the Paṇis were close-fisted and extremely selective in extending patronage to Daiva priests. The invectives, which surface in relation to Paṇis in different portions of the text are evidently the compositions of those poets whom the Paṇis refused to oblige.

The term *paṇi*, which occurs fifty times in different portions of the text, has been explained by Vedicists and historians as bargainer, miser, trader and as one who does not patronize sacrifices. Since the *Ṛgveda* has a separate word for trader, 'Vaṇik', which occurs in two different passages of the text, there is no point in explaining the term *paṇi* as trader.

The term *paṇi* is derived from *paṇa*, which means a bet or a wager, gambling, playing for a stake. A banker or usurer also does this when he loans out a principal amount for a higher return in terms of interest together with a part of the principal or just accumulation of interests far surpassing the principal. The term Paṇa occurs once in the *Ṛgveda* (8.66.10) in the sense of *paṇi* or people making stakes for higher return. The term *paṇān* is accusative plural, just as *paṇin*, which occurs elsewhere in the same sense. This meaning of the term *paṇa* also agrees with the term *grathinaḥ* used in connection with the Paṇis (7.6.3). The passage describes the Paṇis as ill spoken (*mṛdhravācaḥ*) and crooked (*grathinaḥ*), fit to be suppressed by Indra.

From *grath* (cl.9 P. *grathnāti*) meaning tie, string together, connect in a regular series, fasten, arrange, the term *grathinaḥ* would mean a people who amassed wealth by calculating accumulations over days, months and years. The term *ahardṛśaḥ*, which occurs elsewhere in connection with Paṇis, also signifies a people who multiplied their wealth in this manner. This should be read in the light of another passage (8.47.17), which refers to the practice of clearing the principal amount by paying interest along with a part of the principal in mutually agreed instalments. The passage has *sapham* for principal, *kalām* for interest and *ṛṇa* for loan. The repayment of loan may have involved both cash and kind. Interestingly, the term Bṛbu, which is the name of the chief of the Paṇis and Beknāṭā, which means a usurer are of un-Vedic origin and may have been adopted by bardic composers from erstwhile traders and bankers of the Indo-Iranian subcontinent during the decaying stages of the Harappan civilization.

Bhalanas, Gāndhārīs and Tṛtsus (Vasiṣṭhas)

In some of the examples, ethnic identity is represented by the territory inhabited by a particular group like the Bhalanas or people of Bolan valley and Gāndhārīs or the people of Gāndhāra region (North West Frontier province of Pakistan). The Gāndhārīs are further distinguished as the people of the wool country, which is the precise significance of the simile 'like the ewe of Gāndhāra people' (*gāndhārīnām iva avikā*). In some other examples, the ethnic identity is flaunted by certain outward physical features like the Vasiṣṭhas, who wore matted locks and the Viṣāṇin or the Śṛngin, meaning the horn-hooded people or chief. The Vasiṣṭhas and their clients Tṛtsus are twice described as white-robed (*śvityañcaḥ*) and wearing braided and knotted hair (7.83.8; 7.33.1—*kapardinaḥ*). One of the two passages is more specific in stating that the Vasiṣṭhas wore the topknot of hair on the right side of the head (7.33.1—*dakṣiṇataskapardāḥ*). Such characterization is a rarity in the text and may suggest some sort of ethnic dress code followed by an erstwhile Dāsa community coming over to the Ārya fold by accepting the practice of Daiva religion and patronage of Daiva chantsmen. Turning to the Harappan context, carved stone sculptures depict elaborate styles of braids and finely combed hair that was often tied into a double bun or a twisted single bun at the back of the head (Kenoyer, 1998, 136). The bun hair style can also be seen on a miniature Harappan bronze sculpture of male spear thrower or dancer. The Vasiṣṭhas might be anticipating the Kacchis of the time of Pāṇini, who also wore a top knot of hair (Kācchikā Cūḍā) as a characteristic ethnic marker.

Viṣāṇin/Śṛngin

As for the Viṣāṇin and Śṛngin, the two terms may not be really different, although Viṣāṇin appears in connection with the battle of ten kings (7.18.7) and the Śṛngin in two passages of the first book (1.32.15; 1.33.12) apparently without any relationship with the ten kings' battle. Both Viṣāṇin and Śṛngin mean horn-hooded people, at first hostile towards the promoters of Ārya religious beliefs but later subdued by the latter. This seems fairly evident from two allusions to Śṛngin, one of which states that Indra pierced the strong enclosures of Vṛtra (1.33.12—*ilī biśasya dṛlhā indraḥ ni avidhyat*) and also the horn-hooded enemy who caused aridity by damming the reverse (1.33.12—*Śṛngiṇam Śuṣṇam vi abhinat*). The other passage (1.32.15), which was a subsequent composition, describes the horn-hooded people as the subjects of Indra.

Judging by the historical records of mid-first millennium BC, the horn-Hooded people may not be too difficult to identify. Two of the several groups of Scythians are described as Śaka haomavarga or the Soma-sacrificing Śaka and Śaka Tigrekhuda or the horn-Hooded Sakas, both mentioned in Achaemenian records of sixth-fifth centuries BC. The Bisutun Inscription of Darius I (522–486 BC), which is inscribed on a cliff overhanging a high hill-road in western Iran shows the Persian chief seated on a high throne and the conquered chiefs standing in front of him tied by a rope. Among the captive chiefs, one can clearly notice a person flaunting a hooded headgear slightly curved backwards at the top. During the seventh century BC, Śaka Haomavarga lived north of Afghanistan and Śaka Tigrekhuda a little north-east of Śaka Haomavarga. Archaeological discoveries have also brought to light the tomb of a Śaka Tigrekhuda chief at Issyk in Semirech South of lake Balkash in Kazakhastan (Akishev, 1978; Skjaervo, 1995/97). During the second millennium BC, both the Śaka groups may have occupied the Indo-Iranian borderland itself. The Swat Necropolis evidence of late second millennium BC relating to the burials of complete horses may also signify the presence of Śaka peoples on the Indo-Iranian borderland during the Ṛgvedic timeframe. Since hegemonic conflicts on the Indo–Pak borderlands involved neighbouring peoples, it is not unlikely that one of the Śaka groups participated in the battle of ten kings fought on the banks of Ravi.

Śuṣṇa and his Mobile Homes

The name Śuṣṇa is the central figure in the account of a group of desert nomads, who were distinguished by their lifestyle, particularly their mobile homes. The term *śuṣṇa* may not however denote a non-Vedic personal name as in the case of Cumuri, Dhuni, Pipru or Namuci. It seems to be one of the several bardic coinages based on certain physical conditions of life. Accordingly, Śuṣṇa would relate to some desert tracts, highlighting conditions of water scarcity, just as Vṛtra would relate to mountain tracts and barrages frequently blocking the passage of streams and rivers.

The filling up of the well (8.51.8), which followed the defeat of Śuṣṇa by the Vedic-speaking hero Kutsa may signify the capture of some scarce water resources in a desert or semi-desert region. Likewise, the nocturnal movements (*tamogama*) mentioned in a passage of the fifth book (5.32.4), also seems to refer to a hot-dry country where nights are preferred for movements. The priest Uśanā, who is familiar to both Old Avestan and the Ṛgvedic tradition, is said to have conducted a group of Vedic speakers against Śuṣṇa, the demon of drought (4.26.1; 5.29.9). Since deserts can be comfortably negotiated during the night, the priest's expertise must have involved some amount of stargazing and correct reading of the position of cardinal stars.

From these details, it would appear that Śuṣṇa was a nomadic chief of semi-arid tracts with acute scarcity of water and pastures. The bracketing of Śuṣṇa with Kuyava, the demon of bad harvest also signifies a country frequently afflicted by drought. Some sort of carriage drawn by either horse or camel may have been used by Śuṣṇa and his men for transporting goods and people from one place to another. The term *puram cariṣṇavam,* meaning 'mobile cities or townships' appears in a passage of the eighth book (8.1.28) and may suggest that certain groups of desert or steppe nomads on the Indo-Iranian borderlands use to move about from place to place, lock, stock and barrel in carts drawn by horses or camels. Four wheeled camel-carts in south central Asia are known to archaeologists from the mid-fourth millennium BC (Masson, 1992), though it is not known whether these carts were meant for occasional transport or served as mobile homes of the concerned people. As for horse-drawn wagons serving as homes, Herodotus refers to certain steppe Scyths, who had no permanent homes and who lived in wagons in which women and children spent their lives (Sulimirski, 1985).

Śivas and Pakthas

Among the several non-Aryan peoples converted to Ārya religiosity, Śivas and Pakthas deserve special mention. Śivas or the Siboi of the Greeks lived between the Indus and the Chenab. They may refer to the ancient inhabitants of Sibi, about 100 km south-east of Bolan Pass. The place name Sibi might be a modern form of Śiva. Through friendly interaction with Vedic speakers, some of the Śivas may have adopted Vedic rituals and speech. In the tenth *maṇḍala* (10.179), Śibi Auśīnara is mentioned as a poet-priest, who composed three stanzas in which he urges the Ṛtvij priests to carefully prepare oblations for offering to Indra as mid-day oblation (10.179.1-3).

As for the pakthas (Greek paktues), it may be a Ṛgvedic version of paẍtō or paśtō, 'the name of an Iranic dialect and its speakers' traditionally inhabiting South and Southeastern Afghanistan besides recent settlers in northern Afghanistan, Pakistan, Baluchistan and eastern Iran (Farhādī, 1985, 516). The term Paktha appears in quite a few passages and in particular relationship with Trasadasyu and Kaṇva, the ruler and the priest respectively of the Swat valley people. The Swat region lies just east of eastern Afghanistan, which is today inhabited by the Pakhtoons who lend their name to the Pakhtoonistan area. The Pakthas appear to have slowly adapted themselves to Vedic ideology and bardic dialect. In a Dānastuti passage of the eighth *maṇḍala* (8.22.10), the paktha chief is eulogized along with two other chiefs. The bard here is Souvari Kāṇva and the gods who are requested to protect the Paktha chief are Aśvins.

Śambara and his Pit-dwellings

The nature of habitation can also sometimes be a marker of ethnicity like the hill-dwellings of Śambara and his people, who are always described as pit-dwellers, the trait being of an exclusive nature. The chief determinants of Śambara episode furnished by the second book are: (i) association with a mountain country [2.12.11; 2.24.2], (ii) seeking out of śambara from his mountainous hideouts [2.12.11], (iii) a forty-year search launched to this effect [2.12.11], (iv) destruction of 99 Śambara houses [2.14.6; 2.19.6] and capture of the hundredth dwelling [4.26.3; 7.19.5], (v) use of missile fire [2.24.7] to raze the Śambara houses, and (vi) bracketing with Varcī [2.14.6], another detractor of the Gṛtsamada bards. A seventh determinant is the association of Indra with the north-bound course of the Indus [2.15.6]. In all passages relating to fights between Indra and Śambara, the latter is said to have been killed in a mountainous country (*parvateṣu*).

Looking for pit-dwellers in north-western South Asia during the second millennium BC, attention must converge on Karewas of the Jhelum valley in the vale of Kashmir. Excavations in the Neolithic Karewa settlements of the third and second millennium BC bring to light three stages of occupation, of which the second phase ranging between 1800 BC and 1200 BC appears to conform to the Ṛgvedic timeframe and the heroic exploits of Indra in Baltistan and in the Karewa habitation in the vale of Kashmir (Nandi, 2001).

Two other features of the Śambara episode, which are well supported by textual and archaeological data, relate to a forty-year quest of Śambara in a mountain country and the destruction of Śambara houses by missile fire. The pit-dwellings dug deep into the Karewa mud are interconnected with one another facilitating the escape of the enemy from one pit to another in times of an external attack. The manner in which Indra razed the ninety-nine houses is also exclusive to the episode of Śambara in the second *maṇḍala*. This related to the use of the flaming-missiles hurled from a distance (2.24.7). The excavations of 1960-61 also brought to light a crescent-shaped pit separated from a wider pit by a wall of natural soil. The former, which was perhaps used for storage purposes, revealed burnt birch, charred hay and burnt clay. The possibility of the superstructure consisting of wooden posts and thatched roof covered with birch having been reduced by fire cannot be ruled out (*Indian Archaeology—A Review*, 1961-62, 17).

Persians and Parthians

The Persian contexts surface in connection with the gift collection missions of South Asian and Iranian bards, who frequently exchanged positions, temporarily or permanently. The Persian contexts also figure in relation to chiefs in hot pursuit of their enemies, like Cāyamāna Abhyāvartin or the enemies trying to escape such pursuit, like Turvaś. There are altogether four references relating to Persian chiefs and Persian peoples. The Persian people (*parśavaḥ*) appear in the compositions of two important bards, Trita Āptya (1.105.8) and Kavaṣa Ailūṣa (10.33.2). Both the passages are similar and refer to the Persians (*parśavaḥ*) tormenting the poets like co-wives. Perhaps underlining professional jealousy among competing bardic groups. The former poet, probably an innovator of the Soma cult in north-western South Asia, may have fallen victim to professional jealousy and left for greener pastures, finally landing in neighbouring Iranian territory. Professional rivalry continued to haunt him in the new region, which is what he describes in his composition. The other poet also appears to have spent a good deal of his time among the Persian rivals.

Of the two Persian chiefs who figure in the text one was Tirindir and other Cāyamāna Abhyāvartin. The latter participated in the battle of Hariyuppiyā and stationed his protegies Sṛñjaya and Devavāta in the area after winning the battle (6.27.8). The battle over, the Parthian chief showered huge bounties on priests and benefactors and this is what a Bharadvāja composer of the sixth book glorifies through the expression '*pārthavānām mahadakṣinā*' or 'the fabulous prestation gifts offered by the Parthain chief'. The Parthian king here is named Cāyamāna Abhyāvartin, meaning 'the son or descendant of Cāyamāna'. A chief named Cāyamāna actually figures in relation to the battle of ten kings described in the seventh book (7.18; 7.83). The suffix Kavi attached to this chief's name may suggest that like many of the Avestan chiefs, he too was a poet of considerable merit. In all likelihood, Cāyamāna Abhyavartin of the sixth book (6.27) was a descendent of Cāyamāna Kavi and probably ruled his kingdom from Hariyuppiyā and that a Parthian dynasty was well entrenched in the Ravi valley, in the vicinity of Harappa.

As for Tirindir, he did not come to South Asia in pursuit of his enemies, but his charities are praised by both Persian and South Asian poets (8.6.46-48). Two other chiefs, whose Iranian connections can be suggested on the basis of circumstantial evidence, were Yadu and Turvaś. Yadu, who is frequently bracketed with Turvaś, was a fugitive member of Yādava family, whose wealth was captured by the Persian chief Tirindir (8.6.46) and distributed among Iranian bards like Pajra and South Asian bards, like Vatsa Kāṇva (8.6.46; 8.6.48). Turvaś already figures in the battle of Hariyūppiyā as being suppressed by the Parthian chief Cāyamāna Abhyāvartin.

Incidentally, Pajra, who flourished in Iran under Tirindir was an ancestor of Kakṣivān (1.116.7; 1.117.6). Kakṣivān, an important composer of the first book was originally associated with Iṣṭāśva, who may be identical with Kauui Vistaspes of the Old Avesta, the patron of Zarathustra and the Mazdiān faith. If this is so, it may provide a fitting backdrop to a tiff (1.122.13; also 1.122.9 and 1.122.15) between Kakṣivān, a Daiva worshipper and Vistaspa, a Mazdiān patron leading to the migration of the poet's family to South Asia. Probably, Kakṣivān accompanied by his merchant poet father, Dīrghaśravas, spent a long time at different royal codes in South Asia particularly that of the ruler of Sind, whose charities are so graphically recorded in a portion of the first book (1.126). The wealth and arms, manpower, chariots and horses, which he collected in the course of his prestation missions, may have subsequently raised the poet to the position of a king (*rājā*). This seems to be reflected by a composition of Ghoṣā Kakṣivatī, who describes herself as Rājñaḥ Duhitā and prays for the acquisition of horses and chariots to defend her territory (10.40.5).

Ethnic Identity: Physical Features

The materials examined above seem to suggest certain basic criteria, physical, religious and dialectal for identifying diverse ethnic groups on the Indo-Iranian subcontinent. The physical markers relate to skin colour and facial index, neither being exclusive to the Vedic speaking or non-vedic speaking comunities. As for the vedic speakers, there were dark-skinned people as well as light-skinned people. This may also have been the case with the non-vedic people though the bardic documentation, which is clearly one-sided always describes non-vedic people as dark-skinned. Another biolgogical feature relates to facial appearance, which was characterized by the shape of the nose and the jaw. The Vedic speakers sometimes distinguished those with beautiful jaws (*suśipra*-1.99.3) and those with the jaw of the bull (*vṛṣaśipra*–7.99.4). In one instance, a poet refers to a vṛtra as noseless or Faceless (*anāsa*). However, considering the fewness of such references, and the inclusive nature of vedic ideology, it is extremely unlikely that such facial markers were always exclusive to the non-vedic speaking people.

Ethnic Identity: Religion

There are other terms, which denounce opponents not so much for divergent physical features as on account of reluctance to appreciate bardic prayers and honour the bards with gifts. To this category belong terms like *adeva* (without gods, 5.61.6), *amanta* (mindless, 10.22.8), *arādhas* (uncharitable, 5.61.6), *atrātar* (not protecting, 5.61.6), *ayajñyān* (not sacrificing, 7.6.3), *aśraddhān* (disrespectful, 7.6.3), *avṛdhān* (not enriching 7.6.3), *amitra* (unfriendly, 1.133.1) *anindra* (disrespectful of Indra, 1.133.1), *akarma* (non-sacrificing, 10.22.8), *apavrata* (followers of false beliefs, 1.51.9), *anyavrata* (practising other rituals, 10.22.8), *śiśnadeva* (worshippers of the phallic god, 7.21.5; 10.99.3). Where the opposition was more pronounced, the bards used terms like *devakilviṣa* (offence against the gods 10.97.16), *devaninda* (haters of gods, 1.152.2; 2.23.8) and *devaśatru* (enemies of gods, 6.59.1). There are still other words, which are much aggressive in denouncing certain peoples, as *piśācin* (wicked, 1.133.5), *piśangbhṛṣṭin* (with reddish spikes in their hands, 1.133.5), *amānuṣa* (sub human, 10.22.8), *yātumati* (practitioners of witchcraft, 1.133.2-3) and *ambhṛṇan* (hefty, 1.133.5).

These expressions, when examined in their particular contexts, would show that there were several affluent and powerful chiefs who did not care for bardic practice but whom the bards frequently approached for gifts of cattle, horses, gold and other valuables. For instance, the terms *aśraddhān*, *ayajñyān* and *avṛdhān* are used in relation to Paṇis in one passage. Panis, some of whom lived in highland strongholds were frequently approached by bards for gifts. But every time, the requests were turned down. Such refusal may have prompted occasional thefts of the cattle particularly when the Paṇis were away from their homes. But when such lifting was not possible, the bards could only curse the Paṇis by using the choicest of abuses. The Paṇis are also described as Dasyu or enemies and Mṛdhravāca or speaking an uncouth dialect. This is also because of the disfavour meted out to the poets.

Ethnic Identity: Dialect Use

More interesting information surfaces at the level of dialect differentiation. Three key expressions to this effect are *mṛdhravāca, vadhṛvāca and vivāca.* The term *mṛdhravāca, which* occurs several times in the *Ṛgveda*, once in relation to the Paṇis [7.6.3], once in relation to an Ārya chief Puru [7.18.13] and four times in relation to non-Vedic speaking enemies, means a person of hostile, corrupt or uncouth speech. In the case of non-vedic speakers, Dāsa or Vṛtra, the expression is sometimes associated with a term of abuse like in *anāsa mṛdhravāca viśaḥ* (5.29.10) or *vabhram apādam mṛdhravācam* (5.32.8). In the tenth *maṇḍala*, Indra is stated to have destroyed thousands of turbulent enemies (*pura sahasrā aśivā jaghān* 10.23.5), who spoke diverse dialects (*vivāca*) all of the perverted type (*mṛdhravāca*). The speakers of uncouth diverse dialects once again surface in a passage of the third book, which refers to Indra's overcoming the arch enemy Vala, suppressing the proud people and driving away the speakers of perverted dialects (*vivāca nunude*, 3.34.10).

The poets of Swat Valley also spoke a deviant form of the Vedic dialect. Clearly, the term *mṛdhravāca* was used in relation to both non-Vedic speakers of local dialects as well as the speakers of deviant forms of the Vedic dialect. In the first case, the term signified unfamiliar speech. In the latter case, it signified the corrupt form of a familiar dialect. In either case, the dialect was more than one. This is precisely what the term *vivāca* would mean when compounded with the expression *mṛdhravāca*. With the preposition *vi* prefixed to *vāca*, the term denotes diverse forms of speech.

Compared to *mṛdhravāca*, the term *vadhṛvāca* occurs only

once (7.18.9) in the text. The prefix *vadhṛ* means castrated or emasculated, as in Vadhṛyāśva meaning 'a castrated horse' or the owner of a castrated horse and Vadhṛmatī, meaning the 'wife of a sterile husband'. Vadhṛvāca would, accordingly, mean persons with barren speech. The passage in which the term occurs can be meaningful only when it is examined together with another passage (7.18.7) which mentions five non-Vedic peoples who participated in the ten kings' battle against Sudāsa. The nominative plural *vadhṛvācaḥ*, which fits with accusative plural *sutukān* and *amitrān* suggesting thereby more than one non-Vedic dialect probably, five non-Vedic dialects spoken by five groups of non-Āryan peoples, namely Pakthas, Bhalanas, Alinas, Biṣāṇin and Śivas. Since these non-Vedic dialects were unfit for saying the prayers or offering sacrifices, these could not ensure the granting of wishes by the gods and therefore fit to be denounced as unproductive or barren.

As among the non-Vedic speakers, there were distinct dialectal groups within the loose framework of people who subscribed to the Deva ideology and spoke the Vedic dialect. These variants of Vedic dialect were the products of several parallel processes of bilingualism going on in different sub-regions of north-western South Asia. A Bhāradvāja poet of the sixth book refers to different bardic groups (*cārṣaṇāya* 6.31.1) speaking diverse dialects (*vivāca*) and offering prayers (*vi avocanta,* 6.31.1) for water resources, wealth and prosperity of sons and grandsons. The term *cārṣaṇāya* may be a mistake for *carṣaṇaya,* a nominative plural of *carṣaṇi,* which makes the sense appropriate. The expression *vivāca carṣaṇaya* figures once again in the sixth book (6.33.2), where the poet invokes Indra for protecting the speakers of diverse Vedic dialects in their war against enemies. Incidentally, *carṣaṇī* is one of the five terms, which are invariably suffixed to the prime number pañca as in *pañca carṣaṇayaḥ, Pañca kṛṣṭayaḥ, Pañca Śreṇayaḥ, Pañca kṣitayaḥ* and *pañca janāḥ*. In all these cases, the expressions are exclusive to bardic groups and no non-Vedic groups are intended. Pañca or five is a conventional number and may simply mean the existence of diverse bardic communities differentiated from one another on the basis of dialect variation and variations in lifestyle.

Chapter 11

Ethnicity and Dialect Variation

The variations in Vedic dialect noticed in different portions of the Śākalya text may have been the result of parallel bilingual processes involving a colloquial Vedic dialect confined to the families of priests and a more widely spoken non-Vedic dialect. In the process of these interactions, words and idioms from non-Vedic dialect found their way first into the colloquial Vedic dialect and finally to the dialect of the hymns. The other way round may also have been a linguistic reality but the elements are not easily determinable. The lexical and structural elements of colloquial Vedic dialect were also considerably influenced as some more literate persons from among the non-Vedic speakers tried to speak the colloquial Vedic dialect in an attempt to sanctify their position and legitimize their claim to participate in some of the rituals. The declensional variants, Prakriticisms and Dravidian substrates which appear in different portions of the text may have been the result of such a process of upward mobility.

Synonyms of House—Context and Connotation

Turning to the synonym aspect of dialect variation, one might draw attention to different synonyms of the term 'house', of which there are more than a score in the present Śākalya recension of the text. Some of these terms are fairly recurrent in all portions of the work. But, there are others, which seem to be exclusive to certain portions composed by particular bards probably exposed to region-specific dialectal features.

Gṛha, Chadis, Chardis

The term *gṛha*, which in some languages of northern and eastern India is Prakriticised as *ghar*, is a good example of the former category. The word appears in as many as seventy passages of the *Ṛgveda*. As for the later *Samhitā* texts, it occurs uniformly nearly 150 times. Compared to *gṛha*, the term *chadis* occurs only twice in the *Ṛgveda*, once in the eighth *maṇḍalā* and once in the tenth *maṇḍalā*. Another term which sounds like *chadis* but is actually an aberrant form of it, is *chardis* which occurs as many as twenty-one times in the text. The term *chadis*, which is derived from *chad* meaning to cover', fits in well with the sense of a shelter or house. But the term *chardis* which derives from *chṛd*, meaning 'to vomit' is nowhere near the sense of a house though it occurs frequently in the sense of a house. The aberration may have been peculiar to the speech of particular composers. It may also have been an attempt to Vedicize a word borrowed from some non-Vedic dialect with the help of an intrusive 'ṛ'. However, unmindful of this, Old Indo-Aryan (OIA) speakers of the later *Samhitās* continued to use this aberrant form which makes as many as twenty-five appearances in different texts. At the same time, other bards appear to show considerable preference for the correct form *chadis* which makes nearly 30 appearances in later *Samhitā* texts. In the *Brāhmaṇā* texts, which represent the Middle Indo-Aryan (MIA) dialect, both *chadis* and *chardis* passed out of usage. Etymologically, *gṛha* (*grah*, to receive) suggests a structure which received goods collected or generated by the people. But, *chadis* (*chad*, thatching) refers to thatched roofs supported by some sort of posts with or without doors. Joining of large and parallel branches of a tree by a thatch of grass, reeds or leaves, as at Paisra, a small tribal village in the present Munger district of Bihar during the prehistoric time may have been a proto-type of *chadis*. Chadis may also refer to rock shelters of prehistoric times which provided a roof cover against lashing rains, extreme cold or heat. Since roof is the most operative part of housing, it was easily adopted as a synonym of house in succeeding literatures. In the New Indo-Aryan (NIA) languages of northern and eastern India, it continues to simply mean a roof as *chat* in Hindi and *chād* in Bengali.

Dur, Durya and Duroṇe

Three other terms, viz., *dur, durya* and *duroṇe* occur in the sense of a house in different portions of the text. Of these, *dur* and *duroṇe* make 24 and 36 appearances respectively. Durya, which is an adjective of *dur,* makes 10 appearances and means 'relating to the house'. Duroṇe seems to have been formed by prefixing *dura* to *oṇe*. Dura already means house in *Ṛgveda* and *oṇe* means to remove, take away, drag along. From this, *duroṇe* may suggest a house that removes or prevents danger. The term occurs thirty times in the later *Samhitā* texts and thereafter it passed out of usage.

Pur, Durga, Vṛjana

Defensive structures, variously described as *pur, durga* and *vṛjana* occupy considerable space in the bardic compositions and almost always as the foci of armed conflict involving Vedic and non-Vedic speakers. The importance given by the bards to these structures can become meaningful only in the context of the Harappan civilization, probably towards its decaying stages. The whole of north-western South Asia during the Early Bronze Age abounded in a large number of fortified settlements made from mud or mud bricks, burnt bricks and stones. Turning to textual evidence, one might notice that the most frequent of the three terms representing a defensive structure is *pur,* which acconts for over eighty appearances. Pur means citadel, a rampart, stronghold, fortress, town or wall, the last suggesting a walled settlement and not just a wall. The term *durga,* which appears twenty times in the text, means difficult to access, narrow passage, citadel, stronghold, rough ground. Sometimes it appears as adjective, like in *puraḥ durga* (1.41.3), or *duroṇe durge* (4.28.3) meaning strongholds, difficult of access. When used as a noun, the term signifies stronghold or citadel, like Indra capturing all the enemies inside the citadel (7.60.12). Sometimes the term *durga* itself meant fight, as in *ajredurge* (8.27.18) meaning 'In the battle for the capture of an inaccessible fort'. The other term *vṛjana* is formed by prefixing *vṛ,* meaning to cover, enclose to Jana, meaning people. Vṛjana would thus refer to people living in enclosed settlements. The term occurs sixty-three times in the *Ṛgveda* generally in relation to conflicts for the possession of these settlements. In several passages, the poets express desire to capture enclosures (*vṛjana*) belonging to the enemies and lodge themselves in these places (1.51.15; 1.128.7).

Dama, Kṣaya, Sadana

The term *dama* (*dam*, to restrain or control) may have originally meant a chief's house, which functioned as the source of subsistence and authority. In later dialects, the term *dama* became synonymous with wife and the compound *dampati* signified wife and husband, literally 'lord of the house'. In the NIA dialect, *dama* means self control and not 'a house'. The term occurs fifty times in the *Ṛgveda* and fourty-nine times in the later Vedic *Samhitās*. The term *kṣaya* (*kṣi*, to possess, dwell) on the other hand was a normal expression for 'house' in the *Ṛgveda* although its use considerably declined in the *Brāhmaṇa* texts. It occurs fifty-eight times in *Ṛgveda* and 100 times in the later Vedic texts. As for *sadana* (*sad*, to sit), it denoted a place where bardic groups settled down temporarily or permanently to perform sacrifices.

Varutha, Śarma, Gaya

Three other terms which deserve attention, are *varutha, śarma* and *gaya*. Of these, *gaya* is a regular term for house, but it also means household, family, goods and chattels, contents of a house, property, wealth. The use of the term *gaya* (for which several derivations are suggested) in the sense of a house or dwelling is confined to the OIA dialect only, occurring nineteen times in the *Ṛgveda* and thirty-three times in the later *Samhitās*. The term *śarma*, which is derived from *śṛ*, signifies protection, safety, shelter, or refuge. In some passages, it simply means protection or well-being as in *varuthyam śarma*. But in *achidrā puruni śarma dadhire*, the poet is explicit in demanding houses of a compact nature. The term *achidrā* may also mean houses free of damages. The term *varutha*, which is derived from *vṛ* meaning 'to cover', denotes protection, shelter, defence, abode. It occurs twenty-four times in the *Ṛgveda* and twenty-nine times in other *Samhitās*.

Oka and Okas

The term *okas* appears three times in the *Ṛgveda* and thirteen times in the later *Samhitās*. But its position declined with the growth of Middle Indo-Aryan (MIA) speech and its use was confined to certain schools only. It is thus left out by all the *Brāhamaṇas* and *Āraṇyakas* of the Atharvanic and white Yajus schools. More interesting is the case of *oka,* which was fairly popular in the OIA speech, occurring as many as sixteen times in the *Ṛgveda*. In the later Vedic *Samhitās*, which are more numerous and extensive, the word finds place in only ten passages. As for the *Brāhmaṇas* and *Āraṇyakas*, it is altogether discarded. Perhaps this is how a word entering the OIA speech through interaction with indigenous people passed out of use as the liturgical mentors encountered new areas new peoples and new situations.

Harmya and Dhāma

The term *harmya,* which in later historical literature signified a mansion or a part of it has a limited sense in the *Ṛgveda*. In certain passages of *Ṛgveda*, *harmya* means prison. *Harmya* in this case may be a synonym of *gharma,* which among other things, means cauldron or boiler. Accordingly, *harmya* may be an underground chamber, probably circular and certainly dark, simulating thereby the inside of a cauldron, devoid of any ventilation. Such a basement room could be very hot. Kaṇva is said to have been put in a *harmya* of this type and Atri rescued from the scorching heat of a similar basement room. The term *dhāma,* which occurs nearly ninty-nine times in the text, means different things in different contexts. But in several passages, it signifies dwelling place, house, abode, domain. Fervent desire is expressed to occupy ancient dwelling places (*pratnesu, dhamasu*), probably referring to some of the worn-out Harappan diffensive structures during the early second millennium BC.

Varti, Vasati, Pastya, Yoni

Varti, which occurs twenty-six times in the *Ṛgveda* means staying, resting, abiding, living. But in certain passages, it clearly means house or dwelling, as in the episode of Bhujyu

(1.119.4). The term *vasatī*, which is said to derive from *vas*, meaning to dwell, live, stop at a place, stay, occurs twelve times in the *Ṛgveda*. Vasati also means nest, dwelling, abiding, fixing one's residence. The use of the term *vasati* in the sense of a house or dwelling is recorded in the *Ṛgveda* and the later *Samhitās*. Thereafter the term changes its meaning. In the *Manusmrti*, it means 'night' and in the *Raghuvamśam*, the compound *vasati-druma* means 'a tree under which night is passed'. Although it is not clear whether *vasati* survived in the sense of house in historical times, in certain new Indic dialects, like Hindi and Bengali, *vasati* means settlement or habitation of people. The term *pastya*, which occurs sixteen times in the *Ṛgveda*, means homestead, dwelling, household and also the goddess of domestic affairs. The compound *pastya-vat* means having or being kept in a stall, having a fixed habitation. A very uncharacteristic synonym of house in the *Ṛgveda* is *yoni*. The term *yoni*, which occurs nearly 122 times in the *Ṛgveda* means different things in different contexts, like fire pit, furrows in a cultivated field, female reproductory organ and, of course, a house. The fire pit, the furrows and the house were socalled probably because each of these resembled the shape of female genitals.

Swat Valley, Ethnic Kāṇvas and the Eighth Maṇḍala

The interaction of diverse ethnic communities with the Vedic-speaking people in different regions of north-western South Asia is as evident from the dialectal variants within the OIA speech as from a careful sifting of region-specific historical data recorded in the text. But it is quite difficult to mention any such group by name and identify the area inhabited by it. It is all the more difficult to ascribe lexical or structural variants noticed in the compositions of particular bards to any such named ethnic group. The story of Swat valley chief Trasadasyu and his family priest Kaṇva may provide a good beginning from this angle.

The story of the Swat valley chief can be reconstructed from a few passages of the eighth and fourth maṇḍalas (8.19; 4.42; Nandi, 2001, 91) which refer to a group of Vedic-speaking warriors whose number is conventionally given as seven (*sapta-ṛṣayaḥ*) and who attacked the Swat chief, Purukutsa, son of Girikṣita and grandson of Durgaha. The attack was followed either by the killing or captivity (*vadhyamāne*) of the reigning chief. The offensive may have been a sequel to Purukutsa's earlier attack against some neighbouring Vedic people and destroying their autumnal abodes (*śāradīḥ puraḥ*) whose number is once again given as seven. The killing or captivity of Purukutsa left the valley without a ruler and unprotected. The widow of Purukutsa was then advised by the seven bardic heroes to perform Vedic sacrifices in a particular manner in order to obtain a son posthumously. The widow did accordingly and gave birth to a son who was named Trasadasyu or 'the terror of enemies'. Trasadasyu, who is the subject of the hymn, is described as the ruler of Suvāstu, a leader of dark-skinned people (*Śyāvaḥ-praṇetā*) and an Ārya (8.19.36-37). Kaṇva, who is a major composer of the eighth book, and the first book and who frequently figures in association with Swat valley chiefs, Purukutsa and Trasadasyu, is twice described as *kṛṣṇa* and *śyāva* (10.31.11), meaning a person of dark complexion. In one passage, we also hear of a longish confinement of the Swat valley priest in a dingy house (*harmye*), which resulted in his temporary loss of sight. The plight of the priest may have been the result of the priest's association with Purukutsa, who was deposed and perhaps killed.

Another piece of information which relates to the Swat episode shows that Trasadasyu was a half-brother of Puru. In a passage of the text, Puru and Trasadasyu are described as the two sons of Purukutsa. In another passage, Trasadasyu is seen offering a part of his wealth to Puru. In all likelihood, Puru fled the Swat valley after the debacle suffered by his father rendering the valley without a ruler (Nandi, 2001, 91).

The eighth *maṇḍala*, which seems to be the work of the inhabitants of Swat valley, provides useful information on ethno-political linkage in the area. In one passage, Trasadasyu is bracketed with the Paktha, the Daśavraja and the Gosarya. In the seventh book, the Pakthas once again figure in association with Gosarya, Daśavraja, Śivas, Bhalanas and Alinas in connection with the battle of ten kings. The Śivas could have been the inhabitants of Sibi about 100 km south-east of the Bolan pass while the Bhalanas appear to have been Bolanese people inhabiting the area near the Bolan Pass. The name Paktha, on the other hand, may refer to ancestors of modern Pakhtoons who inhabitat the Pakhtoonistan region in eastern Afghanistan which lies just west of the Swat valley across the Khyber Pass. A paktha chief is also the subject of two dānastuti stanzas of the eighth book.

The linkages between the eighth *maṇḍala*, Swat valley and a dusky ethnic community of this region may be further examined from the association of Kaṇvas, the hereditary priests of Swat rulers with Śyāvāśva. The name Śyāvāśva, which literally means 'dusky horse', may actually refer to the rider of a dusky horse or even a dusky horseman. The trekking missions of this bard covered the entire area from Bactria to Gomal valley through the valleys of Kabul and Kurram, all in the vicinity of Swat valley. No wonder, if Śyāvāśva and other members of his group were interacting with the Swat valley people in some way or the other. The connection between the composers of the eighth *maṇḍala* and the ethnic people of Swat valley may also be evident from the domination of Pragātha metre in this *maṇḍala*. The Pragātha metre, which is seldom found in any other portion of the text, may itself have been the result of the manner in which the priests of the valley went about their compositions. Perhaps this is also why the Pragātha compositions were left out when the Vedic fire rituals and the associated prayers were being formalized and stereotyped. Since the Pragātha compositions did not find a place in this formalized liturgy, the composers also did not get the stature generally accorded to the creators of the family books. No less significant is the concentration of Vālakhilya or Khilasūktas in this *maṇḍala*. The eleven hymns, which surface in the middle of the *maṇḍala* are explained by some scholars as belonging to a later date. Normally, however, interpolations find a place either in the beginning of a work or towards its end. The term *khila* means barren or unproductive and not late. The purpose of an invocation was to influence a divinity with the depth of emotion and correctness of accent communicated by means of certain metrically structured words. The Kāṇva poets of Swat valley may not have been lacking in depth of feeling, but it was the accent and the uncharacteristic metrical structuring of the hymns, which rendered certain compositions of the eighth book as supposedly 'unproductive' and therefore fit to be left out. It is perhaps this lack of proper accent and proper syntax, which marginalized the Swat valley speakers of the Vedic dialect, chiefs and priests alike. For instance, a hymn of the seventh book (7.18) which relates to the ten kings' battle describes Puru, one of the participants in the battle as speaking a corrupt dialect (*purum mṛdhravācam*). The Swat nativity of Puru may also explain the fact that although Vaśiṣtha and Sudāsa confronted several Vedic-speaking Ārya chiefs and non-Vedic peoples in the Dāśarājñaḥ, Puru alone is singled out as *mṛdravācam*.

A recent study (Hemphill, Luckacs and Kennedy, 1991; Kennedy, 1995, 49) shows that ancient Gāndhārans and Harappans shared significant similarities in craniometric, odontometric and discrete trait variables. This may suggest some kind of interaction between the Harappans of the Late Bronze Age and the inhabitants of the Swat valley sometime after 2000 BC. Perhaps the vedic speaking people who invaded and captured the Swat valley may have been refugees from decaying Harappan settlements in the neighbourhood of Swat valley. In a depressing habitat scenario, which characterized almost all Harappan settlements after 2000 BC, the Swat valley, described as a paradise on the earth, appears to have possessed all the potentialities of a vibrant life and accordingly praised by Vedic poets as Suvāstu (Swat) or 'beautiful habitation'. The Harappan immigrants may also have been instrumental in the creation of a new culture format, the Gāndhāra Grave Culture.

In view of the association of some of the composers of the eighth book with Swat valley and its native dialect, it would be no surprise if one comes across a large number of lexical and structural variants of the Vedic dialect in different portions of this *maṇḍala*, some of which are exclusive to this book.

Declensional Deviants in the Eighth Maṇḍala

(For illustration, see Appendix)

Norman (Norman, 1995/97, 259) has already drawn attention to the presence of declensional deviants in the text and illustrated it by referring to the parallel use of *'ais'* and *'ebhis'* alternately in the instrumental plural of 'a'-ending words both in masculine and neuter genders. According to Pàṇinian rules, *'ais'* is appropriate in the masculine gender of 'a'-ending words. However, this is not of much significance in view of the fact that the two usages are found, though not too many in number throughout the text and it is not possible to ascertain a specific Vedic dialectal group on its basis. The declensional deviants which we propose to discuss below are of far greater significance insofar as these may provide some idea of a Vedic-speaking segment inhabiting a particular territory and indulging in such aberrations as a matter of habit.

The declensional deviants which immediately draw the attention of the investigators relate to nominative plural, accusative singular, instrumental singular, dative singular and locative singular. For a beginning, however, we may take up the example of locative singular 'u' ending and 'ū'-ending words. In the masculine gender, 'u' ending stem becomes 'au' in the singular number of locative case such as *sādhau, viṣṇau, sūnau*, etc. This regular form which is approved by Pāṇini, occurs frequently in different portions of the text. But in the Eighth *maṇḍala*, this form occurs as an Exception rather than as a rule. The composers of this book show a considerable liking for 'i' ending, instead of 'au' endings as in *viṣṇavi, anavi, tanavi, dasyavi, trasadasyavi, druhyavi, sūnavi*, and so forth. What deserves attention here is almost total absence of this usage in any other portion of the text. Probably, *sānavi* is the only exception which occurs in *maṇḍalas* other than the eighth, which too may have been the composition of a bard influenced by the Swat valley dialect.

In other words, the purists of Vedic dialect scrupulously avoided this aberrant form, which may have been exclusive to the Swat version of Vedic dialect. In one passage of the Eighth Book, the composer refers to the locative singular of 'a'-ending words as *pakthe, daśavraje, gosarye* but *trasadasyavi* and not *trasadasyau* for a 'u'-ending word.

Although the Swat deviants of Vedic dialect were avoided in most other Vedic dialects, the composers of the Eighth Book made their impact on subsequent generations. This would be clear from the persistence of these declensional deviants in the later *Samhitā* texts. For instance, the form *viṣṇavi* occurs in the *Mādhayandina* recension of white *Yajurveda, Kauthumīya* and *Jaiminīya* recensions of the *Sāmaeda* and the *Śaunakīya* recension of the *Atharva Veda*. The regular form *viṣṇau* occurs in the *Maitrāyaṇī* recension of the Black *Yajurveda*. Although this black *Yajus* text uses the correct form of *viṣṇu* in locative singular, it diverts to a deviant for the nominative plural of this term, i.e. *viṣṇuni*. The term *viṣṇu* is a 'u'-ending masculine word and needs to be declined as *Viṣṇavaḥ* in the plural of nominative cases. But the author of the *Maitrāyaṇī Samhitā* declines the word as *viṣṇuni*, as if the word *viṣṇu* signified a neuter gender. Evidently, there is hardly any declensional uniformity within a text, Ṛgvedic or later Vedic. This is further illustrated by uses of the term *madhu*, which some composers decline as 'u' ending masculine word as *madhau* in locative singular while other composers decline it as 'u' ending neuter gender as in *madhuni* in the plural of nominative and accusative cases. This duality also persisted in the later *samhitā* text. But the most surprising is the declension of *madhu* like 'u' ending feminine word in instrumental singular, such as *madhvā*. This deviation is quite recurrent in the *Ṛgveda* as well as later *Samhitā* texts. Clearly, the same word *madhu* is sometimes declined as a masculine gender, sometimes as feminine gender and sometimes as neuter gender. These variables need to be explained more in terms of dialect variations peculiar to separate groups of Vedic speakers rather than as aberrations committed by particular composers. For this, the present arrangement of the text may have to be discarded and a rearrangement undertaken on the basis of single compositions indicating deviant forms.

Turning to accusative singular of 'u' ending words, the composers of the eighth *maṇḍala* once again score a point in the matter of deviant usage. The normal declension in the accusative case would have 'um' endings, like tanum for *tanu*, *cariṣṇum* for *cariṣṇu* and *ṛbhum* for *ṛbhu* but the composers of the Eighth Book freely use deviant forms like *tanvam*, *cariṣṇavam* and *subhūvam*. It is interesting to note that 'um'-ending declensions in the accusative singular of masculine gender are frequently met with in different portions of the text including a few passages of the eighth book itself. As for 'ū'-ending words, the declension in accusative singular of masculine gender would have *ūvam* endings, like *vibhūvam* for *vibhū* and not *vibhavam* as noticed in three passages of third, fourth and tenth *maṇḍalas*. This deviant from is once again notice in *subhavam*, the correct form being *subhūvam*. Curiously, some of the OIA bards did not even distinguish between the masculine and feminine genders of accusative singular. For instance, a passage of the tenth book uses the form *vadhvam* in the accusative singular of feminine *vadhū*. The correct declension *vadhūm* is, however, mentioned in a khila passage of the text. Perhaps still more confusing is the practice of declining the same word in two or more genders. A good example is the term *karkandhu*, which is declined as *karkandhum* in the *Ṛgveda*, the accusative singular of both masculine and feminine genders; but as *karkandhuni* in the *Kāṇva* and *Mādhyandina* recensions of the *Vājasneyī Samhitā* in the nominative and accusative plural of neuter gender.

Turning to the nominative plural of masculine gender, one can once again notice the use of a declensional deviant like *avasyuvaḥ* in place of *avasyavaḥ* and *āhuvaḥ* in place of *āhavaḥ*, the radicals being *avasyu* and *āhu* respectively. Once again, the usage is the handiwork of the composers of the eighth *maṇḍala*. Other composers who do not belong to the eighth *maṇḍala* but were influenced by the Pragātha hymners also used such deviants as *āyuvaḥ* in place of *āyavaḥ* in the second *maṇḍala*, the radical in this case being *āyu*. Curiously, the term *āyu*, which, like *avasyu* and *āhu* has been declined as nominative plural of masculine gender though incorrectly, is elsewhere declined as a neuter gender like *āyuni* in the third, ninth and tenth *maṇḍalas* as locative singular of *āyu*. Likewise, the term *bahu*, which is correctly declined in the masculine gender such as the nominative plural *bahavah* in second, fourth, seventh, ninth and tenth *maṇḍalas*, is suddenly declined as *bahūni* in neuter gender by another composer of the fourth *maṇḍala*. Probably, there was no suddenness in such variables in view of the fact that the composers belong to different regions where their Vedic speech was frequently influenced by local dialects and characteristic speech sounds.

Turning to declensions in dative singular, the deviants appear to fall in line with those discussed above and mostly belong to eighth *maṇḍala*. The 'ū' ending words *vibhū* and *viṣṇāpū* are declined in two passages of the eighth *maṇḍala* as *vibhave* and *viṣṇāpave* respectively in place of *vibhūve* and *viṣṇāpūve*. A similar deviant in dative singular occurs in the sixth *maṇḍala* like *subhave* in place of *subhūve*. There seems to be no let-up in the use of declensional deviants during the age of later *Samhitās*. In some cases things went from bad to worse instead of being sorted out and standardized. In the *Śaunakīya* and *Paippalāda* recensions of the *Atharva Veda*, the term *agrū* is declined as *agrūvai* in the dative singular. This form does not conform to dative singular of any of the three genders. Examples such as this underline a free for all situation in the matter of bardic word-use. Compared to 'ū' ending words, declensions of 'u' ending words also betray deviant forms, like *abhibhuve* in place of *abhibhave*, the latter being the regular declension of masculine 'u'-ending words in dative singular throughout the text.

As for the instrumental case, the different passages of the text throw up interesting markers of dialect variation. Consider the word *kratu*, which throughout the *Ṛgveda* and later *Samhitās* is declined in all cases as a masculine 'u' ending word. Alongside this uniformity, the term is regularly declined both as *kratunā* in the masculine gender and *kratvā* in feminine gender in the *Ṛgveda* and later *Samhitās*. Likewise, the term *paśu* is generally declined as a masculine 'u' ending word in instrumental singular and other cases. But certain bards decline it as *paśvā* in the instrumental singular of feminine gender. Similarly, the term *ghṛtasnū* is declined by some bards as *ghṛatasnūvaḥ* in place of *ghṛatasnavaḥ* in the nominative plural of masculine or feminine gender. But more confusing is the declension of the word as *ghṛtasnuvā* in the instrumental singular of masculine 'u' ending words in place of the correct form *ghṛatasnunā* which too occurs in *Ṛgveda*, the former in the third *maṇḍala* and the latter in the sixth *maṇḍala*.

As in the case of radicals, declensions of roots also betray deviant forms in the eighth *maṇḍala*. The normal declension of √*bhid* in the third person singular number of the present tense is *bhinatti*. But in the eighth *maṇḍala* it is declined as *bhedati* (8.40.10; 11). The declension *bhinatti* is not found anywhere in the text, but from the third Preterite *abhinat* in the third person singular number one can be sure about the bardic use of the form bhinatti in the present tense. Interestingly, the form *abhinat* (8.14.7) surfaces in the eighth *maṇḍala* itself. In later *Samhitās* also, *bhinatti* is a common occurrence. Similarly, the √*rudh* is declined by certain composers of eighth *maṇḍala* as *rodhati* in the third person singular number of the present tense (8.43.6). This deviant form also occurs in the *Kāṭhaka Samhitā* (7.16). The normal declension in these cases would be *ruṇaddhi* which already appears in a passage of the Tenth *maṇḍala* (10.42.9) and thereafter regularly in later *Samhitās*.

In the case of indeclinables also, the poets betray a lack of uniformity. The terms *adha* and *atha*, both of which meant the same thing, appear regularly in all portions of the text, though there is a marked preference for *adha* in the eighth *maṇḍala*. However, there is not much textual support for the suggestion (Macdonell, 1916) that *adha* represents an archaic form and *atha* a more recent one. In the fourty-sixth Sūkta of the eighth *maṇḍala*, the form *adha* appears in three passages (8.46.29,31,33) whereas the form *atha* figures in two passages (8.46,15-16). Similarly, in the ninety-sixth Sūkta of this *maṇḍala*, both the forms *adha* and *atha* appear once each (8.96.7; 15).

Appendix

Table Showing Declensional Variation in Old and Middle Vedic Languages (Appended to Chapter 11)

Word (Roots & Radicals)	*Case/ Number*	*Variant Form*	*Normal Form*
Abhibhū (mfn), to overcome, over-power, conquer	I/3 II/1 IV/1 IV/1	Abhibhūvaḥ – Kāṭh-39.1 Abhibhūvam – Śau-9.5.36 Abhibhūve – RV-2.21.2, Mā-22.30 etc. Abhibhave – Mai-2.13.17 etc.	Abhibhuvaḥ (m) Abhibhavaḥ (f) Abhibhuvam(m) Abhibhūm(f) Abhibhuve(m) Abhibhavai(f) Abhibhuve(m) Abhibhavai(f)
Agrū (*mfn*)	IV/1	Agruvai–Śau-6.60.1,6.60.3, Pai-19.14.4, 19.14.6	Agrūve(*m*), Agravai(*f*)
Āhū (*f*), calling, invoking	I/3	Āhuvaḥ - RV-8.32.19	Āhavaḥ
Āyu (*m*), living, moveable, life duration of life Āyu (*n*),	I/3 I/3, II/3	Āyuvah - RV-2.5.5, Mā-18.39 etc. Āyuni–3.3.7, 9.100.1,10.5.7	Āyavah - In all books except 3 (total 32 times), LV-Occurs in all text (total 30 times) Āyūni
Camū (f), soma reservoir	I/3, II/3 VII/1	Camū–RV-5.51.4, 8.4.4 etc.; Mā-8.39 etc. Camvi – RV-10.91.15, Mā-20.79 etc.	Camūḥ Çamvām
Cariṣṇu (mfn), moving, wandering about	II/1	Cariṇavam – RV-8.1.28	Cariṣṇum
Cāru (mfn)	VI/2 VII/2	Cāroḥ – RV-3.50.2 etc.; Mai-4.14.12	Cāravoh(mf), Cāruṇo(n)
Dasyu (*m*) enemy of the god, robber, Name of a man	VII/1	Dasyavi – RV-8.6.14	Dasyau

Devayu (m)	I/1, II/1 VI/2, VII/2	Devayu–RV-9.11.2; Kau-2.2 Devayoḥ–RV-10.106.3	Devayuma – RV-1.83.2 etc.; Kātha-40.14 etc. Devayo – RV-8.31.16; Tai-1.8.22.4; Mai-4.11.2 etc.
Devāyu, Devāyū (f)	II/1	Devāyuvama – Mā-37.16; Kā-1.4.2; Tai-2.5.9.6 etc.	Devāyuma
Druhyu (*m*) pl. Name of a people; sg. Name of a son of Yayāti and brother of Yadu	VII/1	Druhyavi – RV-8.10.5	Druhyau – RV-6.46.8
Iṣu (mfn), an arrow	V/1, VI/1	Iṣo – Śau-4.6.6, Pai-5.8.5	Iṣoḥ – Mai-3.8.1, 3.8.2
Madhu (*mfn*), sweet, delicious, pleasant	VI/2, VII/2	Madho – RV-1.187.2; Kāṭha-40.8; Pai-6.16.2, 12.3.15 Madhoḥ - RV-	Madhvoḥ (*mf*); Madhunoḥ (*n*)
Panasyu (mfn), showing one's self, worthy of admiration, glorious	I/3	Panasyuvaḥ – RV-9.86.17; Kau-2.503; Jai-3.39.2	Panasyavaḥ
Pavīru (*m*), Name of a man	VII/1	Pavīravi – RV-8.51.9; Mā-33.82; Kā-32.6.13; Kau-2.959; Jai-4.19.1	Pavīrau
Ṛbhu (mfn), clever, skillful, prudent, inventive	II/1	Ṛbhavam – Khi-1.2.9	Ṛbhum – RV-4.37.5, 8.93.34
Sānu (*m*), a summit, ridge, surface, top of a mountain	VII/1 V/1, VI/1	Sānavi – RV-4.45.1, 8.103.2 etc.; Kau-2.556; Jai-3.44.2; Pai-20.51.2 etc. Sāno – RV-9.86.3 etc.; Kau- 1.529 etc.	Sānau (*m*) – RV-1.32.7 etc.; Śau-11.7.12 etc. Sānoḥ - RV-1.10.2; Kau-2.695
Sūnu (*m*), one who urges or incites, a son, child, offspring	VII/1 V/1, VI/1	Sūnavi – RV-8.68.15 Sūno – RV-1.58.8, 8.19.7 etc.; Tai-1.3.14.7 etc.	Sūnau Sūnoḥ - RV-1.117.11 etc.; Mā-27.11
Subhū (mfn), of an excellent nature, good, strong, beautiful	VI/2, VII/2 V/1, VI/1 II/1 IV/1	Subho – Kāṭh-4.1 etc. Subhvaḥ – RV-1.52.1 etc.; Kāṭh- 37.9 Subhvam – RV-9.79.5, Mai- 2.1.9 Subhve – RV-6.66.3	Subhuvoḥ Subhuvaḥ – Kau-1.377 etc. Subhuvam(m) Subhūm(f) Subhuve(m) Subhavai(f)
Tanu (*mfn*), thin, slender, delicate, minute	VII/1 V/1, VI/1 VI/3 I/1 II/1	Tanvi – RV-1.55.8, 8.96.11 etc. Tanuvāḥ – Tai-1.5.5.4, 1.5.7.5 Tanuvām – Tai-1.7.12.2 etc. Tanūḥ – Mā-1.15 etc. Tanvam – RV-1.123.11, 8.76.12	Tanvām/Tanau Tanvāḥ – Mā-3.17 etc. Tanūnām – RV-1.5.10 etc.; Mā-25.22 Tanuḥ – Pai-13.5.18

Tanū (f), the body, person, self		etc.; Mā-3.56 etc.	Tanum – Khi. Sā.-29.7
Trasadasyu (m), Name of a person	VII/1	Trasadasyavi – RV-8.49.10	Trasadasyau
Vadhū (f), a bride, young wife, spouse	I/1 II/1	Vadhu – Śau-14.1.58 etc. Vadhvam – RV-10.107.9	Vadhuḥ Vadhūm – Śau-9.3.24 etc.
Vasu (mfn), excellent, good, beneficient	V/1, VI/1	Vaso – RV-1.10.4 etc., Mā-23.29 etc.	Vasoḥ – RV-1.9.9 etc.
Vibhū (mfn), expand, appear, be developed	II/1 IV/1	Vibhavam – RV-3.31.13 etc., Mā-3.15 etc. Vibhave – RV-8.96.11, Mai-3.12.11	Vibhuvam(m) Vibhūm(f) – Tai-1.5.5.1 Vibhuve(m) Vibhavai(f) – Mā-22.30, Kā-24.17.1
Viṣṇāpū (m), name of a person	IV/1	Viṣṇāpve – RV-8.86.3	Viṣṇāpūve –
Viṣṇu (mn), name of a god	VII/1	Viṣṇavi–RV-8.3.8, 8.12.16, Kau-1.384 etc. Viṣṇoh–RV-1.22.19-21 etc., Kā-1.10.2	Viṣṇau Viṣṇo – RV-8.27.8 etc., Mā-33.47 etc.

NOTE: Gender specifications (*mfn*=masculine, feminine and neuter) are indicated on the basis of M. Monier Williams, *A Sanskrit English Dictionary*, which covers the entire Sanskrit literature and for that reason need not always be applicable to the concerned table. The gender of a particular vocable in this table is determined on the frequency of particular declensions, the regular ones outnumbering the variant forms. If a particular vocable is appropriately declined in one or more genders, it would not constitute a variant form. Instead, the word in question would be gender-free. But if a particular word is inappropriately declined in one or more genders, it would constitute a variant form in every case. An appropriate declension of a word in the Vedic dialect is the declension which is most frequently used and therefore has the approval signature of language use.

The determination of gender recorded in dictionaries is actually a postscript based on language use. If a particular vocable is declined in the Vedic dialect in the feminine gender at one place, in masculine gender in another place and in the neuter gender at a third place, the compiler of a glossary or dictionary has no option but to enter the term as declinable in all three genders. A standard gender use is similarly decided on the basis of how frequently a particular vocable is declined in a particular gender. Ultimately the determination of gender turns out to be a number game. The same applies to the declension of verbal roots which have not been covered in the table here, except occasionally.

Abbreviations

RV - *Ṛgveda Samhitā*
Kā - *Kāṇva (Vājasaneya śukla tajurveda) Samhitā*
Kāṭh - *Kāṭhaka Samhitā*
Kau - *Kauthumīya Sāmaveda Samhitā*
Jai - *Jaiminīya Sāmaaveda Samhitā*
Tai - *Taittirīya (Kṛṣṇa Yajurveda) Samhitā*
Pai - *Paippalāda (Atharvaveda) Samihtā*
Mā - *Mādhyandina (Vājasaneya Śukla Yajurveda) samhitā*
Mai - *Maitrāyaṇī Samhitā*
Śau - *Śaunakīya Atharvaveda Samhitā*

Works Cited

Abhyankar, 1969: Abhyankar, K.V., "Accents in Sanskrit", *Annals of the Bhandarkar Oriental Research Institute*, Vol. 50, pp. 41-55, 1969.

Adams, 1998: Adams, Jonathan, "Did Indo-European Languages Spread before Farming?", *Current Anthropology*, MS 6335, Environmental Sciences Division, Oak Ridge National Laboratory, Oak Ridge, TN 37831, USA, 1998.

Adams, 1998a: The radiocarbon time scale V/s the real time scale, compiled by Adam Jonathan, Environmental Sciences Division, Oak Ridge National Lab. 8, USA, 1998a.

Akishev, 1978: Akishev, K.A., *Kurgan Issyk*, Nauka, Moscow, 1978.

Aliyev *et al*, 1981: Aliyev, I. and Pogrebova, M.N., "On the processes in some Areas of the East Trans-Caucasus and Western Iran in the Late second and Early first Millennium BC", *Ethnic Problem of the History of Central Asia, in the Early Period*, pp. 126-137, 1981.

Allchin & Allchin, 1968: Allchin, B. and Allchin, F.R., *The Birth of Indian Civilization*, Penguin Books, Baltimore, 1968.

Allchin & Allchin, 1982: Allchin, B and Allchin, F.R., *The Rise of Civilization in India and Pakistan*, Cambridge, Cambridge University Press, 1982.

Anthony & Brown, 2000: Anthony, David W. & Brown, Dorcas R., "Eneolithic Horse Exploitation in the Eurasian Steppes, Diet, Ritual and Riding", *Antiquity*, Vol. 74, no. 283, pp. 75-86, March, 2000.

Arnold, 1905/1967: Arnold E.Vernon, *Vedic Metre*, Ch. II (The Popular Ṛgveda), first published Cambridge University Press, 1905, Reprint Motilal Banarsidas Publishers Pvt. Ltd., Delhi, 1967.

Atkinson *et al*, 1987: Atkinson, T.C., "Seasonal Temperatures in Britain during the past 22,000 years, Reconstructed Using Beetle Remains", *Nature* 325, pp. 587-592, 1987.

Barth, 1969: Barth, F.(ed.), *Ethnic Groups and Boundaries*, Introduction, Little, Brown and Company, Boston, 1969.

Barth, 1972: Barth, F. (ed.), "Ethnic Processes on the Pathan-Baluch boundary", *Directions in Sociolinguistics*, pp. 454-464, J.J. Gumperz and D. Hymes, Holt, Rinehart & Winston, New York, 1972.

Bisht, 1989: Bisht R.S., "A New Model of the Harappan Town Planning as Revealed at Dholavira in Kutch, a Surface Study of its Plan and Architecture", *History and Archaeology*, (ed.) B. Chatterjee, pp. 397-408, Ramanand Vidya Bhawan, Delhi, 1989.

Bloch,1920/1970: Bloch, Jules, *The Formation of the Marāthī Language*, French original published in Paris, 1920; translated into English Dev Raj Chanana, Delhi, 1970.

Bokonyi, 1997: Bokonyi, Sandor, "Horse remains from the prehistoric site of Surkotada, Kutch, late third millennium BC", *South Asian Archaeology* 13, 297-307, 1996 and 1997.

Bond *et al*, 1997: Bond, Gerard, William Showers, Maziet Cheseby, Lotti Rusty, Peter Almasi, Peter de Menocal, Paul Priore, Heidi Cullen, Irka Hajdas, and Georges Bonani, "A Pervasive millennial scale cycle in North Atlantic Holocene and Glacial Climate", *Science* 278, 1257-1264, November 14, 1997.

Bongard-Levin and Grantovskij, 1981: Bongard–Levin, G.M., and Grantovskij, E.A., *De La Scythie a l'Inde. Enigmes de l'histoire des anciens Aryens*, French, tr., Ph. Gignoux, Paris, 1981.

Boyce, 1989: Boyce, M., "Avestan people", *Encyclopaedia Iranica*, Vol. III, (ed.) Yarshetar Ehsan, Routledge & Kegan Paul, London & New York, 1989.

Brentjes, 1981: Brentjes, B., "The Mitannians and the peacock", *Ethnic Problems of the History of Central Asia in the Early Period*, pp. 145-148, Moscow, Soviet committee on the study of civilizations of central Asia, 1981.

Broecker, 2000: Broecker, Wallace S., "Was a Change in Thermohaline Circulation Responsible for the Little Ice Age?", *PNAS* (*Proceedings of the National Academy of Sciences*, USA), Vol. 97, Issue 4, pp. 1339-1342, February 15, 2000.

Bromley, 1975: Bromley, Y., *Ethnic Processes in the Soviet Union*, Moscow, 1975; quoted by Renfrew, 1987, Renfrew, A.C., Archaeology and Language, the Puzzle of Indo European Origins, Jonathon Cape, London, 1987; cited in Erdosy, 1989, Erdosy, G., "Ethnicity in the Ṛgveda and its Bearing on the Question of Indo-European Origins", *South Asian Studies*, Vol. 5, pp. 35-42, 1989.

Brooks, 1989: Brooks, Ian A., "Early Holocene Basinal Sediments of the Dakhleh Oasis Region, South Central Egypt", *Quaternary Research*, 32, 139-152, 1989.

Brown, 1994: Brown, Dale M., *Ancient India, Land of Mystery*, Alexandria, Va., Time-Life Books, 1994.

Bryant, 2002: Bryant, Edwin, *The Quest for the Origins of Vedic Culture, The Indo-Aryan Migration Debate*, First published in India, Oxford University Press, New Delhi, 2002.

Bryson *et al*, 1981: Bryson, R.A., & Swain, A.M., "Holocene Variations of Monsoon Rainfall in Rajasthan", *Quaternary Research* 16, pp. 135-145, 1981.

Bubenik, 1996: Bubenik, Vit, *The Structure & Development of Middle Indo-Aryan Dialects*, Ch. 1, Motilal Banarsidas Publishers Pvt. Ltd., Delhi, 1996.

Burrow, 1970: Burrow, T., *The Sanskrit Language*, first published London, 1955, revised edition London, 1970.

Burrow and Emeneau, 1960: Burrow, T. and Emeneau, M.B., *A Dravidian Etymological Dictionary*, Oxford University Press, Amen House, London 1960.

Caland, 1896: Caland, W., *Die altindische Todten und Bestattungsgebräuche, mit Benutzung handschriftlicher Quellen dargestellt*, Verhandelingen der koninklikje Akademie van wetenschappen Te Amsterdam, Afdeeling letterkunde I, 6, Amsterdam, 1896.

Caratini *et al*, 1994: Caratini, C., Bentaleb, I., Fontugne, M., Morzaedec-Korfourn, M.T., Pascal, J.P. and Tissot, C., "A Less Humid Climate since ca. 3500 yr BP from Marine Cores off Karwar, Western India", *Palaeogeography Palaeoclimatology* 109, pp. 371-384, 1994.

Chakrabarti, 2000: Chakrabarti, Dilip K., "The Late Harappans", (ed.) Lahiri, Nayanjot, *The Decline and Fall of the Indus Civilization*, pp. 267-281, Permanent Black, New Delhi, 2000.

Chamberlain, 1899: Chamberlain, H.S, *Die Grundlagen des neunzehnten Jahrhunderts*, Vol. 2, Munchen, Bruckmann, 1899.

Chatterjee and Kumar, 1963: Chatterjee, B.K. & Kumar, G.D., *Comparative Study and Racial analysis of the Human Remains of Indus Valley Civilisation with Particular Reference to Harappa*, W. Newman and Co., Calcutta, 1963.

Childe, 1926: Childe, V.G., *The Aryans, A Study of Indo-European Origins*, Kegan Paul, Trench and Trubner and Co., London, 1926.

Clarke and Fontes, 1990: Clarke, Ian D. & Fontes, Jean-Charles, "Palaeoclimatic Reconstruction in Northern Oman Based on Carbonates from Hyperalkaline Groundwaters", *Quaternary Research*, 33, pp. 320-336, 1990.

Crucifix, 1999: Crucifix, Michel "The Holocene Climate Simulated with a Zonally Averaged Model of Coupled Atmosphere-Ocean-Sea Ice System", *Rapport de recherché presente dans le cadre du Diploma d'Etudes Approfondies en Sciences Physiques*, Conseiller, Pr. Andre Berger, Universite catholique de Louvain, Louvain-la-Neuve,

September, 1999.

Dahl & Nesje, 1996: Dahl, S.O. & Nesje, A., "A New Approach to Calculating Holocene Winter Precipitation by Combining Glacier Equilibrium-line Altitudes and Pine Tree Limits, A case study from Hardangerjokulen, central southern Norway", *The Holocene* 6, pp. 381-398, 1996.

Dales, 1966: Dales, George F., "The Decline of the Harappans", *Scientific American* 214, pp. 93-100, 1966.

Dani & Thapar 1992/1999: Dani, A.H. and Thapar, B.K.,"The Indus Civilization", *History of Civilizations of Central Asia*, Ch. 12, pp. 301-302, vol 1, (ed.) A.H. Dani & V.M. Masson, 1992/1999, UNESCO 1992, first Indian edition, Motilal Banarsidass Publisher Pvt. Ltd., Delhi, 1999.

Darmesteter, 1887/1992: Darmesteter, James, *The Zend-Avesta*, part 1, (The Vendîdād), The Sacred Books of the East, Vol. 4, First published by the Oxford University Press, 1887, Sixth Indian Reprinted, Motilal Banarsidass Publishers Pvt. Ltd., Delhi, 1992.

Demoule, 1980: Demoule, Jean-Paul, "Les Indo-Europeens - Ont-ils existe?", *L'Histoire* 28, pp. 108-120, 1980.

Derevyanko & Dorj, 1992/1999: Derevyanko, A.P. and Dorj, D., "Neolithic Tribes in Northern Parts of Central Asia" *History of Civilizations of Central Asia*, Vol. 1, Ch. 8, pp. 185, (ed.) A. H. Dani & V.M. Masson, 1992/1999, UNESCO 1992, first Indian edition, Motilal Banarsidass Publisher Pvt. Ltd., Delhi, 1999.

Deshpande, 1993: Deshpande, Madhav M., *Sanskrit & Prakrit, Sociolinguistic Issues*, Motilal Banarsidass Publisher Pvt. Ltd., Delhi, 1993.

D'iakonov, 1985: D'iakonov, I.M., "On the Original Home of the Speakers of the Indo-European", *Journal of Indo-European Studies*, Vol. 13, nos. 1-2, pp. 92-174, 1993.

Dolgopolsky, 1989: Dolgopolsky, Aron, "Cultural Contacts of proto-European and Proto-Indo-Iranian with Neighbouring Languages", *Folia Linguistica Historica*, Vol. 8, nos. 1-2, pp. 3-36, 1989.

Elphinstone, 1819: Elphinstone, Montstuart, *An Account of the Kingdom of Cabul and its Dependcies in Persia, Tartary and India, Comprising a View of the Afghan Nation and a History of Dooranee Monarchy*, Vol. 2, Longman, Hurst and Ree, Orm and Brown & John Murray, London, 1819.

Enault, 1979: Enault, Jean-Francois, *Fouilles de Pirak*. 2 Vols. Paris, Publications de la Commission des Fouilles Archaeologique, Fouilles du Pakistan, No. 2, Vol. 2, 1979.

Erdosy, 1989: Erdosy, G., "Ethnicity in the Ṛgveda and its bearing on the Problem of Indo-European origins", *South Asian Studies* 5, pp. 35-47, London, 1989.

Esteller, 1968: Esteller, A., "Problems in the Text-Critical Reconstruction of the Ṛgveda-palimpsest", *Annals of the Bhandarkar Oriental Research Institute,* Vols.48-49, pp. 1-16, 1968.

Farhādī, 1985: Farhādī, R., "Afghanistan", *Encyclopaedia Iranica,* Vol. 1, ed. Ehsan Yarshater, Routledge and Kegan Paul, London & New York, 1985.

Farmer *et al*, 2004: Farmer, S., Sproat, R. and Witzel, M., "The Collapse of Indus-Script Thesis, The Myth of a Literate Harappan Civilization", *Electronic Journal of Vedic Studies,* Vol.11, pp.19-57, December 13, 2004.

Foley *et al*, 1994: Foley, J.A., Kutzbach, J.E., Coe, M.T., Levis, S., "Effects of Boreal Forest Vegetation on the Global Climate", *Nature* 371, pp. 52-54, 1994.

Frankfort, 1992: Frankfort, Henry-Paul, "New Data Illustrating the Early Contacts Between Central Asia and the North-West of the Subcontinent", *South Asian Archaeology,* 1989, Papers from the Tenth International Conference of South Asian Archaeologists in Western Europe, Musee national des Arts asiatiques—Guimet, Paris, France, July 3-7, (ed.) Catherine Jarrige with the assistance of John P. Gerry and Richard H. Meadow, Prehistory Press, Madison Wisconsin, pp. 97-102, 1992.

Galili *et al*, 1988: Galili, E, Weinstein-Evron, M., and Ronen, A., "Holocene Sea-Level Changes Based on Submerged Archaeological Sites off the Northern Carmel Coast in Israel", *Quaternary Research* 29, pp. 36-42, 1988.

Gamkrelidze and Ivanov, 1983: Gamkrelidze, Thomas, V., and Ivanov, Vjaceslav V., "The Ancient Near East and the Indo-European Problem, Temporal and Territorial Characteristics of Proto-Indo-European based on Linguistic and Historic-Cultural Data", *Soviet Studies in History,* Vol. 22, pp. 7-52; "The Migration of Tribes Speaking the Indo-Europeans Dialects from Their Original Homeland in the Near East to Their Habitations in Eurasia", *Soviet Studies in History,* Vol. 22, pp. 53-95, 1983.

Ganopolski *et al*, 1998: Ganopolski, A., Kubatzki, C., Claussen, M., Brovkin, V. and Petoukhov, V., "The Influence of vegetation –Atmosphere-Ocean Interaction on Climate during the Mid-Holocene", *Science* 280, pp. 1916-1919, 1998.

Gasse and Campo, 1994: Gasse, F., & Campo, Van E., "Abrupt post glacial Climate Events in the west Asia and North African

Monsoon Domains", *Earth and Planetary Science Letters* 126, pp. 435-456, 1994.

Genning, 1979: Genning, V.F., "The Cemetery at Sintashta and the Early Indo-Iranian Peoples" *Journal of Indo-European Studies* 7, pp. 1-29, 1979.

Ghosh *et al*, 1979: Ghosh B., Kar, A. and Hussain, Z., "The Lost Courses of the Saraswati River in the Great Indian Desert, New Evidence from Landsat Imagery", *Geographical Journal* 145(3), pp. 446-451, 1979.

Ghosh, 1989: Ghosh, B., "Cultures", *Encylopaedia of Indian Archaeology,* vol. 1, Ch. 4, Munshiram Manoharlal Publishers Pvt. Ltd., New Delhi, 1989.

Ghosh, 1989: Ghosh, A., *An Encyclopaedia of Indian Archaeology,* Vol. I, p. 317, Indian Council of Historical Research, New Delhi, 1989.

Giddens, 1997: Giddens, Anthony, *Sociology*, Polity Press, Cambridge, UK, 1997.

Gillespie *et al*, 1983: Gillespie, R., F.A. and Switzur, R., "Post Glacial arid Episodes in Ethiopia, Implications for Climate Prediction", *Nature* 306, pp. 680-683, 1983.

Gills *et al*, 1993: Gills, Barry K. and Frank, Andre Gunder, "World System Cycles, Crises and Hegemonic Shifts, 1700 BC to 1700 AD", *The World System*, Ch. 5, (ed) Frank, A.G. and Gills, B.K., Routledge, London and New York, 1993.

Gimbutas, 1956: Gimbutas, Marija, "The Neolithic, Chalcolithic and Copper Ages in the North Pontic Area", *The Prehistory of Eastern Europe, Mesolithic, Neolithic and Copper Age Cultures in Russia and the Baltic Area,* Part I, (American School of Prehistory Research Peabody Museum, Harvard University, Bulletin No. 20, (ed.) Hugh Hencken), Ch. 3, Cambridge, Massachusetts, USA, published by The Peabody Museum, 1956.

Gimbutas, 1966: Gimbutas, M., "Proto-Indo-European Culture—The Kurgan Culture during the Fifth, Fourth, and Third Millennia B.C.", *Indo-European and Indo-Europeans,* (ed.) George Cordona, Henry Hoenigswald, and Alfred Senn, Philadelphia, University of Pennsylvania Press, pp. 155- 197, 1966.

Giraudi, 1989: Giraudi, C., "Lake-levels and Climate for the Last 30,000 Years in the Fucino Area (Abruzzo-central Italy) A Review", *Palaeogeography, Palaeoclimatology, Palaeoecology* 70, pp. 249-260, 1989.

Gnoli, 1989: Gnoli G., *The Idea of Iran*, Serie Orientale Roma, Istituto Italiano Per II Medio ed Estremo Oriente, 1989.

Gnoli, 1989A: Gnoli G., "Avestan Geography", *Encyclopaedia Iranica,* (ed.) Ehsan Yarshater, Vol. III, pp.44-47, Routledge & Kegan Paul, London and New York, 1989A.

Gonda, 1959: Gonda, J., *Epithets in The Ṛgveda*, Mouton and Co., The Hague, Netherlands, 1959.

Gonda, 1977 : Gonda, J., *Hymns of the Ṛgveda not employed in the Solemn Ritual*, Chs. 5 & 7, Amsterdam, Oxford, New York, 1977.

Grierson, 1907-1909: Grierson, G., *The Imperial Gazetteer of India, The Indian Empire*, Vol. I, Oxford, Clarendon Press, 1907-1909.

Griffith, 1973: Griffith, R.T.H., *The Hymns of the Ṛgveda*, Ch. 5, first pub. 1889, compact second edition 1896, Kotagiri, Nilgiri; revised edition, Delhi, 1973.

Guha and Chatterjee, 1946: Guha, B.S. and Chatterjee B.K., "Report on Skeletal Remains" Part 2 of "A Chalcolithic Site in Northern Baluchistan", *Journal of Near Eastern Studies* 5 (4), (ed.) E. J. Ross., 1946.

Guha, 1935: Guha, B. S., "The Racial Affinities of the Peoples of India", *Census of India*, Vol. 1.3A, pp. 1-116, Government of India Press, Simla, 1935.

Guiot *et al*, 1993: Guiot, J., Harrison, S., & Colin Prentice I., "Reconstruction of Holocene Precipitation Patterns in Europe using Pollen and Lake-Level data", *Quaternary Research* 40, pp. 139-149, 1993.

Gupta and Ramchandran, 1976: Gupta, S. P., & Ramchandran, K.S., *Mahabhartha—Myth or Reality, Differing Views*, Agam Kala Prakashan, Delhi, 1976.

Hankins, 1948: Hankins, Frank H., "Aryans", *Encyclopedia of the Social Sciences*, 1948.

Harmatta, 1992/1999: Harmatta, J., "The Emergence of the Indo-Iranians, The Indo-Iranian languages", *History of Civilizations of Central Asia*, Vol. I, (ed) A.H. Dani and V.M. Masson, 1992/1999 (UNESCO 1992, first Indian edition, Motilal Banarsidass Publishers Pvt. Ltd., Delhi, 1999.)

Harrison *et al*, 1996: Harrison P.sandy, Yu Ge & Tarasov, Pavel E., "Late Quaternary Lake Level Record from Northern Eurasia", *Quaternary Research* 45, pp. 138-159, 1996.

Hegel, 1817: Hegel, G.W.F., *Encyclopedia of the Philosophical Sciences*, A. Osswald, Heidelberg, 1817.

Hemphill *et al*, 1991: Hemphill, B.E., Lukacks, J.R., and Kennedy, K.A.R., "Biological Adaptations and affinities of the Bronze Age Harappans", *Harappa excavations 1986-1990: A Multidisciplinary Approach to Third Millennium Urbanism*, (ed.) R. Meadow, pp. 137-182, Madison, Prehistory Press. 1991.

Hemphill *et al*, 1991A: Hemphill, Brian E. & Lukacs, John R., "Hegelian

Logic and the Harappan Civilization, An Investigation of Harappan Biological Affinities in Light of Recent Biological and Archaeological Research", *South Asian Archaeology,* (ed.) Adalbert J. Gail and Gerd J.R. Mevissen (Stuttgart, Steiner, 1993), 1991A.

Henning, 1947: Henning, W.B., "Two Manichaean Magical Texts", *Bulletin of the School of Oriental and African Studies,* 27, 1947.

Henry 1989: Henry, D.O., *From Foraging to Agriculture: The Levant at the end of the Ice age.* Philadelphia: U of Pennsylvania Press, 1989.

Hillebrandt, 1891/1990: Hillebrandt, Alfred,*Vedic Mythology,* first edition 3 Vols., Breslau, 1891, 1899, 1902, translated from the original German by Sreeramula Rajeswara Sarma, Vol. 1, first English language edition, Delhi, 1980, reprinted by Motilal Banarsidass Publishers Pvt. Ltd., 1990.

Hock, 1993: Hock, Hans Henrich, "Subversion or Convergence? The Issue of Pre-Vedic Retroflexion Reexamined", *Studies in the Linguistic Sciences* 23, No. 2, pp. 73-115, 1993.

Hodge, 1981: Hodge, Carleton T., "Indo-Europeans in the Near East", *Anthropological Linguistics* 23, pp. 227-244, 1981.

Hoernle, 1880: Hoernle, A.F.R., *A Grammar of the Eastern Hindi Compared with Other Gaudian Languages,* Trubner, London, 1880.

Hoffmann, 1975: Hoffmann, K., *Der Injunktiv zu Indoiranistik, Band 1,* (ed.) J. Narten, Wiesbaden, Reichert, (cited by Witzel, 1995/1997: Witzel, M., "Ṛgvedic history, Poets Chieftains and Polities" (ed.) George Erdossy, *The Indo-Aryans of Ancient South Asia,* Ch. 14, pp. 307-340, First published, Walter de Gruyter & Co. Berlin, 1995, First Indian edition, Munshiram Manoharlal Publishers Pvt. Ltd. Delhi, 1997), 1975.

Hoffmann, 1989: Hoffmann K., "Avestan Language", *Encyclopaedia Iranica,* Vol. III, pp. 47-62, (ed.) Yarshater Ehsan, Routledge & Kegan Paul, London & New York, 1989.

Humbach *et al,* 1991: Humbach, H., *The Gāthās of Zarathustra and the Other Old Avestan Texts,* Vol. 2, Heidelberg, Carl Winter Universitatsverlag, 1991.

Huntley & Birks, 1983: Huntley B. & Birks H.J.B., *An Atlas of Past and Present Pollen Maps for Europe: 0-13,000 years ago,* Cambridge University Press, Cambridge, 1983.

Jacobi, 1909: Jacobi, H., "On the Antiquity of the Vedic Culture", *Journal of the Royal Asiatic Society,* pp. 721-726, 1909.

Jacobi, 1910: Jacobi, H., "The Antiquity of the Vedic Culture." *Journal of the Royal Asiatic Society,* pp. 456-467, 1910.

Jarrige, 1984: Jarrige, Jean-Francois, "Continuity and Change in the North Kachi plain (Baluchistan, Pakistan) at the Beginning of the

Second Millennium BC", *South Asian Archaeology,* (ed.) Janine Schotsmans and Maurizio Taddei, pp. 35-68, Instituto Universitario Orientale, Naples, 1984.

Jones, 1789: Jones, Sir William, "Third Anniversary Discourse, On the Hindus", *Asiatic Researches* 1, pp. 414-432, 1789.

Jones, 1790: Jones, William, "On the Chronology of the Hindu", *Asiatic Researches,* Vol. 2, pp. 111-147, 1790a, "A supplement to the essay on the Indian Chronology", *Asiatic Researches,* Vol. 2, pp. 391-403, 1790b.

Keerthi Kumar, 1999: Keerthi Kumar, V., *Discovery of Dravidian as the Common Source of Indo-European— A Linguistic Monograph,* 1999.

Keith, 1921: Keith, A. B., "The Age of the Ṛgveda," *The Cambridge History of India,* Vol 1, (ed.) E.J. Rapson, Cambridge University Press, Cambridge, 1921.

Keith, 1920/1998: Keith, Arthur Berriedale, *Ṛigveda Brāhmaṇas, The Aitareya and Kausītakī Brāhmaṇas of the Ṛigveda,* first edition, London, 1920, reprinted, Motilal Banarsidass Publishers Pvt. Ltd., Delhi, 1971, 1981, 1998.

Kennedy, 1984: Kennedy K.A.R., "Trauma and Disease in the Ancient Harappans", *Frontiers of the Indus Civilization,* pp. 425-436, (ed.) B.B. Lal and S.P. Gupta, Archaeological Survey of India, New Delhi, 1984.

Kennedy, 1995/1997: Kennedy, K.A.R., "Have Aryans Been Identified in the Prehistoric Skeletal Record from South Asia?", *The Indo-Aryans of Ancient South Asia,* (ed.) George Erdosy, pp. 24-35, first published Berlin, 1995, reprinted in India, New Delhi, 1997.

Kenoyer, 1998: Kenoyer, Jonathan Mark, *Ancient Cities of the Indus Valley Civilization,* Ch. 2, American Institute of Pakistan Studies, Oxford University Press, Oxford, 1998.

Klejn, 1984: Klejn, L.S., "The Indo-Aryans: Who and Where", *Bulletin of the Deccan College Postgraduate Research Institute,* 43, pp. 57-72, 1984.

Kohl, 1984: Kohl, Philip L., "Central Asia, and Palaeolithic Beginnings to the Iron Age", *Synthese* No. 14. Paris, Editions Recherche sur les Civilizations (Cited In George Erdossy), *Indo Aryans of Ancient South Asia,* Ch. I, Berlin, 1995, (First Indian edition New Delhi, 1997), 1984.

Kuiper, 1948: Kuiper, F.B.J., *Proto-Munda Words in Sanskrit,* Noord-Hollandische Uitgevers Maatschappij, Amsterdam, 1948.

Kuiper, 1955: Kuiper, F.B.J., "Ṛgvedic loanwords", *Studia Indologica, Fesrchrift fur W. kirfel zur vollendung seines 70 Lebensjahres,* Bonner Orietalischie Studien, Neue serie, Band 3, (ed.) O. Spies, pp. 137-

185, Bonn, Selbstverlag der Orientalischen Seminars der universitat Bonn, 1955.

Kuiper, 1962: Kuiper, F.B.J., *Nahali, A Comparative Study*, Noord-Hollandische Uitgevers Maatschappij, Amsterdam, 1962.

Kuiper, 1967: Kuiper, F.B.J., "The Genesis of a Linguistic Area", *Indo-Iranian Journal* 10, pp. 81-102, 1967.

Kuiper; 1991: Kuiper, F.B.J., *Aryans in the Ṛgveda*, Amsterdam-Atlanta, Rodopi, 1991.

Kumar, 1973: Kumar, G.D., "The Ethnic Components of the Builders of the Indus Valley Civilization and the Advent of the Aryans", *Journal of Indo-European Studies* 1, pp. 66-80, 1973.

Kurochkin, 1990: Kurochkin, G.N., "Zolotoj Sosud iz Marlika", *Sovietskaya Arkheologiya*, pp. 41-50, 1990.

Kurochkin, 1994: Kurochkin, G.N., "Archaeological Search for the Near Eastern Aryans and the Royal Cemetery of Marlik in Northern Iran", in *South Asian Archaeology* 1993. Annales Academia Scienticarum Fennieae Series B, 271, edited by A Parpola and P. Koskikallio Helsinki, Suomalainen Tiedeakatemia, 1994.

Kutzbach *et al*, 1993: Kutzbach, J.E., Guetter, P.J., Behling, P.J., and selin, R., "Simulated climatic changes, Results of the COHMAP climate—model experiments", *Global Climates Since the Last Glacial maximum*, (ed.) H.E.Wright, Jr., J.E. Kutzabach, T. webb, III, W.F. Ruddiman, F.A. Street- Perrot, and P.J. Bartlein, pp. 24-93, University of Minnesota Press, Minneapolis, 1993.

Kuz'mina, 1986: Kuz'mina, E., *Drevnejöie skotovody ot urala do Tjan'-Sana.* Ilim, Frunze, 1986.

Lahiri, 1992: Lahiri, N., *The Archaeology of Indian Trade Routes*, Delhi, 1992.

Lamb, 1982: Lamb, H.H., *Climate, History and the Modern World*, London, 1982.

Lambrick, 1967: Lambrick, H.T., "The Indus Flood Plain and the 'Indus' Civilization", *The Decline and Fall of the Indus Civilization*, (ed.) Lahiri, Nayanjot, pp. 167-187, Permanent Black, New Delhi, 2000, first published in *Geographical Journal* 1, Vol. 133, pp. 483-495, 1967.

Landmann *et al*, 1996: Landmann, G., Reimer, A. and Kempe, S., "Climatically induced lake-level changes at Lake Van, Turkey during the Pleistocene/Holocene transition", *Global Biogeochemical Cycles*, Vol. 10, pp. 797-808, 1996.

Levi, 1915: Levi, S. "Le Catalogue Geographique Des Yaksa Dans La Mahamayuri", *JA* 5, 1915.

MacDonald *et al*, 2000: MacDonald, Glen M., Andri, A.V., Constantine V. Kremenetski, Olga K. Borisova, Aleksandra A. Goleva, Andrei A. Andreev, Les C. Cwynar, Richard T. Riding, Steven L. Forman,

Tom W.D. Edwards, Ramon Aravena, Dan Hammarlund, Julian M. Szeicz, Valery N. Gattaulin, "Holocene Treeline History and climate Change Across Northern Eurasia", *Quaternary Research*, Vol. 53, pp. 302-311, University of Washington, 2000.

Macdonell and Keith, 1912: Macdonell, A.A. & Keith, A.B., *The Vedic Index*, 1912.

Macdonell, 1916/1993: MacDonell, A.A., *A Vedic Grammar for Students*, first published Clarendon Press, Oxford, 1916, first Indian edition, Motilal Banarsidass Publishers Pvt. Ltd., Delhi, 1993.

Magni, 1993: Magni, Michel, "Solar Influences on Holocene Climatic Changes Illustered by Correlations between Past Lake-Level Fluctuations and the Atmospheric C^{14} Record", *Quaternary Research*, 40, pp. 1-9, 1993.

Majumdar and Pusalker, 1951: Majumdar, R.C. and Pusalker, A.D., *The Vedic Age*, Ch. XII, Bhartiya Vidya Bhavan Series on History and Culture of the Indian People, Bombay, 1951.

Malandra, 1971: Malandra, W.W., *The Farvardîn Yast, Introduction, Text, Translation and Commentary*, Ph.D. Ann Arbor, University of Pennsylvania, Michigan, 1971.

Mallory, 1989: Mallory, J.P., *Search of the Indo-Europeans, Language, Archaeology and Myth*, Thames and Hudson, London, 1989.

Mandel'shtam, 1968: Mandel'shtam, A.M., "Pamyatniki epokhi bronzy V juzhnom tadzhikistane", *Materially I isledovaniya po arkheologii SSSR* 145, Leningrad, Nauka, 1968.

Marlow, 1974: Marlow, Elli Pudas, "More on the Uralo-Dravidian Relationship, A Comparison of Uralic and Dravidian Etomological Vocabularies", unpublished Ph.D. Disseration, University of Texas, Austin, Texas, 1974.

Marshall, 1931: Marshall, J.H., *Mohenjodaro and the Indus Civilization*, 3 vols, London, 1931.

Masson, 1992/1999: Masson, V.M., "The Bronze Age in Khorasan and Transoxania", *History of Civilizations of Central Asia*, (ed.) Dani A.H. and Masson V.M., Vol. 1, Ch. 10; "The Decline of the Bronze Age Civilization and movements of the tribes", *History of Civilizaton of Central Asia*, (ed.) Dani A.H. and Masson V.M., Vol. I, Ch. 14, pp. 337-356, 1992/1999 (UNESCO 1992, first Indian edition, Motilal Banarsidass Publishers Pvt. Ltd., Delhi, 1999.)

McAlpine, 1974: McAlpine, D.W., "Towards proto-Elamo-Dravidian", *Language* 50, pp. 89-101, 1974.

Meadow, 1979: Meadow, Richard H., "A Preliminary Report on the Faunal Remains from Pirak", *Fouilles de Pirak*, (ed.) Jean-Francois Jarrige and M. Santoni, Vol. 1, No. 2, Publications de la

Commission des, Fouilles Archaeologiques, Fouilles du Pakistan, 1979.

Mehendale, 1975: Mehendale, M.A., "The Ṛgvedasamhitākāra and Father Esteller", *Bulletin of the Deccan College Research Institute,* Vol. 35, Nos. 1-2, pp.97-116, 1975.

Middleton, 1967: Middleton, J. *Myth and Cosmos,* Introduction, ix-xi, Natural History Press, Garden City, Long Island, 1967.

Mills, 1887/1988: Mills, L.H., *The Zend-Avesta,* Part iii (The Yasna, Visparad, Āfrīnagān, Gāhs, and Miscellaneous Fragments), Sacred Books of The East, Vol. 31, First Published by the Oxford University Press, London, 1887, Fifth Indian Reprint, Motilal Banarsidass Publishers Pvt. Ltd., Delhi, 1988.

Misra, 1977: Misra, Satya Swarup, *The Laryngeal Theory—A Critical Evaluation,* Varanasi, Chaukhambha, Orientalia, 1977.

Misra, 1992: Misra, Satya Swarup, *The Aryan Problem—A Linguistic Approach,* New Delhi, Munshiram Manoharlal s Publishers Pvt. Ltd., 1992.

Misra, 1994: Misra, Satya Swarup, *New Lights on the Indo-European Comparative Grammar,* Sharada, Delhi, 1994.

Misra, 1989: Misra V.N., "Human Adaptation to the Changing landscape of the Indian Arid Zone During the Quaternary Period", *Old Problems and New Perspective in the Archaeology of South Asia,* (ed.) J.M. Kenoyer, Wisconsin Archaeological Reports, Vol. 2, pp. 3-17, 1989.

Misra, 1994: Misra V.N., "Indus Civilization and the Ṛgvedic Sarasvati", *South Asian Archaeology,* (ed.) Parpola, A. and Koskikallio, P., pp. 511-524, Helsinki, 1994.

Mughal, 1992: Mughal, M.R., "The Consequences of River Changes for the Harappan Settlements in Cholistan", *Eastern Anthropologist,* Vol. 45, Nos. 1 & 2, (Reprinted in *The Decline and Fall of the Indus Civilization,* (ed.) Lahiri, Nayanjot, Permanent Black, New Delhi, 2000), 1992.

Muir, 1860: Muir, J., *Original Sanskrit Texts,* Truber, London, 1860.

Müller, 1859: Müller, F. Max, *History of Ancient Sanskrit Literature,* Williams and Norgate, London, 1859.

Müller, 1888: Müller, F. Max, *Biographies of Words and Home of the Aryans,* Longmans Green Longmans and Roberts, London, 1888.

Müller, 1890-92/1966: Müller, F. Max, *Ṛgveda-Samhitā* (The Sacred Hymns of the Brāhmaṇas together with the Commendary of Sāyanākārya), Vols I-IV, Oxford University Press Warehouse, Amen Corner, London, 1890-92, Second Edition, (Reprinted in India), Chowkhamba Sanskrit Series Office, Benaras, 1966.

Naidu, 1998: Naidu, Pothuri Divaker, "Rapid Climatic Shifts and its Influence on Ancient Civilizations, Evidence from Marine Records", *The Indian Human Heritage*, (ed.) Balasubramanin, D. & Rao, N Appaji University press (India) limited, Hyderabad (A.P), 1998.

Nandi, 1993: Nandi, R.N. "Archaeology and the Ṛgveda", *The Indian Historical Review*, Vol. XVI, 1993.

Nandi, 2001: Nandi, R.N., *Aryans Revisited*, Munshi Ram Manoharlal Publishers Pvt. Ltd., New Delhi, 2001.

Nath, 1959: Nath, B., "Remains of the Horse and Indian Elephant from the Protohistoric Site of Harappa (West Pakistan)", *Proceedings of the First All-India Congress of Zoologists*, Part- 2, pp. 1-14, Scientific Papers, 1959.

Nath, 1968: Nath, B., "Animal Remains from Rupar and Bara sites, Ambala District, East Punjab", *Indian Museum Bulletin* 3 (1-2), pp. 69-115, 1968.

Nath and Rao, 1985: Nath, Bhola and Rao, G.V. Sreenivasa, "Animal Remains from Lothal Excavations", *Memoirs of the Archaeological Survey of India* 78, Vol. 2, pp. 636-650, 1985.

Negahban, 1964: Negahban, E.O., "A Brief Report on the Excavation of Marlik Tepe and Pileh Qraleh", *Iran* 2, pp. 13-19, 1964.

Nichols, 1997: Nichols, Johanna, "The Epicentre of the Indo- European Linguistic Spread", *Archaeology and Language* 1, (ed.) Roger Blench and Matthew Spriggs, pp. 122-148; "The Eurassian Spread Zone and the Indo-European Dispersal", *Archaeology and Language*, (ed.) Roger Blench and Matthew Spriggs, Vol. 2, Routledge, London, 1997.

Norman, 1995/1997: Norman, Kenneth R., "Dialect Variation in Old and Middle Indo-Aryan", *The Indo-Aryans of Ancient South Asia*, (ed.) George Erdosy, Ch. 12, (first published by Walter de Gruyter & Co., Berlin, 1995), First Indian edition by Munshiram Manoharlal Publishers Pvt. Ltd., New Delhi, 1997.

O'Dea, 1969: O'Dea, Thomas F., *The Sociology of Religion*, Prentice of India Private Limited, New Delhi, 1969, (first published, 1966, New Jersey, USA).

Oldenberg, 1890/1962: Oldenberg, Hermann., *Ancient India, its Language and Religions*, (Originally published in *Deutsche Randschau*, Berlin, 1890) English edition, Calcutta, 1962.

Oldham, 1893: Oldham, C. F., "The Saraswatī and the Lost River of the Indian Desert", *Journal of the Royal Asiatic Society* 25, pp. 49-76, 1893.

Papajian, 1985: Papajian, H., "Armenia and Iran", *Encyclopaedia Iranica*, vol. II, (ed.) Ehsan Yarshater, Routledge & Kegan Paul, London & New York, 1985.

Parpola, 1995/1997: Parpola Asko, "The Problem of the Aryans and the Soma-Textual-linguistic and Archaeological Evidence", *The Indo-Aryans of Ancient South Asia,* (ed.) George Erdosy, first published by Walter de Gruyter & Co., Berlin, 1995, First Indian edition by Munshiram Manoharlal Publishers Pvt. Ltd., New Delhi, 1997.

Peiser, 1997: Peiser, Benny J., "Comparative Stratigraphy of Late Holocene Sediments & Destruction Layers Around the World, Geological, Climatological and Archaeological Evidence and Methodological Problems", *The Proceedings of the Second SIS Cambridge Conference on Natural Catastrophes During Bronze Age Civilizations, Archaeological, Geological, Astronomical and Cultural Perspectives,* A conference held at Fitzwilliam College, Cambridge, Organized by The Society for Interdisciplinary Studies, 11th-13th July 1997.

Piggott, 1983: Piggott, S., *The Earliest Wheeled Transport from the Atlantic Coast to the Caspian Sea,* pp. 241-242, Thames & Hudson, London, 1983.

Poliakov, 1974: Poliakov, L., *The Aryan Myth,* Basic Books, New York, 1974.

Possehl, 1967: Possehl, Gregory L., "The Mohenjodaro Floods—A Reply", *American Anthropologist* 69, pp. 32-40, 1967.

Possehl, 1999: Possehl, Gregory L., *Indus Age, The Beginnings,* Oxford & IBH Publishing Co. Pvt. Ltd., New Delhi, Calcutta, 1999.

Prasad, 1936: Prasad, B., "Animal Remains from Harappa", *Memoirs of the Archaeological Survey of India* 51, Delhi, 1936.

Raikes, 1964: Raikes, Robert L., "The End of the Ancient Cities of the Indus", *American Anthropologist* 66, pp. 284-299, 1964.

Raikes, 1979: "The Mohenjodaro Floods, the Debate Continues", *South Asian Archaeology,* (ed.) M. Taddei, pp.561-566, Ist. University Orientale, Naples, 1979.

Raja, 1935: Raja C.K., *Ṛgveda Bhāṣya of Skandasvāmin* (First Aṣṭakā), Madras, 1935.

Renan, 1863: Renan, J.E., *La Vie de jesus,* M.Levy, Paris, 1863.

Renfrew, 1987: Renfrew, C., *Archaeology and Language, the Puzzle of Indo European Origins,* Jonathon Cape, London, 1987.

Renfrew, 1999: Renfrew, C., "Time Depth, Convergence Theory, and Innovation in Proto-Indo-Europeans, 'Old Europe' as a PIE Linguistic Area", *Journal of Indo-Europeans Studies* 27 (3-4), pp. 258-293, 1999.

Roberts, 1977: Roberts, T.J., *The Mammals of Pakistan,* Ernest Benn Limited, London, 1977.

Rossignol-Strick & Planchais, 1989: Rossignol-Strick M. & Planchais N., "Climate Patterns Revealed by Pollen and Oxygen Isotope Records of a Tyrrenian Sea Core", *Nature* 342, pp. 413-416, 1989.

Rossignol, 1995: Rossignol-Strick, M., "Sea-Land Correlation of Pollen Records in the Eastern Mediterranean for the Glacial-Interglacial transition, biostratigraphy versus radiometric time-scale", *Quaternary Science Review,* Vol. 14, pp. 893-915, 1995.

Sahni, 1920-21: Sahni, Rai Bahadur Daya Ram, "Excavations at Harappa", *Annual Progress Report of the Superintendent, Hindu and Buddhist Monuments, Northern Circle,* pp.8-26, Civil and Military Gazette Press, 31st March 1921, Lahore, 1920-21.

Sankalia, 1974: Sankalia, H.D., *The Prehistory and Protohistory of India & Pakistan,* Ch. II, Deccan College, Postgraduate and Research Institute, Poona, 1974.

Sarup, 1920-27/1984: Sarup, Lakshman, *The Nighantu and the Nirukta,* first published: 1920-27, Reprinted Motilal Banarasidass Publishers Pvt. Ltd., 1984.

Sastri, 1965: Sastri, K.N., *New Light on the Indus Civilization,* Vol. 2, Atma Ram and Sons, Delhi, 1965.

Schlegel, 1808: Schlegel, F., *Essay on the Language and Wisdom of the Indians* 2, Mohr and Zimmer, Heidelberg, 1808.

Schmitt, 1974: Schmitt, Rudiger, "Proto-Indo-European Culture and Archaeology—Some Critical Remarks." *Journal of Indo-European Studies* 2, 1974.

Sewell and Guha, 1931: Sewell, R.B. Seymour and B.S. Guha, "Zoological Remains", *Mohenjodaro and the Indus Civilization,* (ed.) Sir John Marshall, Vol. 3, pp. 649-73, Arthur Probsthain, London, 1931.

Shaffer, 1983: Shaffer Jim G., "The Indo-Aryan Invasions, Cultural Myth and Archaeological Reality", *South Asian Archaeology,* (ed.) Janine Schotsmans and Maurizio Taddei, Vol. 1, pp.77-89, Instituto Universitario Orientale, Naples, 1983.

Shaffer, 1995/1997: Shaffer, Jim G., "The Concepts of 'Cultural tradition' and 'Palaeothnicity' in South Asian Archaeology", *The Indo-Aryans of Ancient South Asia,* (ed.) George Erdosy, pp. 126-154, first pub. Berlin, 1995, reprinted in India, New Delhi, 1997.

Shaffer & Lichtenstein, 1989: Shaffer, Jim G. and Lichtenstein, Diane, A. "Ethnicity and Change in the Indus Valley Cultural Tradition", *Old Problems and New Perspectives in the Archaeology of South Asia,* (ed.) Jonathan Mark Kenoyer, Vol. 2, Ch. 12, Wisconsin

Archaeological Reports, 1989.

Shaffer & Thapar 1992/1999: Shaffer, J.G. and Thapar, B.K., "Pre-Indus and Early Indus Cultures of Pakistan and India", *History of Civilizations of Central Asia*, (ed.) A. H. Dani & V. M. Masson, Ch. 11, Vol. 1, 1992/1999 (UNESCO 1992, first Indian edition, Motilal Banarsidass Publishers Pvt. Ltd., Delhi, 1999).

Sharma, 1990: Sharma, A.K., "Animal Bone Remains", *Memoirs of the Archaeological Survey of India* 87, (ed.) Jagat Pati Joshi, (Excavation at Surkotada 1971-72 and Exploration in Kutch), pp. 372-383, 1990.

Sheveroskin, 1987: Sheveroskin, Vitaly, "Indo-European Homeland and Migrations", *Folia Linguistica Historica,* Vol. 7, pp. 227-250, 1987.

Sissons, 1979: Sissons, J.B., "The Loch Lomond Stadial in the British Isles", *Nature* 280, pp. 199-203, 1979.

Skjaervo, 1995/1997: Skjaervo, P. Oktor, "The Avesta as Source for the Early History of the Iranians", *The Indo-Aryans of Ancient South Asia, Language, Material Culture and Ethnicity*, (ed.) George Erdosy, first published by Walter de Gruyter & Co., Berlin, 1995, first Indian edition by Munshiram Manoharlal Publishers Pvt. Ltd., New Delhi, 1997.

Smith, 1919: Smith, V.A., *The Oxford History of India*, 1919

Southworth, 1990: Southworth, Franklin C., "The Reconstruction of Prehistoric South Asian Language Contact ", *The Uses of Linguistic,* (ed.) Edward Bendix, pp. 207-234, New York Academy of Sciences, New York, 1990.

Southworth, 1995/1997: Southworth, F.C., "Reconstructing social context from language, Indo-Aryan and Dravidian Prehistory," *The Indo-Aryans of Ancient South Asia*, (ed.) George Erdosy, pp. 258-277, First published, Walter de Gruyter & Co. Berlin, 1995, First Indian edition, Munshiram Manoharlal Publishers Pvt. Ltd. Delhi, 1997.

Spate and Learmouth, 1967: Spate, O.H.K. and Learmouth, A.T.A., *India and Pakistan, A General and Regional Geography*, London, 1967.

Srivastava *et al*, 1998: Srivastava, Pankaj, Parkash Brahma & Pal Dilip K. "Clay Minerals in Soils as Evidence of Holocene Climatic Change, Central Indo-Gangetic Plains, North Central India", *Quaternary Research* 50, pp. 230-239, 1998.

Stack-Kane, 1989: Stack-Kane, Victoria, "Animal Remains from Rojdi.", *Harappan Civilization and Rojdi,* (ed.) Gregory L. Possehl and M.H. Raval, Oxford & IBH Pub. Co. Pvt. Ltd., New Delhi, 1989.

Stager & Mayewski, 1997: Stager, J.C. and. Mayewski P.A, "Abrupt Early to Mid-Holocene Climatic Transition Registered at the

Equator and the Poles", *Science* 276, pp. 1834-1836, 1997.

Starkel, 1991: Starkel L., "Environmental Changes at the Younger Dryas –Preboreal Transition and During the Early Holocene: Some distinctive aspects in central Europe", *The Holocene,* Vol. 1, pp. 234-242, 1991.

Stuiver, 1965: Stuiver, M., "Carbon 14 content of 18th and 19th century wood, variations correlated with sunspot activity", *Science* 149, pp. 533-535, 1965.

Sulimirski, 1985: Sulimirski T., "The Scyths", *The Cambridge History of Iran*, Vol. 2, pp. 149-199, Cambridge University Press, Cambridge, 1985.

Swadesh, 1972: Swadesh, M, *The Origin and Diversifaction of Language,* Ed. J. Sherzer, 1972.

Swain et al., 1983: Swain, A.M., Kutzbach, J.E. and Hastenrath, S., "Estimates of Holocene Precipitation for Rajasthan, India, Based on Pollen and Lake-Level Data", *Quaternary Research* 19, pp. 1-17, University of Wisconsin, Wisconsin, 1983.

Talageri, 2000: Talageri, Shrikant, *The Rigveda, A Historical Analysis,* Aditya, Delhi, 2000.

Tempo, 1996: "Feedbacks between climate and the boreal forest durning the Holocene epoch", *Global Biogeochemical Cycles,* Vol. 10, pp. 727-736, 1996.

Thapar, 1970: Thapar, B.K., "The Aryans, A Reappraisal of the Problem" *India's Contribution to World Thought and Culture,* (ed.) L. Chandra et al., pp. 147-164, Vivekananda Rock Memorial Committee, Madras, 1970.

Thapar, 1981: Thapar, B.K., "The archaeological remains of the Aryans in North western India", *Ethnic problems of the History of central Asia in the early period,* Moscow, 1981.

Thieme, 1960: Thieme, P., "The 'Aryan' Gods of the Mitanni Treaties", *Journal of the American oriental society* 80, pp. 301-317, 1960.

Thompson, 1990: Thompson, John B., *Ideology and Modern Culture,* Polity Press, Cambridge, 1990.

Times, 2006: *The Times of India,* 24 October 2006, P. 7, Patna Edition, (PTI News).

Trautmann, 2005: Trautmann, Thomas R., *The Aryan Debate,* Introduction; "Constructing the Racial theory of Indian civilization", *The Aryan Debate,* Oxford University Press, New Delhi, 2005.

Tossi et al., 1992/1999: Tossi M., Shahmirzadi, Malek, S. and Joyenda, M.A., "The Bronze age in Iran and Afganistan", *History of Civilizaton of Central Asia,* (ed.) Dani A.H. and Masson V.M., Vol. 1, Ch. 9, 1992/1999 (UNESCO 1992, first Indian edition, Motilal

Banarsidas, Delhi, 1999).

Vasu, 1891-97: Vasu, Srisa Chandra, (ed. & tr.), *Asthaādhyāyī of Pāṇini*, vol.-2, Allahabad, 1891-97.

Vats, 1940: Vats, M.S., *Excavations at Harappa*, Government of India Press, Delhi, 1940.

Velichko, 1993: Velichko A.A., *Evolution of Landscapes and Climates of Northern Eurasia, Late Pleistocene-Holocene Elements of Prognosis*, Vol. 2, Moscow, Nauke, 1993.

Wheeler, 1947: Wheeler, R.E.M., "Harappa 1946,The Defences and Cemetery R 37", *The Decline and fall of the Indus Civilization*, (ed.) Lahiri Nayanjot, pp. 50-57, Permanent Black, New Delhi, 2000, first published, *Ancient India*, Bulletin of the Archaeological Survey of India No. 3, pp. 58-130, Manager Publications, Delhi, 1947.

Wheeler, 1968: Wheeler, R.E.M., *The Indus Civilization*, 3rd edition, Cambridge University Press, Cambridge, 1968.

Wind et al., 1994: Jan Wind, Abraham Jonker, Robin Allott and Leonard Rolfe, "Diversity of language", *Studies in language origin III*, Amesterdam, Benjamin, 1994.

Winternitz, 1972: Winternitz, M., *A History Of Indian Literature*, Vol. I, Sec. I, Calcutta 1927, reprinted, Munshiram Manoharlal Publishers Pvt. Ltd. Delhi, 1972.

Witzel, 1995/1997: Witzel. M., "Early Indian history, linguistic and textual parameters", *The Indo-Aryans of Ancient South Asia*, (ed.) George Erdossy, Ch. 4, pp. 85-117; "Rgvedic history, Poets Chieftains and Polities" (ed.) George Erdossy, *The Indo-Aryans of Ancient south Asia*, Ch. 14, pp. 307-340, First published, Walter de Gruyter & Co. Berlin, 1995, First Indian edition, Munshiram Manoharlal Publishers Pvt. Ltd. Delhi, 1997.

Witzel, 1999: Witzel, Michael, "Substrate Languages in Old Indo-Aryan (Rgvedic, Middle and Late Vedic)", *Electronic Journal of Vedic Studies*, Vol. 5, issue 1, September 1999.

Wright, 1993: Wright H.E. jr., "Environmental determinism in Near Eastern Prehistory", *Current Anthropology* 34, pp. 458-469, 1993.

Yashpal et al., 1984: Yash Pal, Baldev Sahai, Sood, R. K. & Agrawal, D. P. "Remote sensing of the 'lost' Saraswati River", *Frontiers of the Indus Civilization*, (ed.) B.B. Lal and S.P. Gupta, pp. 499-504, Archaeological Survey of India, Delhi, 1984.

Zahn, 1994: Zahn, R., "Fast flickers in the Tropics", *Nature* 372, pp. 612-622, 1994.

Index